A QUARTER CENTURY
OF LEARNING

A QUARTER CENTURY
OF LEARNING

1904-1929

AS RECORDED IN LECTURES DELIVERED AT
COLUMBIA UNIVERSITY ON THE OCCASION
OF THE ONE HUNDRED AND SEVENTY-FIFTH
ANNIVERSARY OF ITS FOUNDING

NEW YORK
COLUMBIA UNIVERSITY PRESS
1931

Printed in the United States of America
The Torch Press, Cedar Rapids, Iowa

CONTENTS

EDITOR'S INTRODUCTION

DIXON RYAN FOX

For eight centuries the university has been the energizing center of learning, the treasury of what has been most thoughtfully and finely said, and the observatory of new fact. It has been the interpreter's house where the universe was simplified to fit man's consciousness. It had its predecessors, the monastery, the academy, the lyceum, the inspiring single teacher, all sustained by man's insistent curiosity, but in modern times, up to very recently, it has had no rival in the organization of scholarship. A university in retrospective mood thinks therefore of the continuing process of discovery, not of phenomena in themselves but of the penetrating inquiry by which their range and quality have been determined.

In the autumn of 1929 Columbia University found itself in such a mood, celebrating as it was the one hundred and seventy-fifth anniversary of its foundation. This particular segment in the cycle of most institutions has not called for special mark; but in the history of Columbia it seemed especially significant. It suggested a solid, though a narrow, continuity for a hundred and fifty years and then a swift expansion into a quarter century of university breadth. Growth never comes precisely in this way; the necessary bases of the university had been laid by the previous generation, and, indeed, in elements, long before. But during the past quarter century it was very different in scope and in consequent organization from what it had been. Its concerns were as broad as knowledge. To survey the progress of university learning during that time throughout the world seemed an appropriate project of the celebration.

It was obvious that the survey should be coöperative, not only for the practical reason that no one felt competent to undertake the whole, but because such a partnership of specialists would symbolize the modern university. An ideal design would demand inclusiveness, but since it was planned to make the contribution in a series of weekly lectures and since lectures are best given in the presence of listeners, it was necessary to estimate the endurance of the university audience. The number seventeen was taken as fitting well into the year's program and the subjects were rather arbitrarily selected as contributing a representative sample of the whole. There was no intention to suggest, however, that these were more important, that physics was weightier than metaphysics, economics than mathematics, or architecture than the other arts. The progress of learning in America was to be given special emphasis, though to assess its share rather than to disturb the general scale. Columbia will be recognized as having made its proper contribution and its achievements have been here reviewed along with those of other centers in this country and abroad. Some lecturers, however, realizing that their audience was especially familiar with the scholars of its own faculties have occasionally cited them to illustrate this or that movement or tendency observable in the period, without necessarily implying primacy.

Athwart this quarter century fell the shadow of the World War. Scholars, being citizens as well, rallied to the various flags. In chemistry and in certain other fields important discoveries were made under the pressure of national needs; on the whole scholars acquitted themselves in many responsibilities with unexpected distinction. Yet the atmosphere of war and revolution was scarcely ideal for the dispassionate search for truth. The universities in many places were strange travesties upon their customary selves. In Russia, for example, "academic life was completely dislocated." [1] How many brilliant young light-bearers were snuffed out on the battlefront will never be known. In the dreary days of reconstruction, especially in Central Europe, learning was pathetically undernourished.

Yet, despite the losses, one who reads these lectures will be impressed with the quantitative growth of scholarship in the period as a whole; after all most of the twenty-five years were marked by peace and progress. With the surplus of wealth and time which new industrial methods have produced there has been more leisure for inquiry. Economic surplus and the democratization of learning have between them lengthened college rolls. While in this country the number of colleges has increased less than 20 per cent during this period, their teaching personnel has trebled. In the British Isles the numerical growth has been quite as impressive. In some newer fields, of course, the gains have been enormous; American psychologists have increased sevenfold since 1904. The great increase in the periodical literature of scholarship throughout the world is in itself an indication of the growing number of scholars.

It would be a serious error to imply that learning has ever been confined to academic chairs, but a striking feature of recent times has been the multiplication of other opportunities for the scholar not possessed of private means. Research foundations have multiplied in number, resources and usefulness, especially in the United States. There are some, like the Rockefeller Institute, which have their own buildings and laboratories, colleges of scientists without pupils, a realization of the dream of Francis Bacon in the *New Atlantis*. Others invest in brains wherever they may be, so that the scholar seeking bread while he discovers truth, goes for aid not to a Maecenas as in ancient Rome or to a noble lord as in eight-

[1] P. J. Novgorotsev in *Russian Schools and Universities in the World War* (J. T. Shotwell, general editor, "Economic and Social History of the World War," New Haven, 1921), 223-235.

eenth-century England, but to an advisory board which may
make him a grant. The mounting costs of publication, due to
the larger remuneration of labor, costs which have been an
obstacle to the spread of new truth, have been met at least in
part by the munificence of such foundations. Periodicals devoted to abstracts of scholarly papers have been similarly
financed. These separate endowments constitute an outstanding phenomenon in the organization of scholarship during the
quarter century; what its ultimate effect may be no one can say.
It was apprehended at the start that the prejudices of the
founders might warp the progress of research, at least in
the social and political sciences, but so far, it seems, this fear
has not been justified by the results. The growth of public
libraries, in part by similar aid from private philanthropy, has
been of incalculable benefit to scholarship.

As industry has grown more complex in process and in organization, the well-schooled investigator has been more and
more in request. "No longer," remarks General Parsons, "is
progress looked for in the ingenious and estimable mechanic
with his monkey wrench, but in the trained man of science."
Petroleum operators, notes Professor Berkey, must have their
corps of geologists; the great public utilities, the electric, telephone and other enterprises, and all sorts of industries involving chemistry, physics and metallurgy must be served as well.
Sometimes, if the research problem be special or occasional,
the industry employs the resources of the university, as through
the Mellon Institute at Pittsburgh and in the study of low-
temperature carbonization at Sheffield; but many large corporations have erected their own laboratories and staffed them
with the finest talent they could find, carrying inquiry into
fundamental principles quite as much as into practical expedi-
ents. This commercialization of science raised doubts in the
breasts of some humanists. "Applied science," wrote one of

them,[2] "has lately been entangled at times in serving sordid purposes, so that its own freedom as science has been hampered and its beneficial influence impaired." But that type of industrial research which in the laboratories of the General Electric Company produced the discoveries of Steinmetz, Coolidge and Langmuir has certainly not degraded science. Not alone in the fields of chemistry, physics and geology has science been recruited into economic service; it is significant that the apostle of behaviorism, Professor J. B. Watson, was made a vice-president of the largest American advertising firm. The theorist, long a man of prestige in Continental Europe, has been supplanting the merely practical man even in America. The public has put its confidence in science. The Pure Food Law of 1905, as our lecturer in chemistry points out, was an early example of this trust.

If the laboratory sciences have in these years become more and more involved in industry and commerce, it is also true that scholarship itself has increasingly adopted the technique of the laboratory. Certain arts have become sciences, notably education, with its elaborate schemes of experiment, measurement and induction. Skill gave way to formulae. Psychology has left the arm chair for the laboratory. That medicine has become more a matter of test tubes and cultures may have necessitated the increase of the full-time staff in medical schools in place of occasional lectures by practitioners, as noticed by Dean Darrach. Economics and, in America at least, sociology have become more and more statistical, dealing with modes and means. These social scientists, so called, now work among the clatter of comptometers and Hollerith machines. Even social history, which has grown respectable within this period, attempts to be quantitative and to generalize from many cases. Everything wants to be called scientific.

[2] A. F. West, *The War and Education* (Princeton, 1919), 55.

The differentiation of professional species, which runs through the whole history of civilization, has gone on apace in these recent years. The body of knowledge grows like a coral island into which a myriad of workers build themselves, each in his tiny area. But at the same time the boundaries of the great divisions have frequently been blurred. "One way of expressing the present trend in science," observes Professor Sherman, "is to say that physics becomes more mathematical, chemistry more physical, biology and geology more chemical." Perhaps this renewed sense of the interdependence of the various specialties has had its part in making popular the college survey courses which Dean Hawkes discusses. Perhaps we must evoke from their century-old retirement the natural and moral philosophers and the natural historians to be our specialists in generalization. "The discoveries of the nineteenth century," writes Dr. Whitehead, "were in the direction of professionalism, so that we are left with no expansion of wisdom and with greater need of it. Wisdom is the fruit of a balanced development. It is the balanced growth of individuality which it should be the aim of education to secure. The most useful discoveries of the immediate future would concern the furtherance of this aim without detriment to the necessary intellectual professionalism." [3]

Certainly mere traditionalism has lost much of its authority in universities. Few give their courses in old form and substance simply because the subject matter has always been taught that way. The uninstructed might expect to find traditionalism dominant in the classical studies, but no such notion will survive the reading of Professor Moore's lecture. As the classicists have reached far into medieval literature with one hand and have seized all ancient society with the other, so history and letters and sociology and jurisprudence and what not have invaded each other's fields with utmost freedom, yet without

[3] A. N. Whitehead, *Science and the Modern World* (Cambridge, 1926), 246.

developing much mutual resentment. These lectures will demonstrate how difficult would be the task of defining all these subjects as at present studied.

All this makes coöperation easier, especially in America where organization is a folkway. Scholars work in groups, in teams. But this runs down through the specialties themselves. We have coöperative histories, encyclopaedias, editions. A scientific discovery is the product of a laboratory, not of a single mind.

In these lectures Americans are mentioned much more frequently than a candid estimate would have justified twenty-five years ago. America is playing a considerably larger rôle in scholarship. Yet we must not lose the world view which sets things in proportion. From 1901 to 1928, approximately the period here under review, eighty-three Nobel prizes were awarded in science, of which five came to Americans; of these, one was of European birth and training and another, also born in Europe, received his university education in Germany. France had nearly six times as many per million population, England nearly eight times, and Germany a little more, while the Netherlands had twenty, and Denmark thirty-four times as many. This is not flattering to American scholarship; it constitutes an indictment that cannot easily be explained away. Yet it is scarcely a fair index of American achievement as a whole. The coöperative method which we have mentioned as characteristic of this country, as well as intense specialization, makes for anonymity. Few single names stand out, though the total is impressive. The fact that Dr. Carrel figures as the solitary American in the twenty-six awards in medicine, by no means gauges the importance of this country in that science.

But true scholarship knows no national frontiers. A nation may achieve hegemony in some art or science, as Germany once did in music, or its scholars in a certain field may develop a dominant national peculiarity, as have American psychologists and architects. But, except in the days of war hysteria, scholars everywhere recognize each other as fellow-workers in a common cause. Some periodicals, like *Isis*, publish original articles in the language the author uses, whatever it may be. The distinguished scientist circling the earth finds himself everywhere among understanding friends. This, of course, may seem no more true in the present century than it was four hundred years ago. But in the days of Erasmus the scholarly world was Western Europe. Russia was added long since, but it is only within the past quarter century that easy intercommunication has been brought about between the scholarship of the old western centers and that of Japan and continental Asia, Australia, South Africa and the two Americas. These twenty-five years have seen a growing number of world congresses in most branches of learning; in fact, there were more in the years from 1904 to 1913 than in any previous decade.[3] There has been a like increase of exchange professorships, of fellowships for foreign study, of joint enterprises carried through by men of many nations, a movement recognized and forwarded by the League of Nations Committee on Intellectual Coöperation and various institutes international in name and purpose. With the memory of the World War fresh and poignant in our minds we must speak with caution, but it seems now in retrospect that progress, much progress, has been made during this quarter century in building the world commonwealth of the intellect.

[3] J. C. Faries, *The Rise of Internationalism* (New York, 1915), 76-98.

HISTORY

Carlton J. H. Hayes

I

History is essentially method, not matter. It is a method of studying mankind. It may be applied to any or all subjects. Consequently the historian who would inaugurate a series of lectures on the progress of scholarship in the various arts and sciences during the past twenty-five years might properly proceed to deliver the whole course of lectures himself, or he might with equal propriety content himself with a formal bow and leave to more competent specialists the elaboration of history. In the present emergency the authorities have decreed a middle course for the professional historian. He is to do something more than to bow, and he is not to talk at great length. His task is simply to preface the comprehensive survey of others with some remarks on the progress of history in general.

For we are concerned at this time with the commemoration of historical events which have transformed the King's College of 1754 into the Columbia University of 1929, and this brings conspicuously to mind a peculiar trait of human beings, the universal fondness for recalling the past and celebrating its deeds. Man, it has been remarked, is the time-animal: he possesses a sense of time; and his memory is a basic factor in enabling him to rise superior to other animals, to rationalize his surroundings, and to produce and maintain the arts and sciences which constitute distinctively human civilization.

Some degree of historical mindedness is inherent in all human beings. We are all conditioned individually in our maturity by memories of what befell us in our childhood. Our social groupings are affected by recollection of what our ancestors did or failed to do. Our culture is the remembered product of the past. Indeed, the highest type of historical mindedness is to be found in the genetic reasoning which has particularly distinguished the scientific advance in our modern age and which has certainly been no monopoly of professional historians. Genetic reasoning has been preëminently developed and applied in the domains of geology, botany and zoölogy, with revolutionary consequences not only to these subjects but to all the sciences and arts, including what had long been called "history." All sorts of phenomena are now viewed in their origin and growth, and speculation is rife not only as to what they are but how they have come about. There are scholarly historians of the universe and of the earth, of plants and animals, as well as of human thought and behavior. Each of the traditional disciplines has become, in greater or less degree, consciously historical. This fact will doubtless be amply demonstrated as the present course of lectures proceeds. Mine will be but a curtain raiser to sixteen other histories of recent intellectual development.

Most scholars employ history as auxiliary to other major interests. A certain number — the so-called professional historians — are reputed, however, to make the study of the past their chief concern. It is to achievements of these that I would address myself.

Twenty-five years ago professional historians in Europe and America were trained in the scientific methods and inspired by the scientific ideals which Ranke and his German colleagues and disciples had espoused in the preceding century, but professional historians were hotly debating among themselves what should be the subject matter to which they might most suitably apply their scientific methods and ideals. Probably a majority still believed, or at least acted as if they believed,

with Freeman, that history is past politics and that therefore
the historian should deal only with political history. Against
this belief, deeply rooted in the dominant practice of the nineteenth century, a growing number of dissenters were already
protesting. Advocates of economic and psychological interpretations of history were making their voices heard and were
alarming the politically minded majority. Champions were
appearing of cultural history, of synthetic history, of the "new
history," men like Henri Berr [1] in France or Karl Lamprecht [2]
in Germany or James Harvey Robinson [3] in the United States.
How silly it is, said Robinson, for historians to waste time in
determining "whether Charles the Fat was in Ingelheim or
Lustnau on July 1, 887," when they should be contemplating
the jaw of the Heidelberg Man. The orthodox were scandal-
ized. They denounced Berr and Lamprecht as mere "philosophers of history," and officers of the American Historical
Association pronounced jeremiads against the dangerous novel-
ties of Robinson.

Now, the foremost historians of France are collaborating
with Henri Berr in the production of his hundred-volume
Évolution de l'humanité, and James Harvey Robinson is himself president of the American Historical Association. These
are indications of the progress made by historians during the
past twenty-five years in broadening their objectives. To understand what has happened in this respect, several developments should be mentioned.

In the first place, it must be made clear that the "new history" is not so very "new." It represents less a revolutionary
upheaval in the twentieth century than a reaction against the

[1] Henri Berr (1863-   ) began the publication of his *Revue de synthèse
historique* in 1900.

[2] Karl Lamprecht (1856-1915) published his *Moderne Geschichtswissenschaft*
in 1905 and completed the first edition of his revolutionary *Deutsche Geschichte*
in 1909.

[3] James Harvey Robinson (1863-   ), *The New History* (1913).

narrow specialization of the nineteenth century and a return to
the wider interests of the eighteenth century. It is but a fulfill-
ment of the hope expressed by Herder in 1784 that the genetic
principle might be employed by trained historians as a key to
all problems of human development, anthropological and psychological, as well as economic and political.[4]

Secondly, professional historians of the twentieth century
have access to a much wider range of convenient source material than their predecessors had. Most historians of the nineteenth century, finding that state archives were relatively well
organized, confined their researches largely to past politics.
At the same time, however, economics, anthropology, sociology, philology and psychology emerged as would-be sciences,
and a goodly number of their exponents, discovering the utility
of the genetic principle, turned historians; they amassed much
material of historical character, classified it, and exploited it.
Thereby they provided the professional historians of our day
with convenient sources for, and splendid examples of, the
historical approach to human interests outside of politics.

Thirdly, with the progress of historical and individual
specialization, there has arisen an obvious need for coöperation. Coöperation is, indeed, such an extremely important aspect of contemporary historiography that I shall presently
discuss it in some detail. Here it will suffice to note that political
historians are now collaborating not only with one another but
also with anthropologists, economists and psychologists who
use the historical method.

As professional historians of the present day have reflected
upon the bitter debates in which their predecessors indulged
twenty-five years ago and have become aware of the manifold
contributions made by historically minded colleagues in all the

---

[4] *Ideen zur Philosophie der Geschichte der Menschheit* (1784), Sämmtliche
Werke, edited by Suphan, XIII, XIV. See also F. M. von Grimm, *Correspond-
ance littéraire, philosophique et critique* (1755), III, 20.

social sciences, they have arrived at something like a new consensus of opinion as to what history is. The vast majority of them throughout the world today are convinced, I believe, that history is a method especially applicable to any and all of the humanistic studies. It is not the method of the natural sciences. It deals with phenomena from the standpoint of time rather than from that of space, and the phenomena are human.

Whatever may be the view of natural scientists, man is for historians the center of the universe. Man, we have come to believe, is neither a pure heavenly spirit set off completely from other forms of life, as was commonly imagined prior to the eighteenth century, nor is he a mere plant or animal dependent exclusively on inexorable laws of physical heredity and environment, as was widely hypothesized in the nineteenth century. He is something unique. He has a distinctive curious intellect, and he has evolved an extraordinary culture whose ramifications, if not always obviously heavenly, frequently transcend the "laws" of biology and botany. Man's culture has an existence of its own. And it is with man's culture that history is primarily concerned.[5]

Some contemporary historians still play with the philosophy of history and some even venture to suggest specific "laws" which determine man's cultural development through the ages.[6] But it must be stated that, in the main, professional historians are now more than ever impressed with man's complexity and more sceptical of generalizations concerning his culture. To be sure, they are quite convinced that the painstaking study of the past is highly useful: that it promotes an enlightened understanding of the present, and that it affords examples both

[5] This view has been developed chiefly by the anthropologists. See F. Boas, *Mind of Primitive Man* (1911), 29; R. H. Lowie, *Primitive Society* (1920), 3; A. A. Goldenweiser, *Early Civilization* (1922), 399; A. L. Kroeber, *Anthropology* (1923), 186-187; and especially Clark Wissler, *Man and Culture* (1923), *passim*.

[6] See, for example, E. P. Cheyney, *Law in History* (1927).

of what should be imitated and of what should be avoided. But, while claiming an immediate utility for the historical method, they admit that it does not get to first causes or lead to ultimate results. They question any knowable determinism, any absolute causality, in human life. Though economics has latterly become the chief auxiliary of history, and though we strive more and more to learn how man has reacted to his economic environment, historians as a class certainly reject that form of the "economic interpretation of history" which a generation ago envisaged man as a greedy automaton and his past as proof of economic determinism. Next to economics, psychology has contributed most to history within the last twenty-five years, but psychology has only strengthened the historians' suspicion that the universe is a riddle and that man himself is the greatest of riddles.

In other words, professional historians of the present generation are a chastened lot. They have no proud faith in the supreme importance of past politics or of any other single aspect of human culture. They have no cocksureness about the eternal validity of their findings. Pushed on by other humanists, and especially by other social scientists, they are gradually regaining the breadth of view which characterized the eighteenth century, albeit in a spirit which the historians of that century lacked — the spirit of humility.

II

Despite the doubts that are multiplying about discoverable "laws" in history, historians still claim that their method of investigation is truly "scientific," that it can and should be applied to the study of humanity in such a way as to give a greater certainty to our knowledge of what happened in the past. This scientific attitude of historians antedates the last quarter century, but it is not old. Beginning with the Benedictines of St. Maur in the seventeenth century, when the modern scientific spirit was young, it reached maturity only in the second half of the nineteenth century. Previous to this time, the historian had usually been an artist and a litterateur and frequently a religious propagandist or a patriotic pamphleteer. Such types of historian we still have with us, and probably always shall, for man, being the time-animal, is always interested in whatever purports to come from the past, and, being an art-loving animal, he likes to have his past embroidered. But some seventy-five years ago the professional historian, under the leadership of Ranke, undertook seriously to assume a scientific attitude in his investigations.

He undertook, in the first place, to test and examine his sources of information far more critically than ever before, and rejected partially or wholly many authorities upon which his predecessors had relied implicitly. Secondly, he resolved to tell the truth like a man, regardless of whose feelings it might hurt. Thirdly, he began to realize the overwhelming importance of the inconspicuous, the common, and often obscure elements in the past. . . . Fourthly, he began to spurn supernatural . . . explanations.[7]

The actual result of the new attitude was the rise of a science of historical investigation and a method of training future historians, which has taken complete possession of the contemporary world of historical scholarship. If trained historians of the present day are concerned with a much broader field than those of twenty-five years ago, if they are investigating social and widely cultural phenomena as well as the strictly political, their method and the scientific spirit in back of it remain unchanged.

There have been abuses in the application of the scientific historical method. In the first enthusiasm about it, its high priests fancied they were pure scientists and could use documents as the chemist employs test tubes. In their devotion to documents, they tended to sacrifice essential truth to what

[7] J. H. Robinson, *The New History*, 75.

scribes had said was true; to neglect the spiritual or psychic forces and influences in human life; and to despise any composition that was not jejune or illiterate. But such abuses are now being corrected. Perhaps one of the most significant books in the whole field of history during the last twenty-five years is that of Benedetto Croce, which distinguishes between the historian as chronicler, that is, as investigator and compiler, and the historian as artist, that is, as informed and conscious writer.[8] Croce would exalt the latter without debasing the former; he would superimpose on the most exacting scientific research the artistic presentation of the results of research; and in this, I believe, he is counseling a course which appeals to the most progressive contemporary historians. Though we still have a host of second-rate professional historians who labor under the spell of the earlier illusion and talk about archives as though they were manna in a desert, and who take pride in writing not at all or very slovenly, the leading historians of the present day aspire to be both scientists and artists.[9]

Coöperation among historians has been an outstanding mark of the last quarter century. Twenty-five years ago, as in earlier periods, most historians worked in isolation. A few religious communities had been collecting and editing source materials for some time, and more recently national organizations of trained historians had been effected, and prominent universities had established departments and seminars for the training of historians. But in the main each historian investigated the past by himself and published the results of his research without special regard to the work of others.

During the past quarter century, however, the increasing

[8] Benedetto Croce, *Teoria e storia della storiographia* (1917), Eng. trans. (1921).

[9] See G. L. Burr, "The Freedom of History," *American Historical Review*, XXII, 253-271, January, 1919; and Jusserand, Abbott, Colby, and Bassett, *The Writing of History* (1926).

specialization of individuals, on the one hand, and, on the
other, the growing recognition of the need of synthesis in the
light of the enlarged scope of history, have combined, coinci-
dentally with the development of coöperation among other
scholars, to develop coöperation among historians. It is evi-
denced by the quickening of earlier joint activities, such as the
editing of source-materials by religious communities, by state
governments, by national organizations of historians. It is
exemplified by the steady growth of university departments of
history throughout the world, accustoming most trained historians to well-knit local unions. It is illustrated, too, by the
noteworthy rise of international organization.[10]

The first international congress of historical studies was held
at Rome in 1903; [11] the fifth was held at Oslo in 1928. They
are managed by a permanent international bureau and are
attended by representatives of all civilized countries. It is
significant that at the last three congresses not one-sixth of the
mass of papers presented have related to the old staple of
politics; more attention has been devoted to the history of art,
to the history of medicine, and to economic history.

Historians from most countries, too, have coöperated in the
formation, in 1919, of the International Union of Academies
and in the support of its permanent secretariat at Brussels.
Likewise they are participating in the work of the League of
Nations' International Committee of Intellectual Coöperation
and its Institute at Paris. Historians from many countries are
collaborating in such enterprises as the *Corpus Inscriptionum
Latinarum* and the *Encyclopedia of Islam*, sponsored by the
International Union of Academies, and the *Economic and
Social History of the World War*, patronized by the Carnegie
Endowment. The number of historical societies and journals

10 See F. A. Ogg, *Research in the Humanistic and Social Sciences* (1928).
11 Preliminary international congresses, sponsored by the Société d'Histoire
Diplomatique, had been held at the Hague in 1898 and at Paris in 1900.

has quadrupled throughout the world during the past twenty-five years.

The number of coöperative historical narratives which have appeared during the past twenty-five years is legion. The first volume of the *Cambridge Modern History*, as planned by the late Lord Acton, was published in 1902; since then have been published its eleven other stately volumes, and the even more impressive tomes of the *Cambridge Medieval History*, the *Cambridge Ancient History*, and the *Cambridge History of English Literature*, of *British Foreign Policy*, of *India*, and of the *British Empire*. Within the same period have appeared the monumental *Histoire de France*, edited by Lavisse, and other great coöperative works by Frenchmen, Englishmen, and Germans, altogether too numerous to mention.[12]

III

Political history, which as a whole has suffered a relative decline within the last twenty-five years, is still studied and written extensively and doubtless always will be. Indeed, certain aspects of it have been brought into special prominence by human events and interests during and since the World War. The war has led to much restudy and reappraisal of the political history of the nineteenth century, especially of Germany's and particularly of Bismarck's. The political revolutions at the close of the war have served to open the archives of many a foreign office and to provide historians with unusually rich resources for detailed studies of the official relations between governments prior to the war. The post-war difficulties of democracy and exigencies of dictatorship have interested some historians in the origins of contemporary Bolshevism or Fascism. The establishment of a League of Nations has turned others to the historical study of internationalism.

[12] See *Histoire et historiens depuis cinquante ans: méthodes, organisation et résultats du travail historique de 1876 à 1926*, 2 Vols. (1927-1928).

The post-war emergence of a number of newly unified national states in Europe has tended further to exalt national history. Historians in Poland, Czechoslovakia, Rumania, Finland, etc., are busily engaged in organizing themselves nationally and in collecting and publishing material on the past of their respective peoples. At the same time, the nationalism which is indicated here, and elsewhere in our post-war world, has recently been itself, in many places and at many hands, the subject of critical historical study. Nationalist history may be more intensely prosecuted now than ever before, but it is not new. Historical criticism of nationalism is new, and it is widespread.

The relative decline of political history during the last twenty-five years has been counterbalanced by the rising vogue of *Kulturgeschichte*. Material culture and spiritual culture have alike been stressed. In the realm of material culture, economic factors in man's past provide nowadays the topics for innumerable monographs and the central theme for many a great coöperative publication. In the domain of spiritual culture, the history of art and the history of science bulk large. There is now an international society, affiliating several national organizations, for the history of natural science, and very important contributions are being made to our knowledge of the origins and development of medicine, physics, chemistry, biology and engineering.

Almost revolutionary progress has been made by historical scholars during the last twenty-five years in extending the fields of their researches both spatially and temporally — to distant places and to distant times. Modern historical scholarship arose in western lands and was at first applied primarily to Europe and secondarily to America. Pioneers there were in the nineteenth century who laid foundations for the scientific study of the history of India and the Far East, but only in the twentieth century has such study been prosecuted by a large number of trained historians. New interest in distant places has been stimulated by political and economic developments — the rapid extension of European and American imperialism and the swiftly growing commercial interdependence of all peoples of our globe. Latterly, hundreds of historical scholars have published treatises on imperialism and its relationship to West or East, and hundreds of others have undertaken researches into the history of the internal developments and foreign contacts of far-away nations. Besides, thousands of young men and women from Asia, Africa and Oceania, flocking to the universities of Europe and America, have learned from our historical seminars the scientific method which they have taken home with them and are utilizing for critical work in their several countries. The modern ideals of historical scholarship are now, for the first time, world-wide.

To distant times, as well as to distant places, historians have recently given special attention. Indeed, it is my conviction that archaeological investigations into the very distant past constitute the most fruitful and extraordinary achievements of historical scholarship during the last quarter century. The great antiquity of man, originally established by geologists in the nineteenth century, was speedily recognized in principle by historians, and before the close of that century archaeologists were exploring the ancient monuments of Egypt and Mesopotamia, Greece and the Roman Empire. It is not too much to say, however, that greater progress has been made during the last twenty-five years in adding to and systematizing our knowledge of early civilization than during all preceding periods. To this end, universities, special schools and institutes, private foundations, private benefactors, governments, and a growing number of trained specialists have contributed; and the results are impressive not only for ancient Egypt, Greece, and Rome, but also for Western and Central Asia, India, China, Mexico and Central America.

Thanks to recent archaeological labors, we now know a good deal about the neolithic culture of all the Mediterranean lands; we can trace the material civilization of Egypt back of the first dynasty to 11,000 B.C. and that of Mesopotamia to 5000 B.C.; we can speak with some assurance of the history of India prior to the Aryan invasions; and we can check the traditional literary accounts of China to at least 3000 B.C. The epoch-marking discoveries of Sir Arthur Evans in Crete since 1900 and those of Hugo Winckler in Asia Minor since 1906 have opened new vistas to archaeologists and have enabled historians to reconstruct the civilizations of the Aegean and Hittite empires which flourished in the second millennium B.C. From the excavations at Knossos has been established the essential truth of the old legend of the Minotaur, and from the remains at Boghaz-Keui has been confirmed the historicity of the Homeric poems, even to the names of the heroes.

Less spectacular but hardly less illuminating has been the recent rise of the new auxiliary science of papyrology. Egyptian papyri of the period of the Ptolemies began to be collected on a large scale in 1890, and English and German scholars commenced to publish them in 1901. Since then, the collecting and editing of papyri have been industriously pursued, and they are supplying us with illuminating fragments of the lost literature of the Greeks and with precious details about the political administration and economic system of the Hellenistic world.

All or most of the latest discoveries concerning antiquity have recently been utilized for a number of new scholarly surveys of the whole field of ancient history, such as those of Eduard Meyer, Rostovtzeff and the *Cambridge Ancient History*, which are vastly more authentic and informing than any composed in the nineteenth century. In particular, many of the new discoveries have been utilized for a profusion of detailed critical studies in the field of religion, relating not only to the origins of Christianity and the syncretism of Graeco-Roman pagan cults, but also to the ancient rites of Egyptians, Assyrians, and Hittites, and to Hinduism, Buddhism, and Shinto. It is in our era that such outstanding students of comparative religion as Harnack, Meyer, Duchesne and Cumont have done their greatest work.

There has been, of course, continuous progress in historical study of the more conventional European history of the Middle Ages and modern times. Far more attention has been paid than formerly to the intellectual history of Europe and likewise to its economic and social history. The historical study of Eastern Europe — the Byzantine Empire, Russia and the Balkans — has been stimulated. In the light of new knowledge concerning the Byzantine Empire, as well as concerning the Hellenistic culture of the Roman Empire and the medieval culture of western Europe, it now appears that the so-called Renaissance was far less important than such nineteenth-century writers as Burckhardt and Symonds had supposed, and that even the scientific advance of the seventeenth and eighteenth centuries was not quite so revolutionary as had been imagined. It is within the last twenty-five years, moreover, that the political and social revolutions of modern Europe have received scientific treatment. Far greater quantities of source materials have been collected, far more thorough studies have been made, far more critical histories have been written, than ever before, on the American Revolution, on the French Revolution and on that revolution in the industrial arts which has profoundly conditioned all our contemporary civilization.

IV

The last quarter century has been marked by an extensive popularization of results of historical research. This does not mean that scientific writings of professional historians are best sellers. In spite of rapidly increasing literacy among the masses, few professional historians of the present day can expect any such number of readers of their books as there was at an earlier day for the works of Gibbon, Macaulay or Parkman. There is, however, a growing class of popularizers of history, who, without being specialists themselves, tend more and more to utilize the detailed studies of professional historians for the general historical narratives which, especially when these are dressed in the fine clothes of literature, the public will read today as formerly. A hundred years ago the historian was preëminently a litterateur; he popularized his own work, which was not over scholarly. Nowadays the trained historian is primarily a research-worker, and his findings are popularized by some one else, who may thereby be more of a scholar than many an old-time professional historian. Between the research-worker and the popularizer there is plenty of friction; the former is inclined to despise the latter, and the latter to denounce the former. The popularizer is a little easy-going; he has a flair for imaginative passages and colorful adjectives; in league with his publisher he has an aversion to footnotes. But while he pokes fun at the dons and the "profs," he appropriates their work. He can, of course, scarcely keep abreast of all their latest scientific achievements, but as a rule he can do what they will not do: he can and does communicate to the masses, even if a bit partially and belatedly, the progressive results of historical scholarship. It is unthinkable, for example, that any truly popular narrative of the American Revolution which might be published in 1929 should reincarnate the spirit of Bancroft's or rely exclusively upon materials and studies available fifty years ago.

Popularization of historical scholarship is effected increasingly through the schools. In all civilized countries of the world, history is taught in school and college; and the tendency during the past twenty-five years has been to increase the time allotted to historical instruction, to improve the training of history teachers, and to better the quality of history textbooks.

Nowadays a very large number of history teachers have attended historical seminars at a university, and though few of them may have the inclination or ability to become productive scholars, they have obtained at any rate some idea of what historical scholarship is and some training in the exercise of the critical faculty. Also, the newer textbooks, if still too nationalistic in outlook and emphasis, represent a great advance over their predecessors; most of them are written by trained historians and embody fruits of the scholarship of other trained historians.

Many popularizers of history have latterly catered to an insistent demand for up-to-date surveys of world-history, of all human progress from Nippon to New York, from caveman to Coolidge. Perhaps the most striking example of the popular world histories which have poured from the printing presses within the last few years is the literary tour de force of Mr. H. G. Wells. Numerous sins of omission and commission are chargeable against his *Outline of History*, but two facts concerning it are highly pertinent to us here. First, it displays on almost every page the anxiety of the author to take account of recent historical scholarship. Second, it is itself an index of the contemporary range of historical interest and research.

Another type of popular history at the present time is the intimate biography, as exemplified by such writers as Strachey and Guedalla, Ludwig and Maurois. Biography in some form has always been popular with any reading public, but within the last twenty-five years has emerged a new kind of biography which appeals to a particularly large audience. The new kind is impressionistic, more or less delicately ironical, and pretentiously personal and psychological. It is less concerned with prosaic political and economic conditions than with personal foibles and psychical complexes. Even more than world history, it is an indication of newer developments in historiography; and, despite all its shortcomings, it is serving both to emphasize certain aspects of human behavior which the professional historian has too long neglected and to recall him from the welter of vague social forces to the studied contemplation of individual personality, the essential vital stuff of history.

V

Such, as I see them, are the landmarks in the progress of historical scholarship over the world during the past quarter century: the perfecting of the scientific method of historical investigation and its application by a greatly increased personnel to a vastly enlarged field; the unparalleled rise of coöperative effort among trained historians and between them and their colleagues in the other traditional disciplines; the continuing attention to national history, newly conditioned, however, by the waxing strength of international concerns; the cultivation of archaeology and the resulting enhanced knowledge of such distant places as China and India and of such distant times as those of neolithic Egypt and pre-Homeric Greece; the shifting of emphasis from political history to cultural history, to economic and social phenomena and to the history of science; the effort to reconcile the science of historical investigation with the art of presenting its results; the advance in the teaching of history and in the standard of manuals for its vulgarization; the adoption of new modes in world history and in biography. Such landmarks are not peculiar to Europe; they are strewn about the world, wherever there are historical scholars. And the number of trained historical scholars has grown faster in the United States during the past twenty-five years than in any other country.

When in 1904 I graduated from this college all the professors in its department of history, except two, held degrees from German universities. Now, twenty-five years later, in a considerably enlarged department, only one holds such a degree. What is true of Columbia in this respect is certainly true of all other institutions of higher learning in the United States. It is a sign that in historical scholarship America has come of age during the last quarter century. Though a beginning had been made with the training of scientific historians in the classes of Henry Adams at Harvard in 1874-1876, and in the early eighties in the seminar of Herbert Adams at Johns Hopkins and under the direction of John W. Burgess at Columbia, it was not until the twentieth century that in the United States native-trained historians largely outnumbered the foreign-trained; and it was not until then that Americans were making first-rate contributions to the world's historical scholarship.

All the trends which characterize the latest historical scholarship in Europe are apparent in the United States. Here, as there, every university worthy of the name, maintains seminars for the training of historians; and if the doctoral dissertations of our students leave very much to be desired in respect of originality, importance and form, their average, I assert without national pride, compares quite favorably with that of recent German or French dissertations. In America, too, much attention has been devoted to the accumulation of source materials. Most of our state governments have been induced to make special provision for the preservation of their archives, and, after many years of nagging and expostulation on the part of historians, even our backward Federal Government is at last on the point of erecting at Washington a huge repository for national archives. The rapid growth of urban and private libraries; the amassing of manuscript collections from home and abroad; the enrichment of archaeological materials in our museums; all this has been stimulated by the historical profession and has been made possible by the many Maecenases and Medici of our day and land. Basic guides to the sources for American history in foreign archives have been prepared under the auspices of the Carnegie Institution and the editorship of Dr. J. F. Jameson; and American-trained historians have given to the world the standard guides to the historical literature of medieval England, of medieval Ireland, of the Middle Ages generally and of the Industrial Revolution.

American historians have not been mere followers in the recent worldwide coöperative movement. The American Historical Association, founded in 1884, has always included in its membership the foremost historians of the country, both academic and lay. It has fostered much scientific work, and, with its recently acquired endowment fund and publication fund, it is in a position to do more. Twenty-five years ago, its official journal, the *American Historical Review*, was still in its first decade and was the only magazine in this country devoted to scientific history. Today there are numerous specialized magazines, each conducted coöperatively and functioning in harmony, rather than in rivalry, with the *American Historical Review*. There are now the *Mississippi Valley Historical Review*, the *New England Quarterly*, the *Journal of Modern History*, the *Hispanic American Historical Review*, the *American Catholic Historical Review*, the *Journal of Negro History*, the *Agricultural History*, and a large number of state and local reviews. There is the *Speculum*, maintained by the Medieval Academy; and there is *Isis*, supported by the History of Science Society.

The American Historical Association is now affiliated with the American Council of Learned Societies and with the Social Science Research Council. Through these agencies trained historians in America, collectively and individually, are collaborating with humanists, on one hand, and with social scientists, on the other hand, both at home and abroad. Abroad, they are taking prominent places in international counsels and undertakings. At home they are contributing significantly to the new *Dictionary of American Biography*, the new *Social Science Abstracts*, and the new *Encyclopedia of the Social Sciences*.

The coöperative histories published or projected in America during the past twenty-five years are impressive in number and value.[13] The most cursory survey should notice at least the *American Nation* series, the Yale *Chronicles of America*, the Columbia *Records of Civilization*, and the social *History of American Life*.

In the field of American history novel explorations have been undertaken, with almost revolutionary results. Detailed scientific investigations by a notable group of historical scholars and the employment of economic interpretations by another such group have afforded, within the last quarter century, new materials and new ideas for a more realistic treatment of the American colonies and their separation from England, and likewise for a saner understanding of the Civil War and its aftermath. To a Columbia audience it is gratifying to know that the changed attitude in these respects is attributable in no slight degree to the original labors of two of our own professors, the late Professor H. L. Osgood and the late Professor W. A. Dunning. Thanks also to Professor F. J. Turner of Wisconsin and Harvard, the high significance of pioneering life in the social and intellectual development of the United States has been newly recognized, and novel impetus has been given to fruitful study of the nature and spread of American culture. These outstanding developments, coupled with the steady output of scholarly monographs on other aspects of American history, help to explain why the newest general histories of the United States are far broader in scope and more objective in spirit than the earlier narrative of a Bancroft.[14]

Prior to 1900 American historians made comparatively few contributions to European history. Prescott and Motley, who belonged to the earlier literary age, created no school and had

13 Justin Winsor's *Narrative and Critical History of America*, 8 Vols. (1884-1889), was an important, but almost unique, forerunner of the coöperative history now so common.

14 See T. F. Tout, *History and Historians in America* (1929).

little lasting influence; and Parkman touched Europe brilliantly but only indirectly. Within the last twenty-five years, however, the United States has begun to take rank with other countries in the prosecution of researches in the history of Europe and, indeed, of the whole world. Our universities and museums now foster archaeological fieldwork, and among our historians are leading exponents of Egyptology, Assyriology and papyrology. We have important centers for the training of investigators in the history of Latin America, of the Far East, and of nationalism, imperialism, and international relations generally; and in all these fields substantial work is being done. American scholars, moreover, are rendering distinguished service to the intellectual and cultural history of medieval Europe and are making original contributions to the constitutional and social history of England.[15]

The teaching of history has been widely extended and greatly improved in America during the last twenty-five years. Our textbooks, if still the occasional prey of politicians, are now seldom the arid product of hack writers, but rather the informed work of real historical scholars. And all kinds of popularization of the new history go on apace in America, as elsewhere.

VI

It is vexatiously true that every generation rewrites history. Historiography, like the subject matter of history, is in continuous flux. If historical writings of a century ago seem strange to us today, those of the last twenty-five years will doubtless be quite antiquated a century hence. Yet, so long as human nature endures, so long as man remains the time-animal, historians there will be, and Sisyphean labors they will continue to perform.

Nor is the labor of any age wholly lost on posterity. As the

[15] See C. H. Haskins, "European History and American Scholarship," *American Historical Review*, XXVIII (January, 1923), 215-227.

scientific spirit of the seventeenth and eighteenth centuries is our heritage today, so its more painstaking application in the present age will be an inheritance of the next century. Perhaps when the tercentenary of King's College is celebrated, it will then be said that it was during the first quarter of the twentieth century when professional historians first began to understand that they were students of parts, of phases, of a vast human comedy of reality, — the great human comedy which is history and which is infinitely grander and more complex and more tragic than anything which had ever before been fancied, even by an Honoré de Balzac.

ECONOMICS

I

Whether we call Adam Smith or François Quesnay the "father of political economy," the science is younger than Columbia University. Discussions of various economic problems, it is true, can be traced back to classical antiquity. But a science cannot be said to exist before a considerable body of knowledge has been systematically organized. It was four years after the chartering of King's College that Quesnay published his *Tableau Économique*, exhibiting the circulation of wealth in a nation of farmers, manufacturers, merchants and Sovereign, thus supplying a framework into which a host of problems could be fitted. It was twenty-one years after our charter was granted that Adam Smith organized economics as a discussion of the relations between individual initiative in making a living and national wealth.

Since these beginnings of systematization in the eighteenth century, the nascent science has had an eventful history. Its old problems have multiplied by fission, new problems have appeared, its factual information about the past and present practices of men has grown enormously, its general scheme of organization has assumed various forms.

While Adam Smith had stressed the problem of maximizing the annual production of wealth, Ricardo pushed the distribution of this social income to the fore. "Previous writers," he said, "afford very little satisfactory information respecting the natural course of rent, profit and wages." "To determine the laws which regulate this distribution is the principal problem of political Economy." [1] But to elucidate the distribution of income in a society where men sell their services or the use of their property for money and then buy goods produced by others, Ricardo found it necessary to begin with the problem of value. He thus fixed what still passes as the standard pattern of economic theory — the dominant themes are value and distribution.

Since the eighteen twenties, however, this pattern has been elaborated and improved. Ricardo explained "natural" values mainly in terms of the costs of producing goods. In the eighteen seventies Jevons, Menger, Walras and, a little later, J. B. Clark, each working independently, developed an explanation of values which shifted the emphasis from cost to utility. Then in 1890 Alfred Marshall showed how it is possible to combine cost analysis with utility analysis in a systematic theory of value. He showed also how this theory can be applied to the treatment of distribution. Under his hands the problems of wages, rent, profits and interest became special cases in a general treatise upon value, and economics became a more highly integrated science than Ricardo had conceived.

This line of development from Ricardo through the utility analysts to Marshall may be taken as the main sequence in economic theory. But other ways of organizing economics have been tried and must be mentioned. When the quarter century with which we are concerned opened, several schools of economists were flourishing. In having schools, economics was more like its mother, philosophy, than like its elder sisters, physics and chemistry. There was not one generally accepted scheme of work; there were several competing schemes.

The historical school distrusted the methods and results of classical economics. It proposed to start afresh by collecting a

[1] *Principles of Political Economy and Taxation*, Preface to the 1st edition (1817).

far wider range of observations and in the fulness of time to derive more trustworthy generalizations by "induction." Marxian socialism, which plumed itself upon being "scientific" in contrast to the "utopian" socialism of earlier generations, concentrated attention upon a problem which neo-classical economics slighted. It asked, how are economic institutions changing, and it professed to give the answer. Both of these schools were losing somewhat of their earlier militancy by the end of the nineteenth century. When Gustav Schmoller, the leading figure of the historical school, published his "Olympian survey" of economics in 1901, he made free (and awkward) use of the "deductive" analysis which he had formerly scorned. Meanwhile, Marxian socialism was undergoing a process of revision at the hands of disciples who toned down, explained away, or frankly rejected certain of their master's most distinctive doctrines. But two other schools were coming to the front.

Pareto, an Italian engineer who had turned to social problems, was developing mathematical economics along the lines sketched by Léon Walras. Though Pareto cultivated a fine scorn for "literary economists," the difference between his work and that of men like Marshall was more technical than substantial. While those who followed the classical tradition attacked the problem of value by dealing with one or two commodities at a time and showing how their prices were affected by the prices of other goods, Walras invented and Pareto improved a method for attacking the simultaneous determination of the prices of any number of commodities in a market where every price affects and is affected by every other price.

Less like the standard pattern and more like the historical program, was the institutional approach to economics. Thorstein Veblen published his first critique of economic theory in 1898 and his first constructive study of economic institutions in 1899.[2] A student of Darwin and contemporary psychology, Veblen contended that the conception of human behavior tacitly employed by economic theorists was sadly out of date. Men are creatures of instinct and habit rather than creatures of calculation. Of these two controlling elements, instincts have remained a nearly constant factor in the life-history of the species, while habits have undergone a cumulative development. It is the cumulative change in prevalent habits of thinking — that is, in institutions — which makes the life of man today so different from his life in neolithic times, in classical antiquity, in the Middle Ages, or even in the eighteenth century. Hence to account for modern economic life we must study its evolution. A scientific economics is one which concentrates attention upon the cumulative change of economic institutions. The explanations of behavior which conventional theory offers in terms of choice between opposing motives are curious products of the rationalist fallacy — consistently reasoned deductions from mistaken assumptions concerning human nature. Let us turn from these futilities, urged Veblen, to study the effects which the daily discipline of life in tending machines and making money is producing upon the mass habits of thought inherited from earlier generations.

II

So much by way of background for the period to be discussed. If the background does not seem confused, I have misrepresented it. In his lecture upon economics in the one-hundred-and-fiftieth anniversary series, Henry R. Seager commented forcibly upon the mixture of doctrines which prevailed at that time: "The dogmatic orthodoxy of the past," he said,

[2] "Why is Economics not an Evolutionary Science?" *Quarterly Journal of Economics*, XII, 373-397, July, 1898, reprinted with its successors in the collection of Veblen's essays called *The Place of Science in Modern Civilization* (1919). The book referred to is *The Theory of the Leisure Class* (1899, 9th *reprint*, 1924).

"has been succeeded by an exuberant heterodoxy which gives
so great prominence to the disagreements among economists
that the agreements are easily overlooked." But he went on to
speak hopeful words about the future, which is now the past
we are reviewing: "This disputatious period is gradually passing in its turn and a new body of principles is emerging which
entitles economics to be regarded as the most exact of the relatively inexact social sciences." [3] What has economics accomplished since Professor Seager thus summed up its status and
its prospects?

One thing is certain: the problems with which economists
concern themselves have expanded vastly during our period,
both in the sense that old problems have unfolded new features,
and in the sense that new problems have appeared. Let me
begin with that certainty, and postpone the question how
economics has reorganized its work.

Some problems have been thrust upon us. During the Great
War each of the leading belligerents undertook to mobilize
its economic forces with a drastic thoroughness quite unprecedented in history. Many economists had an active share
in formulating and administering the policies which were
adopted; but they had little time for reflecting upon the implications of the stern work they were helping to put through
with a rush. After the armistice came the problems of economic
reconstruction, with which nations did not deal in so vigorous
a spirit. And as a pendant to the war came the stupendous
experiment which Russia is trying — the effort to establish a
new economic order.

All these catastrophic changes occurred so suddenly, they
constituted such an overwhelming mass of strange experiences,
that economists have only begun to make piecemeal use of the

[3] Henry R. Seager, *Economics: A Lecture Delivered at Columbia University,*
January 2, 1908 (1909), p. 14.

data they offer for analysis. Fortunately, the Carnegie Endowment for International Peace seized the opportunity to compile an elaborate record of what happened behind the fighting fronts. Its *Economic and Social History of the World War* is one of the large contributions made in our period to man's knowledge of mankind. But this factual record consists mainly of raw materials: to work them up and incorporate the results into our social sciences, will take time. From the addition to this series which John Maurice Clark has in preparation on our own country's share in the great tangle, we may expect a beginning of analysis and interpretation. The way in which the volume of physical production was maintained when so many of the most vigorous workers had been drawn into the fighting forces; the social consequences produced by marked changes in the distribution of property and income; the criteria by which national policies of mobilizing economic resources may be guided in war or peace — these are but three of the many significant problems suggested by the war. Perhaps the lecture upon economics delivered when Columbia celebrates her two-hundredth anniversary will deal at length with what has then been learned from the study of the war and the period of reconstruction. Certainly the Russian experiment must have yielded instructive results by that time. As yet there is not much to report beyond the dazed perception that social organization is more flexible for good and ill than we had realized, more amenable to purposeful control and more exposed to man-wrought disaster.

Science deals with humdrum processes more successfully than it deals with dramatic episodes. This general rule applies to the present case. So let us turn from the heady theme of war to developments which get their significance from slow but steady cumulation of results. To stress the transition, take next that workaday matter, the rise of business schools.

For years business has been claiming an ever growing proportion of college graduates in this country, and business has
been making ever more exacting demands upon its leading
personnel. The universities, our own among the leaders, have
responded to the need and begun training students for business
careers as they have long been training men for the church,
for the law, for medicine, and for engineering.

The organization of these new courses was a difficult pioneering job. It was possible in some cases to draw into faculties
experienced business men with scholarly tastes. But for the
most part the universities had to develop teachers. Economists
knew more about business than any other group of accredited
investigators. To them fell the lion's share of the new opportunity and the ass' share of the new labor. As fast as possible,
young economists made themselves specialists in banking, in-
surance, accounting, merchandising, salesmanship, transportation, corporation finance, commercial geography, business statistics, advertising, and the like. All these men owed a certain
loyalty to economic theory; but they did not always find clear
guidance for their new tasks in the standard treatises, and
many went their own way without much regard to what they
had been taught. By this time they have amassed and organized for their immediate needs a vast fund of factual information concerning business problems and business practices.
This knowledge is taking its place in the general stock of data
at the disposal of economists. Much of it is exceedingly difficult
to use for scientific purposes along traditional lines. But its
existence affords an opportunity and a challenge which the
students of economic behavior cannot blink.

In our country there are traces of an inclination to draw a
dividing line between "business economics" and "economics"
proper. Foreign colleagues tell us that this distinction is more
sharply insisted upon in other lands which are beginning to
develop schools of commerce. One of the hopeful expectations

we entertain of the near future is that the two groups of workers will realize the common character of their interests more clearly than they have so far done. As the men in business economics pass beyond the pioneering stage of their work, they will develop standards as scholarly as those cherished by the strictest adepts in economic theory. On the other hand, if economic theorists seek to understand what is going on about them, they can find no more helpful allies than their colleagues teaching in business schools and working in business enterprises. Perhaps many of the most important contributions to economics will come in future from men who carry into business careers the habit of disinterested analysis of social processes for which economic science stands.

A further embarrassment of riches has come to economics from the multiplication of statistical data and the improvement of statistical technique. All of us know somewhat about the debt which the physical and the biological sciences owe to telescopes, microscopes, spectroscopes, and a host of highly specialized devices for peering into matters invisible to the human eye. Until the present time, the social sciences have received but little technical help in observation. Their devotees have had to work mainly on what an individual could see for himself. But the turn of economics and its sisters has come. Governments and business enterprises, mainly for their own ends, are making and publishing an ever increasing array of records touching an ever increasing variety of human activities. These records afford mass observations upon the production and exchange of commodities, transportation, prices, wages, interest, profits, and similar phenomena which economists have long been watching as best they could. The new materials are far from perfect data for scientific analysis; they are laborious to manipulate; but they extend enormously the factual information at the disposal of an investigator. They make it possible in many cases to substitute measurements for the vague distinctions of former days between factors of major and factors of minor importance.

So economists with an aptitude for quantitative work have thrown themselves into statistical research. Their laboratories are beginning to merit the borrowed name; they are real workshops where masses of objective data are subjected to ingenious analysis. This type of work has made such headway that, in the United States at least, candidates for the research degree are commonly required to show proficiency in statistical technique. Outside of the universities several research institutes, well equipped mechanically and well staffed, have been set up since the war, primarily for fact-finding work on a quantitative basis in the social sciences. Examples are the Brookings Institution in Washington and the National Bureau of Economic Research in New York. The high promise of this line of inquiry, and its high cost are winning economics, sociology and political science a place beside medicine and the physical sciences in public estimation as fit objects for endowment. Government departments and business enterprises are setting up research staffs to attack their most difficult economic and administrative problems by collecting and analyzing objective data. Indeed, the statistical movement in economics is proceeding at a pace which leaves many of us rather breathless.

While a series of substantially new problems have been pressed to the fore by the rapid development of business education and by the progress of statistics, many problems long the object of intensive study have expanded enormously in scope. In discussing the past development of economics, for brevity's sake I stressed what have been regarded by successive leaders as the central issues of economic theory. But these central issues have never constituted the whole field of work. Since

Quesnay and Adam Smith organized the science, their followers have continued the old practice of devoting special attention to particular problems of outstanding interest. In the last
twenty-five years specialization has grown so rapidly that it
sometimes seems to threaten the unity of economics.

Public finance is a problem in point. Adam Smith devoted
Book V of the *Wealth of Nations* to "The Revenue of the
Sovereign or Commonwealth." Ricardo discussed the shifting
and incidence of taxation at considerable length. Elaborate
monographs upon public finance have been part of our literature for two or three generations. But never have the problems of public finance received so much attention from economists as within the period we are reviewing. The enormous
expansion of national debts, the heavy taxes imposed during
the period of reconstruction, the huge reparations and indem-
nities, the growth of municipal expenditures, the cost and value
of social betterment programs — these and a host of related
developments have busied our specialists in such matters. And
these economists have been called into council more freely
than ever before by public authorities. Men like Edwin R. A.
Seligman and Robert M. Haig of Columbia, and T. S. Adams
of Yale have been drafted by the League of Nations, by
national, state and city governments to help solve complicated
practical problems. Our specialists in public finance are becoming practicing social engineers.

The field of labor problems has developed in somewhat
the same way. Always deeply concerned with the wage-earning
classes, economists used to preach sermons on the advantages
of limiting families and on the futility of trade-unions. A later
generation became interested in the structure and policies of
labor organizations. In recent years, economists have taken a
wider view of labor problems and a more constructive attitude
toward them. They think of labor not merely as disagreeable
effort undergone to get wages, but as activities which yield

abiding satisfaction and personal development, if the worker is adapted to his job. How to get men of varied temperaments and capacities into positions which suit their personalities; how to arrange working conditions so as to minimize fatigue and irritation; how to enhance output per man-hour by eliciting interest in the work; how to fix compensation in ways which appeal to the employees' sense of fairness; how to make all parties feel that they are sharing in a common interest — in short, how to give the mass of the operatives a share in the joys as well as the burdens of work, is the bold program which the specialists in labor problems are daring to conceive.

Needless to say, this program represents more aspiration than accomplishment. To attain their aims, economists are realizing that much more than economic analysis of the problems is required. They are coöperating with business executives, engineers, accountants, psychologists, physiologists, social workers. Some are serving as "impartial chairmen" in plans for collective bargaining; others are employed in the personnel departments of business corporations; a few are retained by trade-unions as advisers. In these varied activities, economists are learning a great deal about behavior which finds no place in their traditional discussions of economic motives.

Third, the problem of money and prices, which has exercised the wit of man for many centuries, has entered upon a new phase. Of course the war brought in its train a series of revolutions in price levels, and these startling changes were recorded with unprecedented fullness. Hence the specialists in money have had better material offered them than ever before to trace the relations between changes in the volume of the currency and changes in prices. It was as if the ordinary processes had been placed under a powerful microscope for the benefit of investigators. Into the analysis of monetary experiences in Germany, France, England, the United States and the neutral nations — experiences of a singularly varied character

— Europeans and Americans have thrown themselves with energy. The old debate concerning the validity of the quantity theory has given place to search for the different ways in which money and credit influence prices and the physical volume of trade, and the different ways in which prices and the volume of trade influence money and credit. The compilation of index numbers of prices at wholesale has been supplemented by similar efforts to measure the trends of prices at retail, the physical quantity of goods produced and exchanged, velocities of circulation — indeed all the factors in the "equation of exchange." And each one of these factors is being broken down for more intensive study of its parts. Frederick C. Mills's work on *The Behavior of Prices*, for example, shows how much may be learned by going behind the general index numbers and comparing the diverse movements characteristic of smaller groups of commodities.

Here again, economists are taking an active hand in affairs. Authorities like H. Parker Willis and Edwin R. Kemmerer are being called upon to reorganize the monetary systems of embarrassed countries; a former professor of economics, A. C. Miller, has sat upon the Federal Reserve Board since 1914; others like Sir Josiah Stamp, Cassel, Vissering, Rist, O. M. W. Sprague, Carl Snyder and W. W. Stewart are called to international conferences, or retained by central banks. In this country, the time seems to be near when no self-respecting bank of considerable size will be content until it has added an economist to its staff. A growing group of investigators cherish the daring belief that the world's monetary systems can be reorganized in such a fashion as to "stabilize the price level" — thereby removing many of the business uncertainties which have hitherto been considered inevitable.

Quite a different aspect of the price problem appears in the efforts of business enterprises to control prices for their own profit. Establishing monopolies is an old scheme to that end which keeps developing ever new variants. It is a scheme which has great economic advantages under certain conditions; for there are services which can be rendered to communities more efficiently by a single large concern than by competing companies. How to gain these advantages and yet protect consumers against extortionate charges is a question which grows in scientific and practical interest as society becomes more complex. Study of it leads on to the more complicated cases in which there are a few very large enterprises with some of the attributes of a monopoly, but supposedly competing with each other. Perhaps most characteristic of the day are the efforts of numerous industries to end "price competition," while continuing to compete in quality of service. Not merely economists who take the consumers' viewpoint, but also business men who for one reason or another are forced to buy in a controlled market and sell in a competitive market are deeply interested in these developments. Among the leaders in this intriguing field of study, Columbia has been represented by Henry R. Seager and James C. Bonbright.

To take one more example: It is within the last twenty-five years that the old problem of commercial crises has been reorganized as the study of business cycles, and under this guise has won celebrity. Scientific progress in this field owes much to the increasing volume of statistical data and the refinement of statistical technique. Similarly, the public attention given to the subject owes much to the growing bond between economic research and business practice — or rather, that attention is one of the salient examples of the bond. I have lost count of the number of agencies which are engaged in the hazardous task of business forecasting. And once more we find bold spirits who believe that their studies of business fluctuations have great potential value for society. Insight won by research may make it possible to devise measures which will mitigate the recessions and depressions from which modern nations suffer.

III

If time sufficed, I might comment upon a much longer list of substantially new problems on which economists have begun working since 1904, and of old problems which have expanded enormously under their hands. But I can give a more lifelike impression of the change which is coming over economics if I leave my catalogue of special problems incomplete and turn to certain characteristics of the work in progress which mark it off in a measure from earlier efforts.

In the nineteenth century, economic theory passed through a highly abstract stage. At a time when facilities for observation were narrow, the most effective way of treating many problems was that of setting up in the inquirer's mind an imaginary state of society and considering what would happen under the conditions supposed. These conditions were made simple enough to facilitate analysis; yet the intention was to include among the suppositions the fundamental features of the real world. To make definite analysis possible, these features were usually given an unreal sharpness and rigidity. For example, the wage-earner's standard of living was treated as incompressible, capital funds were assumed to be perfectly fluid, competition was unlimited. Ricardo set this fashion. The most brilliant example of it is Professor John Bates Clark's treatise on *The Distribution of Wealth*, published just before our period opened. I like to call the method in question "imaginary experimentation." Of course it is a favorite and a useful device of other sciences, notably of physics.

The weak point in this method when applied to economics is that one cannot be sure how far conclusions irrefragably established under the imaginary conditions apply to the world we wish to understand. The major economists have sought to explain what actually happens, and have regarded their imaginary constructions as valuable in so far as they shed light upon reality. In this respect, the workers of today are no more

earnest than their predecessors. But many of our contemporaries have gained faith in the possibility of a more direct
attack. Instead of imagining a realm that never was on land or
sea they prefer whenever possible to look directly at Main
Street and see what they can make of the behavior of the
crowd. Current work is decidedly more realistic in form than
the work of the preceding generation. The shift is one in
degree only: it seems to be less marked in Europe than in
America, perhaps because our facilities for observing what is
going on and for utilizing mass observations are better than
those in other countries. And even here, there are individuals,
not all of them elders, who continue to rely largely upon the
method of imaginary experimentation. Also there are problems
which it is still exceedingly difficult to treat realistically. But I
think there is no doubt that the trend of current work sets
strongly in the direction of dealing directly with the concrete
and the actual rather than with the abstract and the imaginary.

Closely related to this shift toward realistic treatment is the
growing emphasis upon measurement. Of course that is made
possible by the increase of statistical data, the refinement of
statistical technique, and the provision of statistical laboratories already mentioned. In a celebrated address delivered
early in our period, Alfred Marshall applied the terms "qualitative" and "quantitative analysis" to economics. He suggested
that qualitative analysis, such as he had himself practiced for
the most part, had "done the greater part of its work," and
that the future task was the more difficult one of developing
quantitative analysis. But "this higher and more difficult task,"
he said, "must wait upon the slow growth of thorough realistic
statistics." [4] In the United States, at any rate, the growth of
"realistic statistics" has been less slow than seemed likely when
Marshall spoke. The new data are not "thorough" in the sense

[4] "The Social Possibilities of Economic Chivalry," *Economic Journal*, XVII,
7, 8, March, 1907.

of covering anything like the whole field of economic behavior, and they do not yet make it possible to reorganize economics as a genuinely quantitative science. But many more problems can now be treated by statistical methods than could be attacked in this fashion in 1904. There is a marked disposition to utilize quantitative analysis just as far as the necessary data are available; also, I think, a growing disposition to prefer problems which can be treated in quantitative terms. Moreover, it is often possible to restate one of the traditional problems of the science, not open to statistical attack as commonly formulated, in such a fashion that existing data can be used. Thus subtly but cumulatively, the character of economics is undergoing a transformation. Out of the statistical laboratories is coming a new conception of what economics should be, as well as a new program of work. Many of our ablest students are attacking "the higher and more difficult task" of quantitative analysis with a faith in its possibilities which may work wonders.

The active participation of economists in practical affairs, of which I have mentioned typical examples, promotes, and is promoted by, the realistic treatment of problems which is coming into vogue, and the increasing emphasis upon statistical observations. One who tries to be of service in business, government or social movements finds himself perforce thinking realistically, or at least shaping his abstract thinking with a definite view to pragmatic testing. Also he is impelled to measure the factors involved in his problems as accurately as conditions permit. On the other hand, interest in what is actually happening, and ability to measure social phenomena make economists more useful in practical affairs and so bring them more openings in business and more calls to public service.

With these changes comes another. The economist who participates in planning policies finds that he must consider factors which are not commonly regarded as strictly economic.

That used to be cited as a reason why economists should stand aloof from practice — they are not competent to advise outside of their own specialty, and their own specialty is never the only thing to be considered. The conclusion now drawn quite as frequently is that an economist should associate himself with men who can supply his deficiencies — engineers, accountants, business executives, lawyers, psychologists and an indefinite list of other specialists. In speaking of labor problems, I have already mentioned one example of such coöperation.

While the need for a combined attack upon social problems may be clearest in practical affairs, it is dawning upon us that the several social sciences must coöperate all along the line. The more realistically minded we become, the stronger grows this conviction. We have no inclination to check specialization; but we wish to know more of one another's viewpoints, methods and results, so that we can utilize more intelligently one another's help. The economic man who buys and sells has a family, he belongs to a political party and votes, he has strictly personal idiosyncrasies and yet shares in the ideas of his generation, he is an historical product. All these characteristics affect his behavior whether we look at him from the economic, the sociological, the political, the psychological or the historical angle. Quite literally, we cannot understand any phase of social behavior apart from all the other phases. It is easy to make this admission — ours is not the first generation to do so; but to accept its consequences in practice and to develop a genuine program of coöperation among the social sciences is hard. On that constructive task our generation has made a beginning — but no more than a beginning.

Tangible evidences of a widespread desire among social scientists to learn from one another abound. Half-a-dozen books have appeared in the last five years designed to interpret the several social sciences to one another. The titles and authorship are indicative of the contents: *The History and Prospects of the Social Sciences*, 1925, written by ten specialists upon subjects ranging from history and human geography to jurisprudence and ethics; *A Gateway to the Social Sciences*, 1926, by a political scientist, an economist, a sociologist and an historian; *The Social Sciences and Their Interrelations*, 1927, to which thirty-two specialists contributed; *Recent Developments in the Social Sciences*, 1927, by a sociologist, anthropologist, psychologist, geographer, economist, political scientist and historian; *Research in the Humanistic and Social Sciences, Report of a Survey Conducted for the American Council of Learned Societies* by F. A. Ogg, 1928; *An Introduction to Social Research* by Odum and Jocher, 1929; *Methods in Social Science*, edited by Stuart A. Rice, 1930. A much larger undertaking in the common interest is the fifteen-volume *Encyclopaedia of the Social Sciences* which E. R. A. Seligman and Alvin Johnson are editing.

Still more significant of the effort to see social problems in the round and to pool the resources of the several social sciences for work in common is the organization of the Social Science Research Council in 1923. This Council is composed of three representatives each, elected by the national associations of the economists, political scientists, sociologists, statisticians, anthropologists, psychologists and historians. To extend still wider this intellectual league, members-at-large have been added to represent jurisprudence, public health, human geography and psychiatry.

The general purposes of the Council are to promote researches in human behavior, especially researches which require coöperation by two or more of the disciplines represented, by planning and sometimes subsidizing important pieces of work, making grants-in-aid to scholars of established position, awarding post-doctoral fellowships to younger people of marked promise, reporting current work through a monthly journal, *Social Science Abstracts*, holding conferences, and effecting coöperation with other agencies whose interests overlap upon its own. Nor does the Social Science Research Council stand alone. The American Council of Learned Societies is another national organization with an even wider constituency; for the humanities are represented side by side with certain of the social sciences in the narrower sense of the word. And several of our leading universities have recently organized social-science councils of their own. In a sense the Faculty of Political Science at Columbia has long been such an organization; but we have set up the Columbia Council for Research in the Social Sciences to bring together representatives from law, medicine, education, psychology, anthropology and business with representatives from the departments of public law, history, sociology and economics. Chicago, Stanford, Virginia, North Carolina and Minnesota have councils of the Columbia type; somewhat similar organizations exist at Harvard, Tulane and Texas; Yale is launching an Institute of Human Relations, and other universities are planning to join this procession.

In short, economists in common with other students of social problems are realizing that to get the best results specialization and coöperation must walk hand in hand. Yet those who are most serious in this endeavor best realize how hard it is really to fuse the knowledge won by different groups. To make mutual understanding easier for our successors, we are introducing courses on social science at large into the high schools and colleges. The boys now being brought up on books which treat human geography, political institutions, social organization and economic activities as parts of a single subject should be free from some of the limitations which still hamper their teachers.

IV

The developments of the last twenty-five years in economics which seem to me most characteristic of the time are the developments I have been describing — expansion of the problems upon which investigators are working, and changes in the spirit and technique of treating problems. What has been happening meanwhile to economic "theory"? That strikes me as a rather outmoded question; but let me discuss it first in old-fashioned terms.

Since 1904 no systematic treatise upon economic theory has appeared which exercises an influence comparable to Marshall's *Principles of Economics*, to J. B. Clark's *Theory of Distribution*, or to Schmoller's *Volkswirtschaftslehre*. There have been significant treatises such as Pareto's *Manuel d'économie politique*, and Cassel's *Theory of Social Economy*, improving upon the mathematical theory of pricing which Walras started; von Wieser's *Theorie der gesellschaftlichen Wirtschaft*, a comprehensive presentation of marginal analysis; Schumpeter's *Theorie der wirtschaftlichen Entwicklung*, attributing economic change to the restless activities of a small class of imaginative innovators who leaven the inert mass of routineers; Pigou's *Economics of Welfare*, building upon the foundations laid by Marshall; Sombart's *Der moderne Kapitalismus*, painting upon a broad canvas the development and the workings of capitalistic institutions; Fetter's *Economics*, seeking to re-establish economic theory upon a sounder psychological basis; Davenport's *Economics of Enterprise*, confining economics to the theory of prices and seeking to get rid of psychology.

I might double this list of examples, and illustrate an even wider range of experimenting with different ways of systematising economics. Experimenting is the significant point, I think. In dealing with specific problems we are realizing the limitations of our older framework; the systematically inclined among us are trying out various methods of conceiving the subject as a whole; the rest of us are watching their efforts with varying degrees of attention, crossed by sympathy or scepticism, while absorbed primarily with problems of detail. There is no consensus of opinion that any of the types of theory suggested are wholly satisfactory or that any is futile. The German historical school seems to have collapsed largely for adventitious reasons, and Thorstein Veblen died in August, 1929, leaving no real successor. But surely there is no diminution of historical interest among economists — quite the contrary. So, too, the institutional approach to economic problems is adopted by many who suppose they are following the lead of common sense rather than the lead of Veblen.

A significant sign of the experimental temper of the time is the subsidence of controversy about the larger issues of economic theory. Turn over the old volumes of our technical journals and you will find them featuring papers dealing with methodology and fundamental concepts. Not so today. The acrimonious quarrel between Schmoller and Menger over the merits of deduction and induction, and the courteous exchanges between Clark and Böhm-Bawerk over the nature of capital, have few recent parallels. This slackening of doctrinal controversy is not a symptom of declining fervor; on the contrary, it seems to me that economists are more heartily interested in their work at present than they have been at any time since the generation of Malthus and Ricardo. The science has greater vitality and cherishes larger expectations than in the quarter century which closed in 1904. I think that we debate broad issues less, because increasing concern with factual observation is breeding in us a more scientific and a less dialectical temper. Also, we are rather bewildered by the multifarious extensions of our tasks, and scarcely know how to conceive of our science as a whole.

The generation to which I belong was brought up on some

system of economics — most of us on classical political economy as modernized by Marshall. We learned to draw a line between economic theory and applied economics. Supposedly, our central body of theory held together our wide-ranging studies in public finance, money and banking, agricultural problems, tariff problems, labor problems and the like. But now that the problems upon which we specialize have grown so numerous, now that each of them has been subdivided for more detailed inquiry, and now that we are so immersed in factual researches, we often feel, as said above, that the science is disintegrating. Frequently a specialist will say boldly that he gets little help from economic theory. Our monographs confirm that impression. Writers upon the money market seldom take their cues from Böhm-Bawerk's, Fisher's and Fetter's disquisitions upon the theory of interest. Writers upon labor problems do not often start their discussions of wage rates with the general theory of value and distribution. And when definite contact is made between factual investigations and economic theory, it is rather to test theory than to verify it. That change in wording from "verification" to "testing" is significant.

The declining authority of what still passes as economic theory *par excellence* over many of the factual investigators, its lessened prestige, is explained by doubts which are spreading concerning the scientific significance of what I have called the main sequence in the development of the subject. From Ricardo to Marshall our masters have explained how rational beings conduct themselves in seeking to minimize the sacrifices of labor and waiting, to maximize the satisfactions of consumption — or, rather, to maximize the net balance of satisfactions over sacrifices. Now the tacit assumption that men value goods according to the pleasures or the gratifications these goods will yield; that they work and save up to the points at which further effort or parsimony will impose pains just equal to the anticipated pleasures, has been vigorously challenged by a line of critics who knew how hedonism has fared at the hands of psychologists. More influential in discrediting the old assumptions has been the increasingly realistic work with concrete problems. The man who studies strikes and lockouts, the shifting fortunes of business combinations, modern methods of overcoming "consumer resistance," or business booms and depressions, does not confirm the impressions of human rationality conveyed by our theoretical treatises. Economists who find themselves working with political scientists are infected by skepticism of the average voter's intelligence. Those who consort with psychologists hear more about habits, conditional reflexes, action patterns, configurations, complexes — a score of fluctuating terms — than they hear about the felicific calculus, declining utility or curves of indifference. Those who deal with international problems find themselves ascribing potency to suspicions, rivalries, fears, hatreds and stupidities which do not yield to reason.

Granted the artificiality of old notions about "the springs of action," what shall we do to mend matters? That has been a puzzling question for economists.

One answer is to substitute a more modern brand of psychology for hedonism. Thus Schmoller gave a list of human instincts, just passing out of fashion in his prime, and proposed to work with them in explaining economic actions. More recently Fetter has offered "a quite new statement of the theory of value, one in accord with the modern volitional psychology." [5] Still later writers flirt with psychoanalysis upon occasion. The trouble with this solution is, of course, that psychology gives no finished answer to the question about human motives which the economist can borrow.

A second escape which has been tried is to throw psychology out of economics. In practice this means abandoning the theory

[5] *Economic Principles* (1915), Preface, ix.

of valuation, which has passed as the very cornerstone of the whole structure. That resort is recommended by Pareto, Davenport and Cassel, for example. These innovators hold that it is none of our concern, as economists, why people attach importance to commodities, or why they will not work or save beyond vague limits. All that economic theory needs as a foundation for its work are schedules of demand prices and supply prices — that is, supposedly objective statements of how many units of different commodities people will buy and sell at various prices within a given time and market. That sounds innocent enough until someone asks what justifies an economist in supposing that people have such schedules in their minds. If that question incites inquiry into the actual behavior of consumers, the psychological unreality of the whole assumption of definite demand schedules becomes uncomfortably clear. Nor is the theory of value the only part of our traditional doctrines which rests upon psychological premises. The whole structure is in the same precarious position. For one cannot reason about how men will behave without making tacit assumptions concerning human nature — and assumptions about human nature are psychological assumptions.

A third way of dealing with our quandary about psychology remains open. It is the one which I think economists find themthemselves taking in their current work — usually without thinking much about the significance of their procedure. The business of the economist is to gain understanding about a certain type of human activities. He does not need a set of preconceived or borrowed notions about the character of human motives for this undertaking, provided he takes human behavior as the problem to be studied. Instead of starting with a set of motives and showing how human beings thus constituted may be expected to act, he can inquire how actual men conduct themselves. Knowledge of current psychological viewpoints and methods improves his equipment for this task and safeguards him against making naïve errors; but he should not expect the psychologist to solve the riddle of economic behavior. The economist must himself contribute toward the understanding of human nature. Economic theory, thus conceived, becomes part and parcel of the social psychology which we are gradually developing through the coöperation of all the social sciences. And not of the social sciences alone; for all the sciences which deal with living matter and with man's environment have their contributions to offer.

This analysis of the changing attitude of economists toward their share in the problem of human nature suggests the way in which we seem most likely to work out a new framework for our science. That framework is quietly developing out of our studies of specific problems. In any growing science there is a continual give and take between system making and fact finding. Systematic ideas keep suggesting new relations, and new facts to be looked for; in turn, new facts as they are established confirm or modify systematic ideas. There are periods in which a system is elaborated which embraces and accounts for all the known phenomena in so consistent and comprehensive a fashion that factual research seems for the time being a hunt for further decimal places. There are other periods in which new factual discoveries discredit the systematic notions in vogue and call for radical reconstruction. Various schemes of organizing the materials old and new are tried; finally there emerges some system which serves the intellectual needs of the workers until they come upon more things in heaven and earth than are dreamed of in their philosophy — and so realize that they need a new system.

In economics we are now passing through one of these periods when factual investigations are straining the framework which is supposed to contain them. As already said, the work in business economics, in statistical laboratories, in realis-

tic studies of many kinds is being pushed forward with little
reference to the lines marked out by economic theories which
are themselves systematizations of an earlier and a less comprehensive body of factual knowledge. Our current monographs
contain within themselves, not only the data, but also the
tentative outlines of the new generalizations which will reorganize the science for further work. No one yet knows precisely
in what form this outline will crystallize; but I venture a sur-
mise, which may seem very quaint in twenty-five years more.

Years ago John Dewey pointed out the path on which all the
social sciences seem to be entering. In his Chicago days he was
preoccupied by the problem how we think. That was part of
the broader problem how men behave. In describing the rôle
of thought in practical life, Dewey revealed the rôle played
by other modes of acting. Also he made it clear that his inquiry
is one in which not only the philosopher and psychologist, but
also the educator and all the social scientists are engaged,
whether they realize the fact or not. Doubtless this philosophic
formulation of the proper study of mankind remained unknown to the vast majority of economists, political scientists,
sociologists and anthropologists. But what a prescient philosopher could glimpse a generation ago has grown clearer in the
course of experience. Many a worker in the social sciences has
discovered for himself that his technical problems of pricing,
constitutional law, imitation, kinship systems, or what not, are
really bits of the great problem of human behavior. Dewey
interprets to ourselves what we are doing in the social sciences,
much as Adam Smith showed his law-flouting generation that
they had been building up unwittingly a new economic polity.
Our adumbrations of what we are about explain that rapidly
expanding coöperation among the several social sciences of
which I have spoken. The Social Science Research Council on a
national scale, its counterparts within several universities, the
Encyclopaedia of the Social Sciences, Social Science Abstracts,

and the coöperative books of interpretation manifest a growing comprehension of common interests and a desire to become equipped through mutual learning for work on the common task.

What is true of the social sciences as wholes is true likewise of the numerous sets of specialties within each social science — economics among the rest. The fears that economics is disintegrating are well founded from the viewpoint of one who takes conventional economic theory to be the common bond. But if we think of economics as concerned with human behavior, all the specialists however schismatic, are enclosed within the fold. Studies of marketing, of personnel administration, of business cycles, of public-utility regulation, of any special problem in the long and shifting list, deal with some aspect of the mundane task of getting a living. Everyone who throws light upon these activities is contributing to economics — indeed, he is contributing to economic theory.

Thus the old distinction between economic theory as a peculiar avocation and the study of special problems is wearing thin, like the walls which shut off one social science from another. This does not mean that there is less specialization in current work than there used to be. Quite the contrary, the expansion of factual knowledge and the refinement of technical methods makes whatever problem a man feels drawn to a more exacting mistress. But in dealing with his special problem, however intensively, the man who grasps the modern view sees how the bit he is doing fits into the program as a whole. Thus specialization gains in significance, while coöperation among the specialists, like coöperation among the several social sciences, becomes easier.

The acceptance of this conception of economics as one of several sciences of human behavior does not lead to the rejection of any of the several types of theory now current. Rather, this conception unites, interprets and gives fresh meaning to these types. Obviously, institutional economics, such as Veblen stood for, has a conspicuous place in the study of human behavior. Widely current habits of thinking play a leading rôle in social activities; we must learn all we can about the cumulative changes which have brought these habits to their current form and about the trend of the further changes they are now undergoing. In the work of economic historians like Vladimir Simkhovitch, the fusion of history and economics is so thorough that one cannot separate the two. As economics becomes increasingly realistic, historical studies of the most varied sorts are absorbed into its working program. But the rationalizing type of work practiced by economists of the main sequence does not drop out. Among the most significant institutions of the current age are the highly elaborated habits of thinking about making and spending money. All of us acquire perforce something of these habits and in so doing we standardize and rationalize our behavior in some measure. Even as consumers, we count the costs of different goods offered for sale and make dim comparisons of benefits expected. In business we carry this rational scheme of control to a point which we often feel paradoxical — our absorption in the technical game may defeat the ends for which we suppose ourselves to be striving. The exploration of this rational aspect of social life is in no danger of suppression; rather it gains fascination when we see the part of life which the orthodox economist sketches in black and white, side by side with life as the modern novelist paints it with his lurid palette. There is a place in the behaviorist setting even for that most abstract type of economic speculation — the mathematical theory of general equilibrium. For our pecuniary institutions really make every price dependent upon every other price, directly or through devious and tenuous connections. It is important to explore these bonds which unite all prices in a system. If Henry L. Moore and his co-workers succeed in getting their equations

into a form which permits them to use statistical data, this
type of work will appeal to the most realistically minded
inquirer. For it, too, sheds light on social behavior.

Thus the constructive work of various schools of economic
theorists promises to combine harmoniously in the framework
which is becoming visible. Nor is the combination an eclectic
affair. On the contrary, each contribution gets whatever place
it can hold on its merits, as an aid to understanding social ways
of thinking and acting. That is a severe test, and doubtless
many of our traditional speculations will undergo considerable
revision in passing it. Imaginary experiments will still be made,
but more distinctly as steps toward understanding actual processes. The fiction of the static state will not lose all its usefulness, though men interested in human behavior will be eager
to find less roundabout and less cumbrous methods of attacking
their problems whenever possible. So too, the notion of equilibrium between opposing forces, and the method of variations
appropriate to it, are not likely to disappear wholly from
economic analysis; but they will be used with a keener sense of
their limitations. Human behavior is such a complicated affair
that those who seek to understand it can ill dispense with any
line of attack.

The parts of our past work which have poor prospects of
survival are the negative parts — the attempts to prove that
there is no value or no place in economics for methods and
results which differ widely from one's own. The men who
prefer some single line of work will have a clearer view of the
value of what their colleagues with different interests are doing
as they come to understand better the bearing of their own
contributions. For example, the critics who have said that,
whatever else it may be, Veblen's analysis of institutions is not
economic theory are right when economic theory deals with
the way in which a general equilibrium is attained between
marginal sacrifices and marginal satisfactions. People who

think of economic theory as dealing with human behavior in getting a living will take no such exclusive stand. Nor does the effort to read the theory of value out of economics fit into the new perspective. Certainly the question how men have come to attach such varying scales of importance to different commodities and different activities in successive generations is one of the problems which must intrigue the student of economic behavior. Contemporary aspects of that problem keep thrusting themselves forward. How does an advertiser influence willingness to buy? How do new products find their way into the standard of living? What reactions do the demands which develop produce upon the old demands? These and the similar questions I might put are questions which realistic students of the present day must face, and such questions concern social processes of valuation. It is vain to tell one of our colleagues who teaches marketing in the School of Commerce that these problems lie outside the pale of economics; that in touching them he is trenching upon psychology which he is not licensed to practice. You will not shake his confidence that he may learn something about the behavior of consumers which is not in the books on psychology and which belongs in books on economics. But when we recognize that all of us are working at problems of human behavior, who will raise such issues? The decline of controversies on doctrinal issues is quite in line with the gradual emergence of the behavioristic conception and is likely to persist as that conception gains ground.

All this talk about the future framework of economics is speculation. In the nature of things, it must be colored by my personal equation. I see what I take to be tangible evidences of the movement, and in many quarters. Yet there are economists who would challenge my forecasts. There are others who would say that the conception of economics as a science of behavior is too vague to give us guidance, whereas my expectation is that it will prove a vigorous organizer of working programs. In view of these differences of opinion, you will do well to take this part of my lecture with caution. One thing, however, admits of little doubt. Economics is developing its old problems, attacking its new problems, improving its technique and widening its alliances with vigor. If we do not reorganize the framework of our science as we move forward, it will be because the scheme excogitated by our predecessors proves more adaptable to changing needs than many of us now venture to believe.

SOCIOLOGY

ROBERT M. MACIVER

There is always a fascination in the exploration of a new territory, the penetration into new regions which the eye or the mind of man has never surveyed before. To certain bold and adventurous spirits of the nineteenth century it came as a revelation that the things most near to us, human nature itself and the human society which it unknowingly creates, remained, from the point of view of the scientific explorer, practically virgin lands. So the pioneers of psychology and of sociology went forth on their allied missions. They brought back maps of their territories which already are beginning to remind us of the symmetrically simple charts in which the discoveries of Cartier and Champlain were presented to their generations. For the days of these pioneers, to whom all honor is due, are past. Nothing is ever so simple in reality as it is to our forerunning imagination. It is one thing to discover the land, another to possess it, and the latter is an unending task. There are swamps and deserts and mountain barriers. There are unrealized obstacles and unexpected defeats as well as triumphs. In the last twenty-five years sociology has been seeking to gain possession of its territory. It has learned something of the difficulty and the magnitude of its enterprise. It has made gains but it has also lost assurance of some of the gains which it formerly claimed. In the devious way so characteristic of human endeavor, sometimes advancing prematurely and sometimes unduly retreating, it has nevertheless made perceptible and definable progress. The main directions of its efforts during this period, the nature of its gains and, so far as one observer can evaluate them, also of its shortcomings — these form the subject of the present review.

During this period new light has been thrown on many of the specific subjects and problems in which sociology is interested. If one were to enumerate the investigations which have added to our knowledge of various aspects of society it would make an excellent showing. But I propose to follow another road. I shall be concerned with sociology as a whole, with its claim to be a distinctive science, with its endeavor to create a systematic body of knowledge, with its purposes and with its methods, with its central problems, with its doubts, and with its pathfinding achievements. How far has the claim of sociology to be an integral science been substantiated since the beginning of the twentieth century? This is the more controversial question which I shall seek to answer. But in seeking to answer it I would ask the reader not to forget the more limited but more indisputable achievements of a thousand patient investigators. Whatever conclusion we come to touching sociology as a science we must surely admit this much, that it has uncovered much interesting and useful information about institutions and organizations, about crowds and social classes, about nations and races, about the family, about processes of social assimilation and conflict, about the movements of population, about rural communities and urban communities, about custom and fashion, about delinquency and crime. I am tempted to proceed with this catalogue and to mention the names of many good and true workers in these fields. But to dwell on individual contributions in particular fields would be more apt to vindicate the work of sociologists than to justify the claim of sociology. This must be my excuse for omitting, within the short space available, many promising and worth-while achievements and confining our attention to the broader issues involved.

In so doing we shall have to submit to a further limitation.

Sociology, in its youthful endeavors to find its place among the sciences, is still so far from being a catholic and unified discipline that it finds very different interpretations in different lands. It is not yet international. It still tends to mean one thing in Germany, another in France, something different in England and in Italy and in Russia, while again in the United States it follows a distinctive road. A partial explanation may be found in the fact that in most of these countries the number of professed sociologists is very small, and that therefore the particular approach and the particular interest of one or two leading representatives in each determines the character of the contribution of a whole country. At the same time the lack of an international basis indicates a defect from which in truth the other social sciences are by no means wholly free. It is rather sociology than society which means one thing in Germany and another in the United States. The indication is that sociology has not yet firmly established that definite body of principles, that common ground of ordered knowledge, which in every science is independent of the divergent interests of its various practitioners. The problem can be set most sharply if we center our interest on the two countries which have done most in the latest period to develop the subject, the countries in which the most intensive struggles are being fought around the standard of sociology. These are Germany and the United States. The reasons for this choice will be best seen if we premise our comparison of the developing estates of sociology in these countries with a brief survey of the situation elsewhere.

We shall take England as our first example of a country in which the paucity of academic recognition has thrown upon the shoulders of two or three men the burden both of interpreting a youthful science and of vindicating its *bona-fides*. Under these conditions a whole subject is judged by the quality of a handful of exponents so that the inadequacies of even one of them are reckoned against the subject he represents, a kind of

test to which fortunately no representative of the more sea-
soned sciences is exposed. The latter borrows prestige from his
subject, the former must lend to his such prestige as he himself
can muster. In England during our period sociology has meant
the kind of thing that L. T. Hobhouse and Graham Wallas
were doing. There were contributions made to sociology by
men whose main work lay in other fields, such as the anthropologist Edward Westermarck, the psychologist William Mc-
Dougall, the economist J. A. Hobson, and the biologist and
erratic genius Patrick Geddes. But it was Hobhouse and Wallas who stood for sociology, and, so far as two solitary men
could, they made a valiant and distinguished stand. Wallas was
a shrewd and sympathetic observer rather than a systematic
scientist. His chief constructive effort was the book entitled
The Great Society, but he was more happy in presenting the
problem of the adjustment of human nature to the sociological
and technological conditions of urban and industrial life than
in formulating a solution of that problem or more generally in
building up a coherent body of doctrine or an orderly arrangement of sociological facts. His most characteristic contribution was expressed in the phrase "balked dispositions," meaning
thereby the drives or "instincts" of human nature which in the
process of long ages were accommodated biologically and
socially to conditions of life alien to those of the "great
society." There are hypotheses underlying this interesting
theory which Wallas never had the opportunity or the scientific
equipment to investigate. He was more interested to follow
up his open-minded observations by practical suggestions
than to carry forward either theoretical construction or elaborate investigation. In this respect he differed greatly from his
companion in arms, Hobhouse, who was a large-scale system-
builder.

The main interest of Hobhouse was in a broad evolutionary
synthesis. It was not so much the evolution of social institutions

themselves which concerned him, but the correlation between the growth of mind and the growth of society. Interrupted as it may be by historical vicissitudes and by temporary necessities, such as the sacrifice of freedom in the expansion of efficiency, there is nevertheless a large harmony between the demands of emergent mind and the conditions of what Wallas called the great society. There are manifold aspects of the development of life and though one may advance beyond another and even for the time at the expense of another, nevertheless they belong together, and in the historical process they reveal, in part at least, their essential harmony. In principle they are elements in an organic unity. The scale of society, the efficiency of its control over inner conditions and over outer nature, the degree in which through coöperative activity it satisfies the various needs of its members, and the degree in which it provides opportunity and stimulus for personal liberty and individual fulfilment — these aspects are not only reconcilable but in the long run they are interdependent. Hobhouse is sometimes accused of being more a philosopher than a sociologist, especially by those American sociologists who regard philosophy as the last refuge of the scientifically incompetent. Philosophy seems to mean, when used as a term of abuse, the tendency to theorize without adequate regard for facts, though the chief sinners in that respect are called practical men and not philosophers. At any rate Hobhouse was deeply interested in learning the truth of things. As his former pupil Dr. Ginsberg has pointed out, "Hobhouse has sought to consolidate his position by painstaking and detailed study of a very wide range of facts; and he was ever ready to revise his views in the light of advancing knowledge." [1] It is true that he did not do much in the way of actual research, in the sense of gathering new facts; but the architect of a building cannot spend all his time cutting stones, and in a science we need the

[1] Article in the *Journal of Philosophical Studies*. October, 1929.

architect as well as the stone-mason. There were no doubt some defects in his system. He did not distinguish clearly enough the ethical principle of progress from the scientific principle of evolution. His desire for synthesis sometimes outran his power of analysis. He was more skilful in revealing the concomitance or correlation of factors than in dealing with the more difficult problem of causal relationship. But to those who envisage sociology as a coherent science which shall bring order to the bewildering array of social facts his work is both stimulating and illuminating.

We cross next from England to France. On the whole France has been more receptive to sociology. In England it would scarcely have existed academically had it not been for an endowment given for the purpose to the University of London. In England sociology can scarcely be said to have developed any "schools" or sects. Hobhouse has at least one valiant successor in Morris Ginsberg and there is a rudimentary group of regional sociologists, inspired by Patrick Geddes, of a somewhat temperamental and somewhat amateurish character. But in France sociology has both traditions and schools. France has strong claims to be the birthplace of sociology. Its interest in regional or geographical sociology may be traced back beyond Le Play to Montesquieu and exhibits a strong continuity right up to the present. The tradition of Comte, though much modified, may still be discovered in the approach of Durkheim and Levy-Bruhl, of Hubert and Mauss. For these later thinkers also believe in sharply contrasting stages of social development, regarding primitive mentality as being differently constituted from that of civilized man. The subtle distinction which they draw between the "collective representations" of the primitive group and the individualized conceptions of modern man is far from being established and may have led along a false trail, though it has stimulated some valuable investigations, particularly in the study of early customs and early forms of religion. It is closely associated also with the French interest in social psychology, represented by the school of Tarde and Le Bon. Another related group is composed of the writers who have sought to discover the principle of social solidarity, including Fouillée, Bourgeois, Hauriou, Gide, and Bouglé. There is no doubt, therefore, that France is richly supplied with schools of sociological thought. But these schools were well established by the commencement of our period. They have revealed no large development in the past quarter century. Solid work has been done by the regional sociologists, and a group of social geographers, led by Brunhes and Vidal de la Blache, has applied their principles on a more extensive scale. An occasional brilliant or original contribution has helped to sustain the faith of the more theoretical schools, such as Halbwachs' *Les Cadres sociaux de la mémoire*, in which the doctrine of a social structure of memory is expounded. But it is from other sources that the newer currents have flowed into the main stream of sociology and since it is these we are in search of we must pass on.

In the earlier part of our period Italy exhibited a ferment of sociological thinking which promised to contribute much to the development of the science. That promise is less in evidence at the present day. The social sciences — and this is peculiarly true of sociology — cannot prosper within a governmental structure which forbids the free play of critical discussion. Under such conditions it reverts to dogmatic ideologies. Before this situation arose at least one outstanding Italian sociologist made his appearance, though his own teaching happened to be largely in accord with the now official sociology of the new Italian régime. Pareto is the cool anatomist of society, penetrating beyond our rationalizations to those original drives of human nature which in his rather uncouth phraseology he names "residues." Pareto is eminently a social dissector, a keen and ruthless analyst. He is always seeking to discover the motivations that lie beneath our social conformities and social conflicts, tracing them back to certain isolable "dispositions" which are native to humanity and which exhibit themselves through a thousand guises. In this he shows his kinship to a school of social psychologists which has representatives in many lands and whose viewpoint is characteristic of an age rather than of a country. But Pareto carries out his principle with unusual thoroughness and with a cogency of illustration and of application which sets him apart. One result is that he suffers gravely from the defects of his qualities. Not only does he decry all evaluations as pernicious to the business of the social scientist but he is scornful of the evaluations which are themselves part of his data, the evaluations which are built into and around social institutions and relationships.

Pareto's seeming absence of temper is itself a temper. It is not scientific to be contemptuous of ingredients in the object you are studying. A contrary dogmatism, that of the mechanist, easily creeps in. This is perhaps noticeable in his famous doctrine of the "circulation of the élites," in which he explains the succession of aristocracies and maintains that the strength of each is a factor of its overbearing display of forcefulness. His refusal to recognize the trends of social evolution and his resort to a barren cyclical theory afford other examples of his dogmatism. His atomistic conception of society is in keeping with his hard quantitative formulations but it reveals its inadequacy at many points, and especially when he deals with the problems of social solidarity and social process. He expresses to the full an important tendency of the age, and his main treatise has been very influential since it first appeared in 1915.

But we cannot linger over it in this cursory survey. We must proceed to those countries which are in the forefront of sociological activity. For reasons already suggested Italy is no longer one of these. If we carried further our process of elimination we would discover that the countries which at the present are of central interest to the sociologist are Germany and the United States. The conditions of the two are in some respects extremely dissimilar. The degree of recognition given to sociology in the academic system is very different in the two countries. The content of the subject, the whole method and approach, are curiously disparate. Yet each is astir with sociological interest, and a comparison of the two will reveal, perhaps better than any other treatment, the existing position of sociology, its recent advances and its present perplexities.

The contrast between American and German sociology at the present time is certainly more obvious than the resemblance. In saying so we are leaving out of account an occasional heretic in either country who has crossed over into the intellectual camp of the other. In Germany, for example, von Wiese and his Cologne disciples exhibit an affinity to American procedures, but they are certainly not typical of German sociology nor are their contributions as yet substantive or particularly important, except as revealing an element of revolt against the dominant trend. It might be maintained that one thing which American and German sociologists have in common is a preoccupation with method. But method means an entirely different thing to American and to German investigators. To the American, method means preëminently research technique, a device for collecting, recording, sorting, classifying, tabulating or counting facts. To the German, method is a principle in terms of which he arranges facts in categories, determines the relation of the categories to one another, analyses a social situation or a large-scale social movement into its essential factors, and offers a synthetic interpretation to the world. In a word, the American is eager for new facts and new verifications, whereas the German seeks new formulations and new thought-constructions. It is not that the German is careless of facts; it is certainly not that he is less thorough. It is that his main objective is different. His voyage of exploration seeks the far horizon of new principles whereas the American does coasting voyages from facts to facts. Consequently, the German is often more preoccupied with the interpretation of old facts than with the discovery of new ones, while the American is often so keen for new facts that he is apt to neglect the established ones. The latter reveals a kind of pioneer spirit in scholarship, working always at the thin line between the cultivated land and the waste, with less interest in the work remaining to be done in the richer fields already explored. American sociologists end where statistics end, and there, one is tempted to say, is just where German sociologists begin. The American makes little use of the work of his predecessors; he likes to start afresh on the raw material, borrowing nothing from his school but his techniques, his tools. The German makes the constructions of his predecessors the starting point of his own work and proceeds to develop and reconstruct them. The American plunges *in medias res*, he conceives his task as a definite project of fact-finding, on which he forthwith embarks. He begins with questionnaires and ends with Hollerith machines. The German has many preliminaries concerning the nature of his project and his approach to it, how it differs from other projects and how it is related to other approaches. He likes to survey his problem from many angles before attacking it. He likes to trace his subject back to the fertilized egg — or beyond it — for he is apt to ponder over the Kantian question, so meaningless to the pragmatic American: "How is sociology possible?" If you asked representative American and German sociologists what the fundamental problems of their science are, they would answer in utterly different terms. In fact, many of the replies which German sociologists actually make to this question would, to us on this side of the Atlantic, seem to be problems that generally need not concern us at all.

One very significant difference between the typical German

and the typical American approach is that the latter rests on the assumption that there are or should be no important methodological differences between the social and the physical sciences. In the recent composite volume *Trends in American Sociology* one of the authors, Professor Read Bain, sets down first among the propositions which according to him represent "the outstanding lines of development in American sociology" the following statement: "Sociology is a natural science." This may not be so innocent a proposition as it sounds, and I shall return to the significance of it at a later stage. But it is certainly characteristic of the more recent attitude within the country. It is in harmony with the pragmatic, behavioristic and mechanistic color of our thinking. We like to externalize our subject matter because we like to measure it, and we like to measure it because we like to externalize it. We like to define the subjective in objective terms, to define an attitude, say, as the "set of the organism." Whether such defining makes the object any clearer is another story. For my own part I think I understand the term "attitude" much more than I understand the phrase, "set of the organism." However that may be, the endeavor to approximate the social to the natural sciences prevails mightily among us. The German, on the other hand, seeks to bring out the distinction between them and to cultivate for the social sciences a methodology correspondent to the nature of the distinctive material with which they deal. He is apt to maintain that a different mode of interpretation is essential, that there are two types of knowledge, one relating to the external objects of perception, the objects of the natural sciences, the other relating to the phenomena of consciousness, including the phenomena of the social sciences. In contrast to the proposition I have just quoted one might set the following statement from some lectures by Franz Oppenheimer on the trends of recent German sociology: "I regard it as utterly essential to discriminate as sharply as possible between the mechanistic procedure of the natural and mathematical sciences and what may be called the psychological procedure, if we are to avoid the logical fallacy of confounding their respective limits." [2] The conflict between these two points of view is perhaps the most significant of all the issues which sociology has to face at the present day.

Enough has perhaps been said to show the marked contrasts between the prevailing attitudes — I refuse to say "sets of the organism" — of American and of German sociologists. I am well aware that the summary characterizations I have given are subject to exception and to qualification. I want therefore to take these two important developments in turn, to examine the general character and direction of the contributions to sociology made in the two countries in recent times. In spite of the antithesis they exhibit, possibly because of it, the next advance of sociology may well depend on the acceptance by each of the gifts which the other can offer.

Sociology in Germany is the offspring of a union between history and philosophy. The earliest child of that union, called the philosophy of history, was of doubtful legitimacy, and indeed there are some who still express their doubts regarding the more recent arrival. That, however, does not prevent it from showing signs of vigor and of growth. German scholarship has been fond of broad historical surveys, and it has also been fond of the application of logical and philosophical categories to the multiplicity of historical phenomena. In the course of these applications it was inevitable that sociological problems, such as the relation of social to cultural phenomena, should emerge. Problems of relationship between social and other historically given aspects inevitably led to investigations into the nature and forms of society itself, and so sociology was born. The sociological thinkers of Germany are still today, as they have been in the past, men who have been led to the

[2] *Richtungen der neueren deutschen Soziologie* (1928).

subject from the special social sciences or from history or from philosophy or some other field. Oppenheimer came from the study of medicine, Sombart and Max Weber from economics, Kelsen from jurisprudence, Troeltsch from history, Vierkandt from anthropology, Scheler from philosophy, and so on. Students do not, as often in America, specialize in sociology from an early stage of their academic career. This outside preparation has not been without its advantages, as helping to give a broader basis to sociology study. It has fostered the contrast between German and American sociology which we have been pointing out.

The main problem to which German sociology has addressed itself was sharply revealed in the writings of Karl Marx. He was responsible too for a certain philosophy of history, the famous doctrine of economic determinism. In his interpretation of the historical process he had reversed the order of causality proclaimed by his master Hegel. To Hegel, history was the unfolding of a great creative design, of the immanent spirit of humanity seeking and finding more and more appropriate embodiment in the structure of society. The forms and processes of production, the relation of the producers to the economic instruments of production, the system in accordance with which land was owned and capital exploited, these were for Marx the essential determinants of the cultural phenomena, of the religion and philosophy and art which Hegel had regarded as the proud free revelation of the reason that is in man. For Hegel, spirit (*Geist*) was the overlord of life. For Marx, "things were in the saddle and rode mankind." By this drastic reversal was the problem set for the thinkers that were to follow. Could one, by scientific investigation, decide between Hegel and Marx? Was either interpretation adequate? Were they both one-sided? It was possible to elaborate impressive ideologies on the lines of either Hegel or Marx, as Spengler did on the one hand and the communist philosophers on the other. It was possible to build whole sociologies on a racial or on an environmental theory of causation. But how shall we decide between them?

A new method was called for, a scientific method to determine the order of social change and to deal with the baffling question of causation in the social process. To the leading German thinkers it seemed a necessary step towards the solution of this problem to distinguish between the sciences of nature and the sciences of man, including in the latter the study of culture and the study of society. Social and cultural forms are in a definite intelligible sense the creation of the human consciousness, and therefore a kind of causality is involved which the natural sciences have no need for, which in fact they must reject if they are to follow objective methods of observation and experiment. But this kind of causality, the activity of the mind aware at once of an outer environment and an inner need, is imminent in the very material of the cultural sciences. It is presented to us in our own experience and it alone enables us to understand the experience of others. It gives to social facts a meaning which physical facts do not reveal. The precondition of German sociology is thus the distinction between the natural and the social or cultural sciences. The road for it was prepared by the writers who, like Dilthey and Husserl and Rickert, developed this distinction. Following this road, Max Weber defined social behaviour as meaningful activity directed towards the meaningful activity of others and thus creating social relationships. It is something not merely to be described in naturalistic terms but to be understood in terms of experience. Following the same road Vierkandt went still further and roundly declared that the business of sociology was the contemplation and analysis of the inner experience of social beings, of the mental relationships which are understood not by observation of the external phenomena of behaviour, not by induction, but by the sheer insight which the mind achieves of the springs of action in other minds. Vierkandt represents the extreme left wing of the German position. He stands at the opposite pole from the prevailing American position. He exposes himself to certain obvious criticisms, though there may still be a core of truth in his insistence on the supreme necessity of insight for the interpretation of social relationships. It is eminently dangerous to slight induction as he does, but on the other hand it is worth pointing out that the most assiduous correlator and fact collector may miss the vital nexus of his facts if he lacks the insight and the direct experience which enables him to penetrate to the motivations of conduct. In fact, sociology demands so wide an experience and so broad an understanding for an effective attack upon its problems that the provision of the appropriate training for students of the subject is beset with unusual difficulty. No laboratory can ever alone supply it.

Having made the distinction between the natural and the social sciences, the Germans sought to delimit the sphere of sociology proper. With their flair for categories it was for them a congenial task to reduce to order and system the multifarious forms and processes of social phenomena. An important step was taken by Tönnies when he drew the illuminating distinction between community (*Gemeinschaft*) and society or social organization (*Gesellschaft*), the spontaneous solidarity of the natural grouping on the one hand and the deliberately created contractual association on the other. But it was Simmel who most rigorously marked out for sociology a province of its own. For him, its distinctive subject matter was the generic forms of social relationship and social situation. His anxiety to assert the claims of sociology to be an independent science led him to stress its concern with pure or abstract forms. Economics for example, studies the operation of competition in the market place, while sociology studies competition as such, a form of social relationship which occurs under every aspect of society. Politics studies the superiority and subordination which is associated with political government, while sociology is interested in these as universal phenomena of social life. Simmel displayed great ingenuity in the analysis of these common forms, but his assumption that the common quality of form must, or should be, examined apart from the special embodiments was logically unnecessary, and proved practically unworkable. The subject-matter of sociology cannot be fenced off in such a manner, whether or not we regard it as a generic or a specific science. None of the sciences of man, whether anthropology or economics or politics or history or psychology or sociology, can stake its peculiar claim over a whole area of phenomena and serve notice that "trespassers will be prosecuted." It is in the last resort the interest, the range, the approach, the focus of investigation which must differentiate between them, for they must all deal with aspects or syntheses of the unity of human nature and of the solidarity of society. The work of Simmel was the origin of great disputations which did little to advance the substance of sociology. Perhaps if Simmel had more clearly realized, as Max Weber did after him, that the common is not divorced from its particulars, that the type contains the varieties of the type, and the one includes the many, much needless debate would have been avoided.

We must not, however, give the impression that German sociology has been exclusively preoccupied with questions of orientation. The discussion of these questions was of value as revealing the nature of some of its major tasks, and to these, especially to the Marxian problem of the causality of social change and the interpretation of social evolution, the more recent sociologists have addressed themselves with fine penetration. In our brief compass we cannot recount or assess their work in this field. A mere reference or two must suffice to suggest the character of their achievements. Sombart illuminated with much mastery of his rich historical material the

social conditions and concomitants of the coming of capitalism.
Max Weber showed another side of the process, the complex
interaction of religious and social changes. In his fine work on
the sociology of religion he brought out the affinity between
the quality of protestantism and the kind of discipline demanded by capitalism. When, for example, Benjamin Franklin
wrote in 1736 a little work entitled *Necessary Hints to Those
Who Would Be Rich*, he proclaimed with quintessential clarity
those hardy virtues of industrious frugality which fostered the
growth of capitalism and were no less in accord with the
world outlook of protestantism. Time is money and money is
fruitful; be thrifty, upright, and a good accountant; act so that
your credit is good; let your creditor hear the sound of your
hammer at five in the morning or eight at night — that will
comfort him more than the sound of your voice singing in the
tavern. Such are the maxims on which capitalism flourishes and
they are the practical applications of the protestant spirit.
Weber shows accordingly how protestantism prepared the
way for capitalism as well as stimulated its growth. This was
part of his great survey of the religions of the west and of the
east, in which he undertook to show not only the interdependence of religious and other social factors but also the specific
contribution of religious ethics in the formation and maintenance of various types of social order. Religious and other
cultural expressions are not, as Marx claimed, merely reflections of the economic order, they are formative influences and
their operation can be traced within the causal scheme of which
any given phenomenon or set of phenomena is a resultant.
Weber was not the only German thinker who helped to clarify
the relation of religion to the whole social situation. Of the
others Troeltsch, for his interpretation of the social doctrines
of the various Christian churches, must specially be mentioned.

The sustained attack made by the Germans on the fundamental problems of sociology is well revealed in the work of

Scheler, Mannheim and Alfred Weber. Faced with the baffling complex of interactive factors in the social process they
addressed themselves particularly to the analysis of the main
lines and streams of tendency within it and to the discovery
of the relations within a whole situation of environmental,
economic, technical, cultural and other factors. Of their various
contributions the one which appeals most to the present writer
is that of Alfred Weber, perhaps for the reason that before
making acquaintance with the formulations of Weber he had
felt the necessity for working along similar lines. Alfred Weber
distinguishes three main processes in the incessant movement
of society. In the first place there are always at work the
innate or essential drives of human nature itself, determining
under the conditions of a particular natural environment,
geographical and climatic, the basic social structure, the elemental system of economic, political, sexual and kinship relationships. This Alfred Weber calls preëminently the "social
process." In the second place there are the techniques, the
utilitarian applications of science, the forms of practical organization, the whole apparatus by which men seek to control
nature and serve their ends. The changes within this system
he calls "the process of civilization." Thirdly, there are the
creative expressions of the human spirit, the fine arts, the
standards of values, the interpretations revealed in philosophies and religions. These together form a distinctive historical
stream which Alfred Weber calls "the movement of culture."
Culture so defined has principles and qualities different from
those of civilization and, though indissolubly bound up with
the latter, is not subject to the same process of cumulation.
To discover the intricate relations of the three great strands
in the web of history is the chief task to which Alfred Weber
has devoted himself. In the accomplishment of this task we get
beyond the one-sided causality both of Hegel and of Marx,
and as we discern in any historical phase the manner in which

the social structure is bound up with the processes both of civilization and of culture the foundations are being laid for a systematic sociology.

This all too cursory survey must here suffice to show the main trend of sociological enquiry in Germany. A fuller picture would include the development of research institutes, the prosecution of social-psychological studies of the phenomena of classes, crowds and other social groupings, and the appearance of various divergent tendencies from the dominant ones on which we have dwelt. On the whole German sociology has been engrossed in the problems of systematization and of methodology. Although notable results have been attained we may feel that there has been excessive argument and dispute over approach and method, that some of the questions much debated — whether, for example, sociology is a generic or a specific social science — are either barren or solve themselves as definite investigations proceed within the field. We may feel that at times scholarship degenerates into scholasticism. These are the defects of the qualities which German sociology has revealed, but both the qualities and the defects provide an instructive contrast to the situation of sociology in America. To this situation we now turn.

A remarkable change has befallen American sociology since the early years of the twentieth century. A movement of revolt, if not of revolution, has gathered headway, mainly an uprising of a younger generation against the ways of an older. It is an iconoclastic movement, a critical break with the past rather than a critical development of its work. This new departure of American sociology is itself a very interesting sociological phenomenon. It is in large measure an expression within the scientific field of attitudes which for long have been characteristic of American life. Sociology is obviously a peculiarly favorable field for the expression of these attitudes, not only because its subject-matter is society but also because, being a

new subject without any body of traditions behind it, it was the
more free to follow the bent of its exponents. Moreover,
sociology as an academic study found its chief expansion in the
less traditionally minded colleges of the West and the Middle
West, which good authorities declare to be the genuine America, the center of its indigenous forces. Be that as it may, the
rapid spread of sociological teaching in the West certainly has
fostered the autonomous development of the subject on this
side of the Atlantic. Twenty-five years ago American sociology
was still colored by the teaching of Lester Ward, who owed
his inspiration to Herbert Spencer and other European sources.
It was an optimistic application to society of the evolutionary
biology of the nineteenth century. Society was a social organism, evolving through its own coöperative activities to a higher
perfection. The end was as clear as the means, so that social
theory and practical diagnosis went safely hand in hand. The
grand scheme of things was unfolded, and there was no dubiety
in the design.

Such was the general situation of sociology until presently
another upstart science, psychology, began to ask disturbing
questions, began to throw doubts on the rationality and the
simplicity of the human mind, began to explain conduct in
terms of bodily functions, interpreting its manifestations by
reference to glands and conditioned references instead of to
ideals, began even, through its more philosophical exponents,
to doubt the very possibility of the attainment of universal
truth or else to define truth as a formulation that works here
and now but is not the same to-day, yesterday and forever. As
these questions grew more insistent, the dominant rôle formerly played by evolutionary biology was assumed by the new
psychology, with its dislike of introspection, with its love of
experiment and measurement and with its increasingly behavioristic temper. No other influence has in my opinion been so
important for the explanation of the character of recent

American sociology as that of the psychological schools of the country. Sociology has in fact become largely social psychology. It has turned away from the study of social institutions, from the investigation of the source implications of religion and ethics, from the use of historical data, from the formulation of broad principles. It has been insisting more and more on concrete studies of adjustment and maladjustment, on the collection of the facts of behavior revealed within given social situations, on the relation between the group phenomena characteristic of particular urban and rural areas and the environmental conditions, on the descriptive exposition of social changes based on statistical enquiry. Accepting from the physical sciences the conviction that the knowable is also the measurable, it proclaims, through the majority of its younger investigators, the supremacy of the quantitative approach.

The result has been the impression on American sociology of an excellent realism. There is no doubt that its feet are on the ground. Through individual and coöperative research, backed by the resources of the various foundations, it has discovered, sorted and correlated an extensive and impressive array of evidences regarding social behaviour. Impatient of theories, it has been diligent in the scrutiny and the verification of facts. It has searched the highways and the hedges. It has studied the hobo and the gangster, the delinquent and the criminal, the pioneer and the peasant, the immigrant of every nationality, each in his social habitat. It has dissected Pittsburgh and Chicago, "Middletown" and the prairie settlement. It has investigated the family and the school, the "culture area" and the geographical region. It has shown a practical interest in the problems of population and of public health, of heredity and of mental hygiene, of poverty, of child welfare, of recreation, carrying out specialized researches in all of these fields. Our knowledge of society has been greatly enriched by these diligent and careful enquiries, and the complexities of social phenomena have been more fully revealed. Behind the attitude of observation and experimentation which they represent there lay a sense of revulsion against the theological and the wholesale reformist dogmas which seemed to infect the earlier American sociology.

On the whole, American sociology had been more subjected to these influences making for quantitative and inductive study than that of Europe, and this fact may help to explain its present tendency to abandon theory altogether. It was necessary to clear the ground, to start afresh, to find scientific salvation, to cling to the facts without predilection, to endeavour to see things as they are without hypothesis as well as without prejudice. The quantitative method seemed most of all to be devoid of bias. Where you deal with qualities you admit some kind of evaluation, and there lay danger. But there is no sentiment about weights and measures, and the adding machine tells you nothing but the truth. So intelligence had to be stated in percentages and attitudes had to be measured along a line. And if consciousness and purpose and all such intangibles resisted our conscious, purposeful, efforts to reduce them to measurable and directly observable phenomena, then we must not, as scientists, talk about them any more. This was the *reductio ad absurdum* at which the extreme behaviorists arrived, but even the behaviorists, though their services have been rather expensive, have made their contribution to the common cause — they have cleared many eyes of the superstition which prevented them from seeing human beings except through the mist of ancient prejudices.

The most distinctive school which has developed under the above-mentioned conditions names itself the "ecological," with its headquarters in Chicago. Ecology in this reference has been defined as "the science of the changing spatial relations of human beings and human institutions." Strictly considered, the spatial area denotes a field of study rather than a mode of study. The locality or the geographical region has been found since the days of Montesquieu or Le Play a convenient basis for social investigation, and it was admirably used for this purpose by the school of Demolins. The chief contribution of the Chicago school has been the detailed descriptive study of particular urban areas and urban types, given by Park, Burgess, Thrasher, Shaw, Zorbaugh, Anderson, and others. The study of rural areas on the same lines is less developed, though interesting researches have been made by Galpin, Kolb, Taylor, Zimmerman and others. We may perhaps include in the same general category the impressive work of Thomas and Znaniecki, *The Polish Peasant*. What is characteristic of all the "ecologists" is that they seek to reveal and illustrate certain social processes which are relative to an environment, though not necessarily a physical one, such as accommodation and assimilation, together with the conflicts and maladjustments that may be involved. It is obvious that the mobility of American life provides excellent material and opportunity for such studies, and good advantage has been taken of them. On the other hand the whole ecological approach is faced with a critical problem as soon as it passes from description to explanation, and here the weakness on the side of theory of present-day American sociology begins to show itself. Can we interpret as well as describe social phenomena in terms of locality? It is undoubtedly a fact of interest, for example, that delinquency rates traced along radiating lines outwards from the Chicago "loop" show a graduated decline, but since locality is a bracket including economic, occupational, national and other selective factors we want some organon for assessing the causal relationship of these factors to the phenomenon in question. This, after all, is the primary scientific problem, and as I shall show presently it is here that the quantitative method fails us. In the whole intricate complex of factors what rôle can we assign to environment, to geographical or social habitat?

The urgency of this question, engrossing to German sociologists but so far neglected by our American schools, is seen when another group appears on the scene, the "culture area" group with its anthropological antecedents, and practically denies the causal significance of the geographical environment. The recent advocacy of the "cultural approach" is to be welcomed, for it brings again to the front this fundamental problem of the interpretation of social change and the validity of the principle of social evolution. So far, however, the adherents of the school have scarcely realized the implications of their position. There is no time to dwell on this point but two comments may be made in passing. In the first place we must distinguish the study of culture as such from the study of society. What the sociologist wants primarily to know is the relation of a given culture to the social organization within which it falls, the relation of cultural change to social change. It has been easy to say to the classical answers to this question that they are inadequate and one-sided, that they contain only a part of the truth. But we seek to know what part of the truth? We talk of the social importance of invention and of the rôle of diffusion. But how shall we estimate the importance of the one, the rôle of the other? Even our best thinkers fail us here. Beard dwells on the economic factors, Veblen on the technological factors. Again we raise the issue, how shall we decide between them, and how shall we include in a reasoned interpretation the various other factors within the unity of a modern culture. This brings us to our second comment. Any study of a culture that is not history or mere description demands, in the vast complex of interactive and incessantly changeful factors, a philosophical-scientific grasp of the unity and equilibrium of manifold related elements, demands principles of significant selection within the array of phenomena, demands in fact not only a very wide knowledge but a rare power of analysis, evaluation and synthesis. Apart from this it cannot discover an adequate scientific basis. Apart from this it is in danger of degenerating into a rather childish search for external patterns, symbols and uniformities.

In short, cultural sociology, or for that matter any other variety, cannot advance far if we reject the possibility of the formulation, application, and discovery of broad principles. There has been a tendency in recent American sociology to affect a scorn of principles. Some say that the business of the sociologist is facts, which usually means figures, not theories, the statement being itself the most absurd of theories, because it would deprive the "facts" of the very quality that makes them facts, their relevance or their meaning. One prominent sociologist declares that the idea of evolution has lost its fascination for contemporary social scientists and "may be enjoyed by freshmen only!" This attitude is of course a reaction against the too simple and too optimistic formulations of an earlier stage. We have discovered that the conditions of what we call primitive life are much more complex than was formerly assumed, and the discovery gives emphasis to the still greater complexity of civilized life. We have discovered the vast heterogeneity of the social institutions of peoples on similar cultural levels, discounting unilineal theories of evolution. From the inadequacy of some theories we rashly conclude against the necessity of any. Current revolts against traditional beliefs and norms of conduct no doubt help to reinforce this attitude. It may even be associated with the post-war disillusionment with the grandiose deceiving doctrines which fed the war-time spirit. A similar intellectual revolt pervades the fiction of our age. I will quote a passage from one of the best of our recent novels to illustrate the similarity. It is taken from Hemingway's *A Farewell to Arms*. "I was always embarrassed by the words sacred, glorious, and sacrifice and the expression in vain. . . . I had seen nothing sacred, and the things that were glorious had no glory and the sacrifices were like the stockyards at Chicago if nothing was done with the meat except to bury it. There were words that you could not stand to hear and finally only the names of places had dignity. . . . Abstract words such as glory, honor, courage, or hallow were obscene beside the concrete names of villages, the numbers of roads, the names of rivers, the numbers of regiments and the dates." A salutary and just reaction, we may well agree. But man's spirit cannot long be content with names and dates, and science cannot long survive on mere facts and figures. If old theories pass, new ones must take their place, for without laws there is no science. If we deny the possibility of them we are but passing from one dogmatism to another. Moreover, in sociology it has been too easily assumed that a few seemingly contradictory facts belied the insight of the greater constructive theories, such as Maine's law of the movement of civilization from status to contract or Durkheim's law of the transition from mechanical to organic solidarity. These and similar theories may require to be restated but they are rejected only by the lesser minds which do not comprehend their truth. The rank and file of sociological workers, themselves incapable of comprehensive insight, may after all take too great and democratic a pleasure in dethroning the intelligence that preceded them.

The false opposition between fact and theory is paralleled by the equally pernicious opposition between theory and practice. Just as facts are futile without interpretation, so is practice unintelligent apart from principle. Sociology in America has always been interested in the investigation of practical social problems. It is still so today, although the procedure and the outlook have been changing. The prevailing attitude is well expressed in the remark of W. I. Thomas, taken from a recent report: "It is evident that all the sciences dealing with man have their attention at present on behavior problems and are more or less concerned with data which may lead to the prediction and ultimate control of behavior manifestations." But there are certain implications of this interest in practice, in control and in prediction, which need to be stressed. The interest in practice must be related to an interest in principle, or it becomes mere empiricism. We must, for example, ask: Why do we want to predict and what do we want to predict? Some principle of selection, of significance, is involved. It is certainly not in order to say after the event, "I told you so," that the scientist wants to predict. For him prediction is either a verification of law, a demonstration of the relatedness of things within their system, or else a means of control — and in the latter case we are at once within the sphere of evaluation. *What* then do we want to predict? Not everything, surely. No doubt if some foundation gave me enough funds to hire enough assistance I could gather the information which would enable me for some time thereafter to predict within a small margin of error what percentage of the population of New York City would go to their beds before midnight and what percentage later, but I feel sure the result would not be worth the expense of time and money. There are so many things we can predict already where the prediction conveys no particular illumination. It used to be said long ago that sociology was no science because it could not predict. What nonsense! It can predict a myriad uniformities. Do we not know that the subways will be crowded at 5 P.M. and empty at 5 A.M.? Alas, what is hard to predict is not uniformity but change — significant change. So once more we are thrust back to the problem of the principles beyond the facts.

It is important, I believe, to insist on these points in the present stage of American sociology. There is today a great devotion to what is called the quantitative method. This devotion is excellent if kept to its proper sphere, which is the preliminary stage of research in those fields where we are dealing with measurable or countable units. But it should be borne in mind in the first place that science and research are not identical terms, that science is a body of systematic knowledge and research a means of contributing to it. It should also be borne in mind that the rather badly named qualitative method is not an inferior and temporary substitute for the quantitative. Just as there is no conflict between collecting and interpreting facts, so there is no conflict between the methods of discovery and the methods of understanding. The one demands the other. It is a mistake to say that interpretation is easy "arm-chair" work and that the real labor is that of the fact-collector. This proletarian philosophy of science is contradicted by the whole history of science. Interpretation is thinking directed squarely upon the facts, and it has been wisely said that most men will do anything to avoid the intolerable burden of thought. I am afraid that this is true of some researchers also, and they are apt to compensate by saying needlessly unpleasant things about theory.

It should be recognized that the degree in which the quantitative method is applicable depends on the nature of the subject. It is of essential importance when we are dealing with questions of prices or of votes, of population or of health. It is of great importance in the detection and measurement of many types of social change. It is less helpful in the study of legal systems or folkways or group consciousness or social motivations. How far it will help us depends on the kind of questions we are asking. It will tell us how many people obey or disobey what laws, but it won't tell us why they obey or disobey. It won't answer our final problems of causation, when we are seeking to interpret a social situation in terms of the complexly interwoven factors involved in it. A method is justified in so far as it enables us to illuminate or to answer our problems, and it is justified in no other way. By their fruits shall ye know them. Cooley, for example, has by non-quantitative means thrown new light on the group process, and Dewey on the ·

relation of custom and habit. Shall we then say that they are not scientists? The extremists of the quantitative method are apt to say so. They are willing to make great sacrifices in the name of science. They'll cheerfully employ definite indices for indefinite things and derive accurate results from inaccurate data. They're ready to measure my precise degree of conservatism without knowing what conservatism is, or my attitude to the church, — as if the church were a single spatial entity.

Not for a moment am I attacking the use of statistics which has given its excellent realism to American sociology. Columbia, with Mayo-Smith, was a pioneer in this field, and his work has been well upheld by Giddings. But Giddings was and is too catholic minded to be at the mercy of a narrow theory or to make a method his master. What I am pleading for is the *use* of statistics. What I am attacking is the false idea that they are self-interpretative, that the job of the scholar is done when the statistics are mustered. In truth it is only begun. How often has one attended meetings to discuss some problem of research where the only thing agreed upon was the need of more statistics. Besides more and better statistics we need more and better interpretations, and the latter need is far less realized. Better statistics are necessary, but this is after all largely a matter of expense, whereas better interpretations must proceed from our intelligence and our social experience. Without these the greater advances are never made, and this has been true in the period we are surveying. As I look back over it the names that stand out are those of men like Sumner, with his intimate perception of the significance of the folkways, like Veblen, with his incisive penetration into the social consequences of the changing industrial arts, like Cooley, with his grasp of the living process of the group, and like our own Giddings, with his flexible synthetic formulations of the conditions and the great phases of social development. Such men as these were both our system-builders and our inspiring influences. Systems change and pass, but they are the intellectual structures within which we must live, and if they pass we must seek to build anew, having learned from the builders who went before. To-day the materials for our building are better and more plentiful — and here we give grateful thanks to the quantitative workers. The bricks and the mortar, the steel and the lumber, are being prepared. The bricklayers and the hodmen, the masons and the carpenters, the riveters and all the rest are ready. Now we must pray that the architects also arrive, and if the gods are kind, perhaps they will send us a genius or two who will erect, for our temporary habitation, buildings that will soar a little nearer to the unfathomable skies of knowledge.

GOVERNMENT

HOWARD LEE McBAIN

I

Thirty-six years ago a distinguished professor of Public Law in Columbia University, Frank J. Goodnow, wrote in the preface to his treatise on *Comparative Administrative Law*: "The great problems of modern public law are almost exclusively administrative in character. While the age that has just passed was one of constitutional, the present age is one of administrative reform." Professor Goodnow could not, of course, have foretold the European cataclysm of 1914 to 1918. He could not have foreheard the crash of thrones that followed it. He could not have foreseen that there would ensue feverish years of constitutional reform — indeed an era of construction-making on a scale never before experienced in history.

But apart from all this there was probably something of exaggeration to write in 1893 that the great problems of modern public law are almost exclusively administrative in character. At the close of the nineteenth and the beginning of the twentieth century there were in many parts of the world rumblings of discontent with existing constitutional arrangements. In the United States our Federal Constitution was being attacked as the citadel of private property, its guns deliberately planted and pointed at the naked breasts of the struggling masses. With almost sinister and cynical design its checks and balances had been planned to thwart the will of the divine majority. Its principle of federalism with resulting political decentralization was wholly out of harmony with the plain facts of our national economy; for industry, labor, transportation, finance, had all become organized upon a nation-wide basis disregardful of state lines. Its applied doctrine of the separation of powers was a stumbling block in the path of needed reforms in the processes of politics. In other words, this hoary eighteenth century document was outworn, outmoded. Moreover, the way of its possible modernization was permanently clogged by its own difficult amending artifice. Such in brief was the nature of the indictment against the fundamental law of the nation that was raised in the periodical literature and books of the first quindecade of the twentieth century. And Professor Goodnow himself gave something in disproof of his earlier view when in 1911 he joined temperately in this chorus of criticism by publishing his significant little volume *Social Reform and the Constitution.*

The gunners who manned the guns in this ancient but impregnable citadel were, strange to relate, nine well-mannered and cultivated gentlemen, well beyond military age, who sat in sombre state and silken robes on the bench of the Supreme Court in the capitol at Washington. In 1895 this high Court handed down decisions in three cases that caused wide popular discussion and much adverse comment. These were the Sugar Trust Case, the Income Tax Case, and the Debs Injunction Case. Ten years later a law fixing a ten-hour day for labor in New York bakeries was declared void in the soon to become famous case of Lochner v. New York. For a number of years thereafter the tide of indignation arose against reactionary courts in general and against the Supreme Court in particular, though, truth to tell, the Supreme Court as compared with the highest courts of certain of the states was a mild offender. The cry of judicial usurpation was raised on high. It was a cry almost as old as the constitution itself; but many of those who now raised it were innocent of history. A veritable warfare of articles and books in criticism and in defense of the courts raged. The doctrine and the practice of judicial review were examined from every conceivable point of view. It was alternately extolled and execrated and, as in times past, a number of proposals were brought forward for subjecting it to the bit.

II

Throughout the nineteenth century the "more democracy" movement in the United States had expressed itself chiefly in adding to the number of electors by removing disqualifications for voting, and in multiplying the number of elective offices. Since the qualifications for national suffrage were determined by the several states, every widening of a state electorate operated also to widen the national electorate in that state. In the forefront now came agitation for the enfranchisement of women. This was less in the interest of bettering democracy than in the interest of bettering the status of women. It was a feminist rather than a democratic movement. There was furious debate, with woman's grievances pitted against her alleged higher duties and political incapacities. If the superb organization of the suffragists could have been taken as a sign or portent mere man should have been more wary than he was. Events have revealed it was not a sign.

While the movement for the enfranchisement of women was gaining impetus everywhere, the movement for disfranchising the Negroes in the South was gaining throughout the North a reluctant acceptance of the inevitable. The Negroes had been blasted into political significance by the upheaval of the Civil War. A generation of election chicanery and fraud had followed. At length the South determined to set its house in better order. By clever legal and administrative devices the Negro vote was destroyed, if not forever, at least until it is resurrected by some succeeding generation. The result was a new emancipation — the emancipation of the southern white man from the fiat of the Fifteenth Amendment. Thereafter there was much talk, but the amendment lay, as it always had been in fact, still-born.

Despite the stupidities of politics it is difficult to believe that many of those who brought about the blight of manifold elective offices in state and local governments in this country, were honestly moved by their devotion to the democratic principle. True, this was the argument and the urge that was used. It was as plausible as it was sophistical. Man is known classically as a political animal. This he has certainly never been except as a last resort in making a choice among evils. Politics lie very far down in the columnated list of his interests, though history has taught him the wisdom of holding in his hand the possibility of governing himself however little he ordinarily avails himself of the opportunity. Here he was asked to perform an impossible chore at the polls. Inevitably his job was transferred to his political bosses. He became a mere rubber stamp but was nevertheless held responsible for the choice he registered by marking his dictated ballot. And I suspect, though this would be difficult to prove, that this was the motive that spread in state constitutions and statute books thousands of provisions of law that increased the acreage and the jungle confusion of American ballots.

Fortunately the national government was spared this deluge. Never dreaming that any such sophistical philosophy of politics would overtake their progeny, the practical wonder-workers of 1787 provided for the election of only a President and Vice-President — and even this by indirection. The indirect method they ordained was shortly bent to approximate directness. But that difficult process of amending the Constitution, which they also ordained and which has so often been deplored by single-eyed reformers, saved us from the popular election not only of a presidential cabinet but also of innumerable postmasters, customs collectors, and other federal officers of local jurisdiction. It seems appalling to us in this age that constitutional amendments to effect this awful purpose were frequently introduced in Congress. Doubtless they would have been thrown to the country and speedily adopted by the necessary quota of state legislatures had not greedy party leaders been better satisfied with the existing scheme. The direct largesse of congressional spoils (permitted, if not compelled, from the presidential table) was preferred, as a certainty, to the transfer of such life-sustaining crumbs to the dubious distribution of national political machines or the changeful charity of state and local organizations. At any rate we escaped. God, apparently, protects not only inebriates and children but also sometimes democracies.

In the opening years of the present century, thinking people awoke. The slogan of the short ballot was hoisted. The capacity of that *homo sapiens*, the average voter, had plainly been overestimated. To be sure, he had not complained. He was merely stupified, and being stupified he had done what he was told to do. He had put his cross — the mark of his political illiteracy — in the circle or square that accompanied the emblem of an eagle or a star or an arm and hammer, or what not. A child of six could have done as much and as well. But intelligent persons had been fed too long upon the fruit of this evil tree. They had sharpened their axes and were laying them lustily to its flourishing roots.

III

While this agitation for scotching a previously heralded reform was under way the "more democracy" idea did not lie fallow. It was still fecund with rosy dreams of its destiny. In the national government was one conspicuous sore spot. United States senators were still chosen by the votes of state legislatures. This system had been denounced and defended for half a century. But whatever its alleged advantages, this indirect method of choice was certainly undemocratic. No body of representatives springing from popular vote would be likely to be dubbed a millionaires' club, though rich men have been known to wrest senatorial togas from the populace as well as from state legislatures. The climax of the long movement for the popular election of senators was reached in the first years of the century. The Senate itself finally succumbed to permit the proposal of a constitutional amendment to effect that end.

Nor was this the only mark at which the "more democracy" idea was firing. In the states the suffrage had long since been extended to practically all adult males. Yet strangely enough democracy had not sufficiently arrived. The will of the people was still flouted by representatives of their own choice. What was the trouble? Why, surely it could be naught but the machinations of these extra-governmental agencies, political parties, upon whom, in point of fact, the whole burden of keeping a ramshackle government going in any sort of unity and harmony had deliberately or unconsciously been placed.

Since the introduction of the Australian ballot in the eighties and nineties of the last century, political parties had been increasingly subjected to statutory restrictions. Now they must be democratized by law. We must compel the voter not only to elect his officers willy-nilly, but also to elect his party candidates for office in a pre-election burst of democratic zeal. It is of small moment that this movement for direct primaries was started in Wisconsin by the late Senator La Follette because he could not dominate his local Republican machine and saw no other way to defeat his opponents and retain himself in power. The fact is that, whatever the reason, talk and writing on behalf of the direct primary system, as opposed to nominations by conventions, occupied an important place in the American political science of the early twentieth century.

But this was not sufficient. No matter how nominated and elected, representatives still, for one reason or another, exhib-

ited a callous indifference to, or defiance of, the people's
wishes. We must have better means of political self expression
and of imposing our wills upon our chosen servants. Hence the
initiative, the referendum, and the recall. How passionately
these nostrums of democracy stirred the minds of politicians
and political scientists only a few years back! What endless
pages were filled with polemical discussions, with attempted
scientific diagnoses of our democratic ills, and with the virtues
of the proposed healing remedies!

And while the common people were thus, as they thought,
shaking off the cruel yoke of machine politics and freeing themselves for a bigger and better exercise of their democratic
powers, cities, too, were to be liberated from the galling burden of legislative interference in their affairs. Municipal home
rule by constitutional grant was being widely mooted.

In the field of social and financial reform numerous proposals were in the offing that raised questions of constitution-
ality. These can not be here detailed. But the need for a federal
income tax was very much in the foreground. And the prohibition of intoxicating liquors was marching majestically on its
way. In 1900 prohibition prevailed in only five states. By 1910
the number was nine. By 1915, it was nineteen, and that number doubled in the next five years.

IV

Such was the constitutional setting in which American political science found itself in the infant and adolescent years of the
present century. Let us briefly assess results.

The marksmanship of the Supreme Court manning the guns
in the citadel of the Constitution is always perfect. It hits
whether its hit be approved or not. Amid all the discussion of
its prerogatives, powers and usurpations, the Court went
placidly on its way. As at other periods a few of its decisions

attracted wide public interest and were hotly debated. These tend to distort the picture of its work as a whole. This at least may be said, that some of the best and some of the worst of our politico-economic writings of the last quarter century are to be found in the pages of its numerous rendered opinions. Regrettably enough, too great a part of this best finds lodgment in dissenting opinions where, nevertheless, it constitutes a very precious national possession.

Woman suffrage was swept into the National Constitution by the Nineteenth Amendment. And Negro suffrage was swept out of National Constitution by various devices in the constitutions of the southern states by which the Fifteenth Amendment was effectually circumvented. The short ballot movement made great gains in a number of states and a large number of cities, with resulting concentration and visualization of responsibility for the conduct of government. United States senators were made subject to direct election by the Seventeenth Amendment — a democratic triumph which has not heightened the mental quality of that body, however much it has altered its spirit and affected its attitude toward public questions. The direct primary has become the general rule for making nominations throughout the country. In actual operation this contrivance of democracy varies so greatly with time, place and circumstance that it is difficult, if not impossible, to estimate its results in terms of gain and loss. By and large, perhaps, it has neither hurt nor helped things much. Certainly it has fallen far short of its advocates' hopes. In a country in which normally it is extraordinarily difficult to develop national leadership, it should have been known in advance that the direct primary as applied to the nomination of candidates for the presidency, as it is by the laws of a score of states, would prove an absurdity. Such it has proved.

By 1912 the initiative, referendum and recall had spread

into most of the states west of the Mississippi and in a few of them, such as Oregon and California, it has been extensively employed. In the East direct government was introduced only in Maine and Massachusetts. It would be difficult to demonstrate that these media of democracy, where they have been made available, have had any significant effect upon our institutions. They have not destroyed or even materially weakened representative government. They have not borne flower in radicalism. Nor can it be shown that the states that enjoy them are either more forward or more backward in their political policies than are the states without them. Only three states have succumbed to direct government since 1912 and none since 1918. Discussion of these ways of democracy has ceased.

Municipal home rule, adopted in four states prior to the opening of the century, is now found in nearly five times that number. Despite its inevitable legal confusions, its net accomplishments have probably been salutary.

That the Constitution of the United States is not unamendable, as commentators had so often contended, was demonstrated by the quick ratification of the highly desirable Income Tax Amendment of 1913. The expansion of the police powers of Congress along the tortuous avenue of the commerce clause has gone steadily, and occasionally ridiculously, forward during the last twenty-five years. This clause, however, was not expansive enough to satisfy the demands of the prohibitionists. Despite the gradual growth of Federal police power, usually exercised as an assistance to the states, the extension of such power as is embodied in the Eighteenth Amendment marked a fundamental change in our constitutional system. The fate of the proposed Child Labor Amendment at the hands of oppositional or hostile state legislatures seems to indicate that there is popular hostility to any such further centralization — at least for the time being.

V

In the light of this brief survey of pragmatic politics since 1900 it can scarcely be said that the present century ushered in an era of quiescence in the matter of constitutional reforms. Nor were we alone in being concerned with political fundamentals. In England the most important constitutional change since the Reform Bill of 1832 occurred in 1911 when, after a bitter struggle between the peers and the common people, the House of Lords, though left with somewhat more than the tinsel of power, was nevertheless relegated to a rôle of relative obscurity in the formulation of national and imperial policies. The Representation of the People Act of 1918, by which women were enfranchised and seats in the Commons were redistributed, was at least as significant as the changes wrought by similar laws in the nineteenth century following the reform of '32.

In France, throughout the period of our survey, electoral reform was, as it still is, a perennial subject of debate and of disingenuous experimentation, while the agitation for regionalism was and is a reality even though its purpose is unrealized. In Germany the Social Democrats strove without surcease or success for genuine parliamentary government, for a liberalization of Prussian suffrage, and for a redistribution of seats in the Reichstag, while Alsace-Lorraine struggled vainly for a self-governing place in the sun of the Empire that was to crumble in 1918.

That curious political, racial and geographic monstrosity, Austria-Hungary, was the scene of almost continuous agitation for constitutional reform in its two grand divisions, the Hungarian Monarchy and the Austrian Empire. In the latter at least one notable reform was achieved in 1907, when the class system of voting for members of the Abgeordnetenhaus was abolished, approximate manhood suffrage was introduced, and seats were redistributed not only provincially but also racially.

In Russia the first flickering candle of constitutionalism was lighted with the call of the Duma in 1905; while from that time down to the opening of the World War, the liberty-loving Finns waged battle royal with the Czar's bureaucrats for constitutional autonomy. Important changes in the constitutional governments of both Norway and Sweden were made in the early years of the present century. In 1910 Portugal became a republic, and the Union of South Africa was born into the family of British self-governing dominions, whose whole status in the British Empire was to be fundamentally altered in the years following the War. In 1912 China set sail upon what has proved to be an almost constantly stormy sea of republicanism.

Of the constitutions that were set up by the political progeny of the Treaty of Versailles there is time for only a word or two. Republicanism had been stagnant in Europe for half a century. For whatever cause — and the cause was probably as much President Wilson as it was irresistible popular demand — it now burst into new bloom. Written constitutions creating institutions to be operated by a wide electorate became the order of the hour. Woman suffrage and proportional representation — proposals that had gained little or no headway through many years of agitation — were adopted almost as a matter of course. Presidential government after the American pattern found no favor. Parliamentary government by a cabinet responsible to a popularly elected assembly was everywhere introduced. Upper chambers, previously thought indispensable to such a form of government, were dispensed with in one or two countries and were elsewhere invariably put in positions of subordination. Federalism after the American pattern was likewise eschewed. Where it was provided, as in Germany and Austria, it is little more than a name, so overshadowing are the powers of the central governments.

The organizations of revolutionary soldiers' and workers'

councils that sprang into being in central Europe on the heels of the war were sufficiently powerful and threatening to cause a system of workers' and economic councils to be anchored in the constitutions of Germany, Austria, Jugo-Slavia and Poland. These constitutional provisions, so pregnant with potential political significance at the time of their making, have borne little fruit. Economic councils have not successfully competed for power with political parliaments constituted upon the usual plan of representation without regard for functional or occupational groups.

In the early years of the present century there were considerable extensions of communal enterprise in the countries of western Europe and in Australia and New Zealand. Apparently, however, this movement had decidedly slowed down when the necessities of the war caused its sudden and swift revival. Government ownership, operation or control of resources, industry, transport, communication, distribution and consumption was established on a scale that had been dreamed of only by the most advanced state socialists. Many signs pointed to a survival of much of this beyond the aftermath of the war. It is not surprising, therefore, that the constitutions of the postwar period not only made provision for, but also positively invited, the nationalization of many enterprises. But hopes and prophecies failed. The pendulum of reaction from the war and all its works made more than a full swing back. There has been little extension of government operation of services in any country and in one or two there has been actual retrogression by way of denationalizing services that were operated by the government prior to the war.

VI

There remains to mention Italy and Russia, though neither the Fascist nor the Soviet régime lends itself to brief characterization. Italy adopted manhood suffrage in 1912 and proportional representation in 1919. Both are now abandoned. That the government inaugurated and dramatically conducted by Signor Mussolini is a dictatorship is not to be denied. It is nevertheless unique among dictatorships in its peculiar relation to industry and labor and in its apparent grip upon the rank and file of the Italian people. The degree to which the nation is regimented is almost unbelievable. The spectacle of eight and a half millions of so-called voters, who in the spring of 1929 marched to the polls to cast perfectly useless ballots for the entire four hundred uncontested candidates for membership in the Chamber of Deputies is surely a spectacle worth recording if only because of its singularity. The Fascist party, enrolling less than a million adult members, is a closed system. Its Grand Council, which hand-picked these four hundred deputies and which has now been made an organ of the government itself, has become for all practical purposes the Italian State.

Strange as the application of the word may seem, the Russian régime is probably best described as an aristocracy of the proletariat. Lenin himself once unhesitatingly referred to it as a "real oligarchy," for, he argued, "the dictatorship of the proletariat through the organization of all proletarians is impossible. . . . It can be brought about only by the small vanguard imbued with the revolutionary energy of its class." The Soviet governmental organization established by a written constitution is itself completely dominated and controlled by the oligarchically organized Communist party which is a law unto itself above all constitutions and laws. The total membership of this monopolistic and tight-held party with its discipline of blood and iron is only about one per cent of the population, while actual political power is completely in the hands of the Politbureau of the party consisting of nine members and eight alternates. Based upon a philosophy of the state and of the relation of the individual to industrial and political society that has never before had concrete expression, the system is unique in so many respects that it defies description in the commonly accepted terms and categories of parliamentary politics.

There is nothing that is new in the principle of dictatorship and little that is new in its methods of strangling opposition. But there are novel elements in the philosophies and purposes of both Fascism and Sovietism. Though democracy has long been adjudged bankrupt by many theorists, Italy and Russia are not theories; they are living and breathing and operating challenges to democracy. Indeed, there is much to demonstrate that events have not been molded by the philosophies of these systems, but rather that their philosophies have been the product of swift moving events.

VII

While all these changes in the fundamentals of political systems have been evolving, there have also been, as Professor Goodnow prophesied, many changes in the field of public administration. In the United States, despite the doctrine and rule of the separation of legislative, executive and judicial powers, government by administrative tribunals that combine these three kinds of power has gone steadily forward. This was made almost inevitable by the increasing complications of a technological civilization in which the individual found himself caught in the vortex of an ever-narrowing corporate concentration and control. Laws and courts were not sufficient to his needs. Agencies that united the functions of rule-maker, detective, prosecutor, judge and jury, seemed best adapted to meet those needs. Yet few will contend that government by administrative commissions has been an unadulterated success. Under commission rule, for example, public utilities have not been transformed into eager and generous servants of a satisfied and grateful public. It should always be remembered that government is itself in considerable part controlled by the very forces it seeks to subjugate. Moreover, among competing and antagonistic interests in an enormously complex and already law-ridden economic world, it is seldom easy to determine what is wisest and most just in public policy. And it is even more difficult to translate determined policy into administered law. The law tends to become as complex as the economic forces it strives to govern. And regrettably enough, those who administer it are not always wise or even honest and are at best humanly frail. There is indeed mystery in the fact that so loose-built a thing as democracy is able to cope as well as it does with the perplexing complicacies of modern civilization.

Improvements in administrative organization and methods, though far from being spectacular, have not been negligible. Budget and other financial reforms have made progress in nation, states and cities. Many state and city governments have been reorganized to the end of centering responsibility and resolving order out of a chaos that was the product of piecemeal and haphazard growth through many unfolding years. Proposals to reorganize the national administration are still, as they have been for a long time, in the bag of politics. In all our units of government the merit system has been extended and dents have been made in the problem of personnel recruitment and management.

Whether as a result of these and other changes government is conducted with greater efficiency and economy today than it was a quarter of a century back is open to question. Americans are more interested in the slogan than in the realities of efficiency and economy. Here and there arrangements certainly have at least the appearance of being better than they once were. But the margin of the unachieved is wide. And despite the penal sanctions with which our numerous laws bristle, corruption in places high and low has probably been as prevalent in our era as in any other of our history. Neither the governors nor the governed have been or can be made good by law.

VIII

In this series of addresses my colleague, Professor Mitchell, has already discussed the growing interrelationships and interdependencies of the several social sciences and the resulting development of coöperative inquiries and researches. Little need be added. As governments have increasingly sought to direct and control economic forces, political science and political economy have been thrust into each other's arms quite regardless of their wishes or natural affections. There is little or no politics that is not concerned with economics and little or no economics that must not reckon with politics. The intimacies between law and politics are too obvious for comment. Since governments are historical developments, however abrupt their occasional revolutionary origins, political science has always leaned heavily upon history. In his study of society, the sociologist can not ignore political society, nor the political scientist the extra-political aspects of society as a whole. In recent years a good deal has been said about the psychological and statistical approaches to the study of politics. But the fact is that there has never been any realistic study of politics that did not take account of what was known or suspected about man's psychology. Not much can be gained for politics by repetitious use of the word "psychology" or by introducing the lingo of psychology into the lingo of political science. The so-called new psychology, whether social, behaviorist, Freudian or Gestalt, has certainly not as yet advanced to the stage in which it can make large contributions toward an understanding of the phenomena of politics or a solution of its many intricate problems. Every intelligent student of politics welcomes every intelligent use of available statistics that throw light upon the processes of government. But political statistics are not only not numerous but are also full of pitfalls for the unwary. The quantitative method has been and can be applied to politics only in limited degree — in far less degree than it has been or can be applied to economics. There are imponderables in every science of human mental action. In no science, perhaps, do these play a larger rôle than in the science of politics.

IX

As governments have set up and placed their hands upon an ever enlarging number of brakes and throttles, there has been insistent need for more and better fact-finding and fact-interpreting agencies. And this need has been met in considerable part. There have been innumerable inquiries by legislative committees and commissions and some of their work has been notable. In addition to these long employed agencies, legislative reference and drafting staffs and bureaus of governmental research have been widely established as parts of the regular machinery of government. These have naturally varied in point of resources, political opportunities and quality of personnel, and, therefore, in point of usefulness. Following the establishment of the New York Bureau of Municipal Research in 1907, a large number of private agencies for governmental research were founded in all parts of the country, some with, and many without, university connections. It is impossible to strike off in a word the measure of their achievements. A few have been little more than paper organizations but some of them have, over a goodly expanse of years, rendered highly significant services to the cause of improved government.

In England and on the continent of Europe there has been no parallel to this American development. In the former the most important researches into governmental problems are still made, as they have been for many years, by royal commissions and departmental or parliamentary committees appointed from time to time to investigate and report on specific topics. The work of some of these agencies has been of extremely high order.

Mention should also be made of the founding of the American Political Science Association in 1903 and the establishment under its aegis in 1906 of the *American Political Science Review*. The Association has had an honorable career and the *Review* has been a most serviceable instrument. The National Municipal League, which came into being in 1895, likewise embarked upon the publication of the useful *National Municipal Review* in 1912. The only important British journals devoted exclusively to the study of political problems have been the *Journal of Comparative Legislation*, established in 1897 (expanded in 1918 to include the subject of international law), the unfortunately short-lived *Political Quarterly*,[1] and the recently launched *Journal of Public Administration*.

X

Concerning the literature of political science in the twentieth century something must be briefly said. Naturally an important part of it has been concerned with the movements and tendencies in politics of which I have spoken. There have been a few worthy treatises of a comprehensive character and an endless stream of monographic studies, good, bad and indifferent. In this field as in every other, millions of sterile thoughts have been put into printed words and a pathetically large amount of labor has been spent to no profitable purpose unless it be regarded as a profitable end in itself to keep composition machines clicking and printing presses flying in the interest of prosperity rather than of posterity. Almost anything that one might say generally of the literature of political science would be either too generous or too grudging. All too frequently the ancient and unproved axioms of this nebulous science have been uncritically reaffirmed. But on the whole there has been a stimulating reaction from stark and fruitless legalism on the one hand and from pure and impure speculation on the other, toward a wholesome realism. The stuff of politics is

[1] Revived in 1930.

neither the dust of law nor the gossamer of dreams. It is facts, however difficult of ascertainment — the facts that go into the making of forces. And more and more have the thinkers and writers of the generation under review essayed the hard task of tearing aside the thick veil of mystery that shrouds the processes of politics in order to discover and reveal the true inwardness of these processes. The result has been helpful. We have at least been given an infinity of details about government — details not only about its osteology and anatomy, but also in respect of its histology and pathology. Nor has all of this literature of description been merely dryly factual. Into some of it have been woven golden threads of philosophy, of critical appraisal and of constructive proposal.

Moreover, apart from this, there has been a lively revival of interest in political theory, led for the most part by philosophical writers who have vaguely envisaged or groped for a new political order founded upon one or another variety of new economic and social orders. Challenging the basic theories that underlie the organization and functioning of democracies through parliamentary institutions, they have found it less difficult to demolish than to erect. This revival, whatever its objections, has been most useful in stimulating reflection upon the fundamentals of politics.

A year or two ago one of the ablest of modern political scientists, Charles A. Beard, ventured to ask "whether, with the possible exception of John Taylor's monumental *Inquiry*, a single immortal work in political science has been written in America since Hamilton, Jay and Madison struck off from the flaming forge of controversy the enduring philippic that bears the title of *The Federalist*." I shall not venture to confer immortality upon any political book of the last quarter century. But I do venture the conjecture that the immortality of the *Federalist*, if such it be, derives not alone from the penetrating profundity of its thought but as well from the fortuitous circumstance that the experiment in government which it analyzed and expounded chanced to endure. The government provided for by the Constitution of the United States had been operating less than two months when Senator William Maclay recorded in his famous Journal: "Get, if I can, *The Federalist* without buying it. It is not worth it. But, being a lost book, Izard, or someone else, will give it to me. It certainly was instrumental in procuring the adoption of the Constitution. This is merely a point of curiosity and amusement to see how wide of its explanations and conjectures the stream of business has taken its course." The dangers of contemporary estimates respecting the immortality of books are fully as great in 1929 as they were in 1789.

JURISPRUDENCE

Young B. Smith

Since the beginning of the twentieth century, approximately a half-million reported cases have been decided by the courts of record in the United States and approximately a quarter-million statutes have been enacted by the legislatures of the forty-eight states. These figures do not include the even larger number of decisions of inferior tribunals nor the ordinances passed by municipalities nor the rules and regulations promulgated by departments, bureaus, commissions and other administrative bodies.

This phenomenal growth and expansion of law has invaded the domain of individual liberty to an extent unknown in modern history, thereby arousing resentment among large numbers of people. Moreover, the rapid increase in the volume and complexity of law has taxed beyond their capacities existing devices for law administration thus impairing their efficiency with consequent delay, confusion and at times complete failure of enforcement. As a result, men are beginning to ask questions about law which are proving embarrassing to those responsible for the administration of justice.

With the view to assuaging the widespread discontent, a multitude of resolutions have been passed by bar associations and other civic organizations; commissions, both public and private, have been appointed to make investigations and recommendations; and more laws have been proposed to correct the actual or supposed defects of existing laws.

The expansion of the domain of law has been both acclaimed and decried, but there is general dissatisfaction with its administration. The difficulties have been attributed to a number of causes, and as many different remedies have been suggested. In the main the criticisms of law and the arguments both for and against actual or proposed changes have rested upon assumptions, often naïve, and frequently without foundation in fact. Nevertheless the dissatisfaction is a fact too evident to be ignored.

Some say there is too much law; the country has gone law mad. Others say there is not enough law; existing rules are archaic and unsuited to the needs of the times. Some say the law is too rigid. Others say it is not certain enough. Some bewail the departure from tradition. Others complain that the law lags behind. Thus the contradictions multiply.

The indictment of those charged with responsibility for the state of the law has most commonly been grounded upon one of three counts: ignorance, cupidity or corruption. Whatever the ground, the idea is implicit in current discussion that some group or groups are to blame. Whether it be the lawyer or the judge, the legislator or the public administrator, the business man or the politician, the laborer or the propagandist, the minister or the teacher, who is assailed, there is a tacit assumption that but for his ignorance or stupidity, his indifference or inaction, his bigotry or avarice, his depredations or other malfeasance or nonfeasance, conditions might have been better. That conditions might have been different is a reasonable assumption. That they might have been better is not so clear. Those who know the history of law are not discouraged by the popular outcry. They know that conditions are much better than they were and there is every indication of further improvement. Indeed the widespread discontent is the most hopeful sign that better days are ahead.

The volume and complexity of law should not strike terror in our hearts. Suppose there are a million laws. No one is affected by more than a few of them. There are thousands of municipalities in the United States. Each has its code of rules and regulations. The total number of municipal ordinances is appalling, but most people are affected only by those of a single city or town. Likewise human relations are legion, but most people are involved in only a few of them. No one is concerned with many of them. Therefore, the law, so far as a particular individual is concerned, is that small fraction of the totality of laws which affects his particular relations with other people. Yet if there were only those few, simple and fundamental laws of which we hear so much, the vast proportion of the numerous relations which go to make up the complex society in which we live would be left to the mercy of anarchy. On the other hand, there is no gain in making laws, whatever their purpose, which in actual operation are of no social benefit. A law without adequate machinery for its administration and enforcement is usually futile, and a law incapable of reasonable enforcement because of social conditions is absurd. Moreover, the attempt to control by law conduct which may be more effectively controlled in other ways is a misuse of law and a social waste. The volume, the scope and the complexity of law are important in so far as they bear upon the effectiveness of law in performing its function in society, but there is no inherent virtue either in a few or in many laws, nor is the domain of law encompassed by fixed and unchanging lines.

It is significant that the recent expansion in the law has been contemporaneous with the rapid advance in the physical sciences and the changes in the social structure which have resulted from the development and the use of the machine. With the rise of the urban communities, the greater interdependence of men due to the specialization of labor, the concentration of wealth through the agency of the commercial corporation, the mass production of goods, the expansion of credit, free schools and increased leisure for the masses, man found himself in a new world. His changed environment made him conscious of needs and desires hitherto unfelt. New interests sprang into being and old interests faded away. The clash of these new interests created new problems of major importance and interest values changed. The rules of law which had developed through the ages to foster or curb old desires were impotent to effectuate the adjustments which had to be made. The revision of legal rules through judicial decisions was too slow to be effective and man seized upon the instrument of legislation to aid in making the necessary changes because he knew of no better way. True he handled his instrument with imperfect skill, but the pressure of circumstances called for the use of such skill as he had. There was little time for experimentation and reflection. Adjustments had to be made. Man acted. Whether he acted wisely remained to be seen. At least adjustments were made. The effects were later observed. Man liked some of the effects, he disliked others. He began to contemplate his work. Further adjustments must be made, but the pressure for action is not so great. There is more time for investigation and meditation. The undesired effects must be obviated and former mistakes must be discovered. Man's interest in legal science and legal philosophy is aroused.

The phenomena which I have described are not without precedent. The rapid expansion of English law following the industrial revolution, and the movement culminating in the Napoleonic Code after the French revolution, are conspicuous instances of wholesale lawmaking incident to upheavals in the social order. Whether law be regarded as a manifestation of something more fundamental and profound, or as a growth evolving out of custom and tradition, or as a device consciously created by man to regulate human affairs, its periods of stability and mobility seem to synchronize with the periods of stability and mobility in the social structure. Long intervals of social tranquility tend to breed respect and reverence for legal institutions with a corresponding diminution of change, whereas major disturbances in the social order are often followed by dissatisfaction with and distrust of law which frequently presage important periods in its development. Once the law is adapted to the new conditions, confidence is restored and change becomes less perceptible with the restoration of social equilibrium. It is also noticeable that man's ideas about the nature and function of law seem to shift with its progress or retrogression. These observations indicate an interrelation between social conditions, rules of law and man's ideas about law. Certainly man's ideas about law affect the rules of law and the rules of law affect his ideas about law. Likewise social conditions affect both the rules of law and man's ideas about law and they, in turn, affect social conditions. It is this interplay of forces which combine to produce the phenomena of positive law and which make the phenomena so difficult to understand.

For more than two thousand years man has speculated about the origin, the nature and the ends of law.[1] Beginning with the discussions of the Greek philosophers, the literature of all ages abounds with juristic thought. Until comparatively modern times, the conclusions arrived at have been largely the product of metaphysics.

Observation [says Korkunov, in commenting upon Greek thinking,] gave only fragmentary science and therefore they filled in with deduction. I can observe only accessible phenomena. Meditation, however, knows no exterior bounds. Everything may be the subject of meditation. Freed from necessity of observation, it can go forward to the establishing

---

[1] The following exposition of various philosophical and juristic ideas is based largely upon: N. M. Korkunov, *General Theory of Law* (Hastings' transl., Modern Legal Philosophy Series, 1922) ; R. Stammler, *The Theory of Justice* (Husik's transl., Modern Legal Philosophy Series, 1925) ; J. Kohler, *Philosophy of Law* (Albrecht's transl., Modern Legal Philosophy Series, 1921) ; F. Berolzheimer, *The World's Legal Philosophies* (Jastrow's transl., Modern Legal Philosophy Series, 1912) ; *The Progress of Continental Law in the 19th Century* (Continental Legal History Series, 1918) ; and R. Pound, "The Scope and Purpose of Sociological Jurisprudence," *Harvard Law Rev.*, XXIV, 591, *Harvard Law Rev.*, XXV, 140, 489, *The Spirit of the Commmon Law* (1921), *An Introduction to the Philosophy of Law* (1922), *Interpretations of Legal History* (1923).

of an entire complete system, to what is called a philosophical system. Since Plato's time the thinkers among mankind have worked out not a few such systems. But their very number and the impossibility of finding a sufficient objective reason for preferring any one of all these different ones, could not fail to produce doubts of the utility of metaphysical paths toward a genuine science of real things, and not merely a collection of opinions.[2]

Among the oldest and most persistent of notions about law is the belief in an ultimate, fixed and unchanging law, in some way discoverable by man, upon which, it is thought, rules of positive law should rest. Appearing first in Greece, it was later expanded by the Roman jurists. In the Middle Ages it "was identified with divine law, eternal and unchangeable, to which were opposed variable human laws." [3] Upon it was grounded the philosophy of the rationalists during the seventeenth and eighteenth centuries. The idea was given its modern impetus in the seventeenth century by Grotius who is commonly regarded as the founder of natural law philosophy. "That is just," proclaimed Grotius, "which is conformed to the nature of society among reasonable beings. Such law is absolutely natural and independent of time and place. No one can change it. It would exist and remain the same even if there were no God." [4] The theory of natural law was transmitted to America by Pufendorf and Blackstone. It was accepted by the French philosophers of the eighteenth century and was used to bolster up the political theories of Rousseau and his followers in Europe and in America. For more than two centuries it dominated the thinking of jurists in two continents until it received its mortal blow in the nineteenth century from the historical school of Savigny.

[2] Korkunov, *General Theory of Law* (Hastings' transl.), 3.

[3] Korkunov, *General Theory of Law* (Hastings' transl.), 118.

[4] Grotius, *De Jure Belli ac Pacis*, Proleg. vii-xi; *Lib.* I c. 1, §10, No. 5; The translation of Grotius' text is taken from Korkunov, *General Theory of Law* (Hastings' transl.), 25; see also Berolzheimer, *The World's Legal Philosophies* (Jastrow's transl.), 115.

According to Korkunov,[5] the belief in the existence of natural law is partly due to man's conception of right and justice and his propensity, observed by John Stuart Mill eighty-seven years ago, "to conclude that wherever there is a name, there must be a distinct separate entity corresponding to the name." [6] So, recognizing by observation variable rules of positive law, man forms in his mind by antithesis the concept of a right and just law to which he unconsciously assigns the attributes of reality. Moreover, the hypothesis of natural law is suggested by the observation that not infrequently the attempts to enforce certain laws are wholly frustrated. This phenomenon suggests, at once, the operation of some force, beyond the control of man, which governs all law. On the other hand, a comparative study of the legal systems of different times and places revealed inconsistent rules operating with equal effectiveness. This observation, made by the historical jurists in the nineteenth century, refuted the hypothesis of natural law but it led to another which was also fallacious. The historical jurists, typified by Savigny, associated these differences in rules of positive law with the differences of race, environment, custom and tradition with the result that they assumed that particular laws were a necessary product of social life; that they evolved from the particular culture of particular peoples.[7] The historical jurists rendered a valuable service in refuting the hypothesis of natural law and in directing attention to the legal past, but they cast no light upon the future. To them law happened and would continue to happen and there was little that man could do about it.

Coincident with the revival of interest in historical study, the idea developed that the processes by which law emerged

[5] *General theory of Law* (Hastings' transl), 116, 134, 135.

[6] Mill, *A System of Logic*, Book V, Chap. III, par. 4.

[7] For a discussion of the Historical School, see Korkunov, *General Theory of Law* (Hastings' transl.), 27, 118, 143; Berolzheimer, *The World's Legal Philosophies* (Jastrow's transl.), 204.

from custom and tradition were governed by principles of universal application and the illusion of natural law appeared in a new form. According to some, these principles could be reached only by philosophical paths. According to others they could be ascertained only by observation. The former approach was adopted by Hegel, the latter by Comte: both were searching for a master control beyond the power of man.

At about the same time, the reaction against the speculations of the philosophical jurists in their quest for the secret of legal phenomena, produced a group of practical minded men who were more concerned with what law is and what it is likely to be than in how or why it came to be what it is or why it should be what it is not. They studied the rules of law rather than their origin, and sought their immediate possibilities rather than their ultimate ends. Although analytical jurisprudence, in its crudest forms, appears among the Romans and among the lawyers of Coke's day, its modern development began with Austin in the first half of the nineteenth century, and characterizes the work of such English scholars as Markby and Holland.[8]

The analytical jurists, like the philosophical and historical jurists, saw only a part of the picture. In the first place, their concentration upon the rules of law narrowed their vision and they lost sight of the fact that rules are but means to an end with the result that the law tended to become arbitrary and technical. In the second place, their disregard of the historical evolution of the rules, gave to the rules an aspect of permanency which made their further adaptation to changing conditions increasingly more difficult. In time, the generalizations about rules and the propositions based upon rules became almost as fixed and unbending as the imaginary principles of natural law or of historical growth. The analytical jurists

[8] For a discussion of analytical jurisprudence, see Pound, "Scope and Purpose of Sociological Jurisprudence," *Harvard Law Rev.*, XXIV, 594.

relied too much upon legislation to bring about change. Legislation failed them in spite of the efforts of such men as Bentham in England and Field in New York.

Apart from the views of the philosophical, the historical and the analytical jurists, it is important to notice the effects upon juristic thinking of the success of objective methods in the natural sciences. During the first part of the nineteenth century the imagination of man was stirred by his discoveries of the physical structure of the universe. By painstaking observation he was piecing together a picture of things as they were and by hypotheses, based upon his experience, he was developing a science of physical laws. It is not surprising, therefore, that the attempt was made by Comte to develop a similar science of law. Although Comte was led astray by the idea that the phenomena of law, like physical phenomena, were governed by laws of nature, he emphasized the necessity of an objective methodology in juristic science the importance of which is only beginning to be appreciated. Moreover, Comte, by stressing the fact that man was distinctively a social being, laid the foundation of the sociological school which later was to overthrow the individualistic philosophy that had developed during the seventeenth and eighteenth centuries.

The second half of the nineteenth century witnessed a number of important developments in juristic thought. The speculations of the philosophical jurists, the fatalism of the historical jurists and the rigidity of the analytical jurists, did not harmonize with the changing outlook of man which was taking place as a result of new knowledge and its application in the natural sciences. Man's improved estate, which followed his triumphs over nature, had turned his attention from the golden age of the past to the millenium of the future. He was gaining confidence in his power to control future events and the notion of progress by conscious effort was taking hold. The growing faith in the "efficacy of effort" was manifested in the increasing use of legislation as a means of bringing about change in the law and accounts for many of the reform movements which later swept both Europe and America. Thus man's interest was diverted from the origin and nature of law to its purpose. This point of view brought forth a utilitarian philosophy of law of which Jhering is the principal exponent. Jhering's views are admirably summarized in the following words of Dean Pound:

. . . For, he says, while we explain events of external nature by "because," human acts are explained by "in order to"; and this "in order to" in the case of the human will is as indispensable as the "because" in the case of a physical object. Hence the law of cause and effect as applied to the human will, that is, the psychological law of cause and effect, is a law of purpose. Upon this basis he builds an utilitarian philosophy of law, challenging the then philosophical position at the outset. "The sense of right," he says, "has not produced law, but law the sense of right. Law knows but one source — the practical one of purpose." In other words, whereas the philosophical jurist, adopting an idealistic interpretation of legal history, considered that principles of justice and right are discovered and expressed in rules, and the historical jurist taught that principles of action are found by experience and developed into rules, Jhering held that means of serving human ends are discovered and are fashioned consciously into laws.[9]

Jhering's jurisprudence was one of realities in which the validity of legal rules was determined by their results. He also recognized the power of man to shape the rules by conscious effort. What is even more important, Jhering, unlike Bentham and other utilitarians, proposed a social theory of law. Prior thereto, the prevailing theories of law had been individualistic. The harmonizing of individual wills so as to preserve the maximum of freedom for each was regarded as the cardinal function of law.[10] The notion that the will of the

[9] Pound, "The Scope and Purpose of Sociological Jurisprudence," *Harvard Law Rev.*, XXV, 141.
[10] Pound, "The Scope and Purpose of Sociological Jurisprudence," *Harvard Law Rev.*, XXV, 143.

individual is important only in so far as its autonomy promotes social interests has developed within the last hundred years and is still regarded as a novel idea by many Americans. What is meant by social interest is not so clear, but it connotes a community of interest, shared by large numbers of people in contradistinction to the interest of a single individual.

It is not without significance that the idea of social justice was born during a period when specialization in labor was gaining momentum and producing large numbers of men laboring under similar disabilities which tended to make them conscious of their common plight and to bring them together into large groups because of their increasing dependence upon other large groups with dissimilar interests. The common interests of those within a group encouraged collective action and the interdependence of groups with conflicting interests necessitated coöperation which accentuated the importance of group or class interests as distinguished from individual interests.

According to the eminent French jurist, Duguit, "the division of social labor is the paramount fact of our time; it is the pivotal point, as it were, upon which the law of today is revolving and accounts for the conception of social function as the only sound basis of law." [11]

The social utilitarians affected man's ideas about law in several ways. They brought purpose into legal thinking; they affirmed the power of man to control the development of law; and they emphasized the conception of law as a means of social ends.

Jhering's ideas have been referred to by Kohler as "amateurish platitudes" [12] and Berolzheimer has argued that "psychologically, man is not a coldly calculating machine regulated by utility, but an emotionally responsive being"; that "utilitarianism fails to account for government or law, not alone by

[11] Duguit, *Les Transformations générales du droit privé depuis le Code Napoléon.* (See transl. *Progress of Continental Law in the 19th Century*), 76.
[12] Kohler, *Philosophy of Law* (Albrecht's transl.), 11.

reason of the many residual phenomena that refuse to tally with this view, but because of the inherent difficulty of reaching an acceptable definition of utility." [13] Nevertheless the increasing efforts of man during recent years to bring about desired results through legislation bear witness to the fact that the ideas of the social utilitarians have not been without effect.

With the appearance of Darwin's *Origin of Species* there followed a widespread interest in biology and the hypothesis of evolution. This prompted a study of primitive society which resulted in a biological explanation of law. Likewise the influence of Karl Marx led to an attempt to explain law as a by-product of economic conditions. Also with the rising interest in psychology, men observed that social phenomena were partly the result of psychic forces and men like Ward and Tarde perceived law as an expression of the group will.[14]

While the acquisition of new knowledge and its application during the nineteenth century coupled with the changes which were taking place in the social structure affected man's ideas about law in many ways, his ancient propensity to wonder about the place of law in the scheme of things was not wholly dead. Moreover, the rigorous disciplines of the natural sciences and their requirement of purely objective methods, had not completely rid man of his idealism. Secretly he still yearned for justice even though he confessed that it was a myth. Actually he continued to enact laws and to repeal laws with the hope that life would be made more bearable. It was to be expected, therefore, that the twentieth century would witness a revival of interest in philosophical jurisprudence. Old ideas had to be revised in the light of new knowledge, but a creed there had to be and a number of creeds appeared.

The first to appear is the creed of the Neo-Kantians which

[13] Berolzheimer, *The World's Legal Philosophies* (Jastrow's transl.), 76.

[14] For an excellent discussion of these and other interpretations of legal history, see Pound, "Scope and Purpose of Sociological Jurisprudence," *Harvard Law Rev.*, XXV, 162, 495, 503; Pound, *Interpretations of Legal History*.

is embodied in the work of Stammler. He accepts the principle of evolution and concedes that there is no fixed and unchanging justice. On the other hand, he proclaims absolute and eternal principles for determining justice whatever the conditions, the time or the place, "A law of nature with changing content." [15] He recognizes the errors of the historical jurists and admits the power of man to affect the development of law by conscious effort. Also he substitutes for Kant's individualism a social theory of justice with the proviso that the will of the individual is not to be arbitrarily restrained.

Following shortly after Stammler came the monumental work of Kohler which sets forth the creed of the Neo-Hegelians. After roundly condemning the views of the Neo-Kantians because of their alleged disregard of the facts of history, Kohler builds an imposing philosophy upon the premise that law is a cultural phenomenon which is ever changing. That is just which accords with the culture of the particular time and place. Unlike the historical jurists who thought legal development was beyond the control of man, Kohler concedes the efficacy of human effort in adjusting law to the prevailing culture. He too repudiates the extreme individualistic philosophy of the eighteenth century and places law upon a social base although he insists that the advance of culture is dependent upon the fullest possible development of the individual.

"Humanity," says Kohler, "is destined to a deep knowledge of the world and of the supermundane. It is destined to form and to rule, to form in the sphere of art, to rule over the earth; and, perhaps, by virtue of technical science, over further fields of the universe. The totality of humanity's achievements is called culture; and in this culture, it is the part of the law to promote and to vitalize, to create order and system, on the one hand; and, on the other, to uphold and further intellectual progress. . . . Thus the history of humanity shows a constant

[15] Stammler, *The Theory of Justice* (Husik's transl.), 107.

tendency toward individualization, and again an unceasing pressure toward collectivism; the development of legal principles corresponds to both these movements, immeasurably increasing the forces of the individual, on the one hand, and, on the other, promoting unity so that the achievements and the activity of the individual may benefit mankind." [16]

There also grew up a body of thinkers whose only creed seems to be that they have no creed. They claim to know nothing except what they perceive, and such generalizations about law as they admit are confessedly mere hypotheses for experimental purposes. They wholly reject metaphysics, and are skeptical about ethics. Their interest seems to be in observing where observation is possible and rejoicing in such understanding as their experience permits. To them man's ideals of right and justice or his theories about law and its function are but phenomena, like his behavior, to be observed and reckoned with in relation to other phenomena. They are more interested in a science of law than in legal philosophy. In so far as they are philosophers at all, they reflect the ideas of James and Dewey. For lack of a better name, they are called Positivists, because of their objective methods and their empirical ideas.

What is more important than their differences is the agreement among Neo-Kantians, Neo-Hegelians and Positivists alike that the individualistic conception of law is no longer tenable. While the echoes of this eighteenth century idea are still heard, the events of the last fifty years have disclosed its fallacy. The conception of the inalienable rights of man was a valuable aid in the revolt against tyranny, and it was suited to the needs of the pioneers during the periods of conquest, of colonization and adventure. But with the rise of present day society, these same inalienable rights became obstacles in the path of progress. They stood in the way of important changes

[16] Kohler, *Philosophy of Law* (Albrecht's transl.), 59, 54.

in the law made necessary by new conditions. Thus the same idea which had once aided in the struggle for freedom was now operating to enslave mankind. A new conception of law was needed and sociological jurisprudence came into vogue.

While most of us are disdainful of the philosophical and juristic ideas which I have described, it is surprising how, unconsciously, our reactions to questions of law and government are controlled by them. We cannot escape them. They are an important part of our intellectual inheritance. They are transmitted to us in different forms by our parents and our teachers. They permeate the books which we read and the discussions which we hear. In time they become deeply rooted in the subcellars of our brains. Start a discussion of constitutional law and you will hear much about the fundamental law and the rights of man. The natural law philosophers are not all dead. Consult a lawyer about your business affairs and you will find that the analytical jurists are with us still. Propose a repeal of the Workmen's Compensation Law and you will be surprised by the number of sociological jurists who dwell in our midst. What is more important is the fact that most of us do not belong exclusively to any one of the schools. At different times the same man speaks the language of one and then the language of another. It would be most instructive if, instead of contrasting the reactions of one man to those of another, we began comparing the different reactions of the same man. Stop contrasting Holmes with McReynolds and begin comparing Holmes with Holmes and McReynolds with McReynolds.

We are living in an age of reconstruction. Our system of law is being made over in order to meet the requirements of a vastly changed society. Out of the maze of ideas about law which have evolved during the ages, there is one to which man is holding fast: that is the idea that he can influence its development by conscious effort. The enormous amount of legislation which has been enacted during the last quarter century is ample proof of this fact. It is also evidence that man's efforts to manipulate the law have not always been directed by an enlightened intelligence.

Progress has been made but much remains to be done. Among the outstanding achievements of the century, forced by this age of specialists, has been the use of specialists in connection with law administration. Through the establishment of numerous commissions, bureaus and departments, as parts of the executive branch of government, with power to make rules and regulations and to enforce them in the various fields of human endeavor, it has been possible to make use of specialized knowledge in the regulation of specialized activities. Thus, we have doctors in charge of health bureaus, engineers in the departments of building, and experts in transportation on railroad commissions. Moreover, the development of administrative agencies has turned law into a preventive as well as a remedial device. Men are no longer compelled to endure a danger until they are hurt and then sue for damages. The administrative tribunal may prescribe regulations calculated to prevent dangers and proceed immediately to remove them when they arise. Also in the fields of commerce and trade there has been a decided movement towards uniform laws in the different states. The Uniform Negotiable Instruments Law, the Uniform Sales Act, the Uniform Bills of Lading Act and the Uniform Warehouse Receipts Act, are statutes of this type. Similarly, through the expansion of the Act to Regulate Commerce, the transportation facilities of the country have been largely placed under a single control thus avoiding the confusion which formerly resulted from the simultaneous control of a single trunk line railroad by the utilities commissions of a number of states. Furthermore, a vast amount of constructive legislation, such as workmen's compensation acts, the Federal Reserve Act, child labor laws, and the like, has been enacted, thus demonstrating that man can make laws which promote the general welfare. These achievements have not been accomplished without a struggle. At every step the theories of natural law and the inalienable rights of man have blocked the way but the will to progress has prevailed. On the other hand, many blunders have been made. Foolish laws have been passed and good laws have been abused or overturned. Blunders will continue to be made so long as the various and inconsistent ideas about law are the masters rather than the servants of men. If man would make better use of these ideas in determining the course of his conduct, he must first become conscious of them and of their influence upon his reactions. He must seek knowledge wherever he can find it and strive to be guided by experience rather than by emotion.

With these multifarious ideas and an elaborate system of laws fashioned largely after a culture which had passed, man has labored during the last quarter century. At the same time, he has carried the burden of the most complex civilization in the history of the world. Is it surprising that the law is no better than it is? Is it not remarkable that it works as well as it does?

PSYCHOLOGY

Robert S. Woodworth

Over twenty years ago, when I had the privilege of address-
ing this body — or its predecessor — and presenting a sketch
of the then state of the science of psychology, what loomed
largest in my presentation, according to the record preserved,[1]
was a certain cleavage within the ranks of psychologists. "Two
standards are displayed," I told you, "two parties are in the
field." The one party consisted of the introspectionists, who
defined their goal as the description of consciousness. The
other party had no special name, but might be called the
objectivists, since they doubted the value of introspective observations, and were not interested in the description of consciousness as such, but used objective methods in the effort to
understand what might roughly be designated as the mental
functions of the organism.

It was a surprise to me, just the other day, on reading over
this lecture of 1908, to find the cleavage of the introspective
and objective wings of psychology so much to the fore, several
years before the emergence of behaviorism. We may rightly
think of behaviorism as an outstanding characteristic of the
past twenty-five years, but we have to remember that it was
very fully prepared for, on the positive and constructive side.
Objective methods for studying learning, memory, emotion,
and motor reactions were already well developed and much in
use. Tests for measuring individual abilities and performances
had been in use, though not in wide use, for a decade or more.
Animal psychology, which also made use exclusively of objective methods, had developed very rapidly in the preceding few

[1] *Psychology* (1908).

years. Objective psychology was a fact, a going concern. It is true that it had made no claim to be the whole of psychology. The spirit of the objective psychologists of that day was well expressed by Cattell, in 1904: "There is no conflict between introspective analysis and objective experiment — on the contrary, they should and do continually coöperate. But the rather widespread notion that there is no psychology apart from introspection is refuted by the brute argument of accomplished fact." [2] What has happened since that time is that a considerable number of active young psychologists have not only adopted the objective method for their own researches, but have gone further and insisted that the introspective method is essentially futile and unscientific, and that scientific psychology must be based wholly on objective observation.

If that were all that behaviorism had done, it would deserve only passing mention in the story of the past twenty-five years. As a matter of fact, it is difficult to demonstrate any pronounced effect of behaviorism upon the methods and actual research work of psychologists. Behaviorism did not open the door to radically new types of investigation, nor did it effectively close the door to the introspective type of work. It did not convert the introspectionists — fortunately, for they have made valuable contributions in recent years, especially to the study of sensation. The most that behaviorism did to the introspectionists was to arouse them to more vigorous efforts to hold up their end. Behaviorism has, however, been espoused, almost religiously, by many of the younger psychologists, as they came along, and thus has shifted the center of gravity of psychological study away from the introspective and towards the objective side. It has perhaps delayed progress as much as it has furthered it, by filling the atmosphere with unnecessary discussion, and holding psychology in the debating-society stage of its development. Good or bad, it has been and is a striking

[2] *Popular Science Monthly*, LXVI (1904), 176-186.

phenomenon. Whatever the individual psychologist's attitude in the matter, he must admit that the appearance of behaviorism is a sign of the times, and something that psychology has to explain to its sister sciences.

Behaviorism is rather a puzzling phenomenon. Had it really made the discovery that psychology could study human and animal behavior, and had it originated the objective method in psychology, then the enthusiasm with which many have greeted it would be easily understood. But behavior study was already in full swing, and in fact gave birth to behaviorism — not the reverse. As to methodology, while several of the behaviorists have been active in incisive research, their methods have not been radically new, and their contributions in this respect have been on a par with those of other psychologists, rather than revolutionary or distinctive. Perhaps more can be claimed for the movement on the side of concepts and theories than on the side of method. There has certainly been much less said in late years of consciousness. This change, however, like the increased use of objective methods, is at most an accentuation of a tendency that was already visible, rather than a revolution due to a single group.

Starting with the impression that all the traditional terms of psychology, consciousness, sensation, perception, emotion, learning, memory, thinking and the rest, were tainted beyond recovery by the subjectivism of the past, the behaviorists have little by little taken most of these terms back into their vocabulary, by giving them a behavioristic definition. Behavior includes not only the overt movements of arms and legs, but also, of course, the movements of speech, even when these become so reduced as to be inaudible. And it includes movements of the internal organs, as well as the secretory activity of the glands. Behavior is conceived as motor and glandular activity of every sort, and the fundamental hypothesis of behaviorism seems to be that all activity of the organism, in-

cluding whatever we ordinarily call "mental," is really motor
and glandular activity. Emotion is said to be visceral activity
— a theory of emotion which amounts to the old James-Lange
theory minus any reference to the sensations which James and
Lange supposed to result from the visceral activity and to
make up the feeling of the emotion. Thinking is said to consist
of speech movements — of slight, "sub-vocal" movements only
to be observed by the aid of refined apparatus which has yet to
be devised. Memory consists in the retention of verbal habits.
Conscious behavior is verbalized behavior, that is, behavior
accompanied by telling oneself what one is doing; and the
unconscious is the unverbalized. Thus the behaviorist has succeeded in admitting to his psychology several topics which at
first he left out in the cold. He has succeeded in formulating
theories of several types of mental activity — theories worthy
of consideration, even by those who are not behaviorists, but
theories the chief value of which, to the behaviorist himself,
is that they allow him to cover the ground of psychology without lapsing into subjectivism. The particular theories so far
put forth may be hasty, and not destined to endure; but it is
an achievement and a contribution to have formulated these
activities in terms of behavior.

Yet I do not believe that we have put our finger on the real
claim of behaviorism. I do not believe its appealing character
rests upon saying "subvocal speech" when you mean thinking,
or "visceral behavior" when you mean emotion. This phenomenon called behaviorism seems, rather, to consist mostly
in the fearless, iconoclastic spirit of its promulgators. They
call a spade a spade; they handle everything without gloves.
They are tough-minded, hard-boiled. They are foes of
anything "traditional," and willing to entertain the most
unsettling possibilities, such as that it might be better
if children never knew their own parents. They abhor
mystery and especially any explanation that leads into mystery.

Consciousness smacks of the mind, the mind of the soul, and the soul of old theological mystery. Therefore away with consciousness! "With the advent of behaviorism in 1913," writes Watson,[3] "the mind-body problem disappeared. . . . The behaviorist finds no mind in his laboratory." "The unverbalized of the behaviorist is a natural science substitute for the unconscious of the psychoanalysts. The mystery of the unconscious then straightway disappears." Behavioristic psychology is a simplified psychology, simplified largely by elimination. Though what is thus eliminated may later reappear, there can be no doubt that many problems inherited by modern psychology could well be ignored, for the time at least, and that this spirit of fearless breaking with the past has scientific value as well as popular appeal. Thus psychologists in general, while not converted to behaviorism, look with some favor on its adolescent temerity and exuberance.

Though behaviorism, under that name, was and is a distinctly American movement, it obtaineed its best ammunition from Russian sources. Just about the beginning of the period we are considering, the physiologist Pavlov [4] and the neurologist Bechterew,[5] both working in what was then St. Petersburg, and working independently, or in rivalry rather than in coöperation, discovered how to produce in the laboratory what Bechterew called associative reflexes, and what Pavlov called conditioned reflexes. Bechterew devoted the efforts of his laboratory to motor reflexes, and showed how a breathing movement, an avoiding movement, or a reaching movement, could be attached to an indifferent stimulus simply by combining this latter with a stimulus which naturally aroused the response. Pavlov preferred to work with the flow of saliva as the response, and showed how to tie this response to the sound of

[3] In E. Dummer, *The Unconscious: A Symposium* (1928), 93.
[4] I. P. Pavlov, *Conditioned Reflexes* (1927).
[5] W. von Bechterew, *Objective Psychology* (1913).

a bell or metronome, a touch on the skin, or any originally
indifferent stimulus. Each of these laboratories, believing that
an important clew to the understanding of human and animal
behavior had thus been found, devoted itself with great energy
to following up the lead. Bechterew called the subject objective
psychology, or reflexology. Pavlov called it cerebral physiology, and has always insisted that his work was physiological
and not psychological in any sense. He insisted that such terms
as desire and expectancy, applied to the experimental animal,
simply led to confusion, and that physiological concepts alone
were of any service. Of late, however, becoming acquainted
with the American animal psychology, which started in 1898
with Thorndike, he has recognized it as quite harmonious with
his own work. As a matter of fact, Pavlov's conditioned reflex
work has meant more to American psychology than it has to
the physiologists. It has been a godsend in two ways to the
behaviorists. The notion of a conditioned reflex has been
taken as furnishing a fine behavioristic key to all learning; and
the conditioned reflex method has been accepted as a great
addition to the stock of objective methods. The most striking
application of this method was Watson's experiment in which
he showed how the fear of a furry animal could be generated
in a baby by presenting the animal along with a loud noise that
frightened the child. This experiment put into circulation the
notion of conditioned fears, and of conditioned likes and dis-
likes and conditioned emotions in general.

But, some one may query, exactly what has been achieved by
this work? No one ever supposed that *all* fears were instinctive; it was obvious to common sense, and well recognized in
psychology, that many fears were acquired by association.
Also the mouth watering at the dinner bell was obviously an
acquired response. Is it so important to know exactly how the
fear of furry animals is, or may be, acquired? Well, the
achievement seems to be twofold. The conditioned reflex is

thought of as a learning process at the bottom level, and as not demanding any elaborate intellectual work, such as would be involved in "seeing the connection." To be sure, the inner process of forming a conditioned reflex may really be very complicated, since we know, from Pavlov, Bechterew and others, that it depends on activity of the cerebral hemispheres. But the name, conditioned reflex, carries a physiological atmosphere, and so leads us towards elementals. "To be conditioned" sounds more scientific than "to have learned." The gain, up to date, is rather illusory, and consists mostly in an increasing *demand* for fundamentals in psychology.

It is a very definite gain, however, to have experimental evidence of the conditioned or associative response, even though we were practically convinced of the thing all along. It is a gain for psychology to get away from the arm chair and from what "we know," though it must be admitted that many who talk glibly about "conditioning" are still comfortably ensconced in the arm chair. All in all, however, and from many causes, psychology has certainly made progress during the present century in the direction of demanding clean-cut evidence for its conclusions.

Behaviorism is a logical development of the association psychology, which has flourished for the past two centuries. For the phrase, "association of ideas," it has substituted the more modern "connection between stimulus and response," which certainly has the advantage of bringing motor activity into the picture. The conditioned reflex may be thought of as association in its lowest terms. Where, then, did behaviorism start, the fact rather than the name? Shall we reckon Thorndike, certainly a pronounced associationist, with the behaviorists, and shall we perhaps call him the real leader of the movement? He never sought to read the introspectionists out of the party, and so far he obviously is not a behaviorist. He spoke of the satisfyingness and annoyingness of the outcome of an act as factors in stamping the act into or out of the system; and in other details his terminology is not altogether free of the subjectivism which the behaviorists abhor. But I suspect that, in the perspective of later years, his work and conceptions will appear to be part and parcel of whatever is positive in the behavioristic movement. In fact, already, from the perspective of spatial distance, that is, from the viewpoint of European psychologists,[6] Thorndike is sometimes singled out as the typical American behaviorist.

If behaviorism is radical in pushing the association psychology to its limit, another school, taking shape among the younger German psychologists almost simultaneously with the emergence of behaviorism in this country, may be called still more radical, since it rejects the whole association psychology as a hampering tradition. Though the Gestalt psychology had its forerunners, it emerged into sudden prominence in 1912 with a vigorous protest against the "brick and mortar psychology" of the associationists. The great difficulty of the association psychology had always been to find the mortar that held together the supposed sensory elements into the complex patterns of tune and rhythm, visible forms and objects. Psychology had conceived its task to be analogous to that of analytical chemistry. It had sought for the elements of experience and of behavior, and had found them, so it believed, in elementary sensations and feelings on the one side, and in elementary reflexes on the other. But it had to admit that these elements were somewhat abstract, if not unreal. The elementary sensations and feelings do not occur in neat isolation, but always in patterns and configurations; the concrete, observable datum being the pattern and not the elements. So, on the motor side, the simple reflex was admitted to be an abstraction, convenient for purposes of analysis, but not occurring in isolation. The

[6] See, for example, K. Bühler, in *Bericht über den IX. Kongress für experimentelle Psychologie* (1926).

organism, so the Gestalt psychologists insisted with new emphasis, was a dynamic system, not a sum of separable parts. It was not a closed system, since it was in constant interaction with the environment, but it behaved as a whole system and not as a mere aggregation of parts. The task of psychology, accordingly, was not to break this totality into artificial elements, but to take the system as a whole, and to study the patterns of its activity and the conditions under which each pattern arose. The patterns are primary, and not to be understood as products of some sort of integration of separate elements. For example, motion as we see it in the moving pictures, in spite of the fact that there is no physical motion on the screen, but only a rapid series of stationary snap shots, cannot be explained as built up out of the stationary views as elements, but indicates a primary motion-seeing response of the organism; and what psychology has to do is to discover the conditions under which this response pattern is aroused to activity, as against the conditions under which that other type of response pattern, seeing a sequence of still views, is called into play.

Behaviorism erased from its slate the analysis of conscious experience which had been proclaimed as the task of psychology. Gestalt psychology further erased the motor analysis which behaviorism advocated. It would seem that the psychological slate should thus be left fairly clean; and so it would, except for the fact that the actual research of psychologists has all along been largely devoted to studying the conditions under which different reactions occurred — under what conditions two lights could be distinguished in brightness, under what conditions a poem or a skilled movement would be learned, under what conditions a conditioned reflex would be established. A case could be made for the assertion that we had been Gestalt psychologists all along, without knowing it.

Of all the work done by the Gestalt psychologists — and

they have been exceedingly active in research — most general interest attaches to their studies of the learning process, especially in animals. Where Thorndike had spoken of learning by trial and error, with the gradual and automatic stamping in of satisfying responses and elimination of annoying responses — and where the behaviorists had sought to go him one better, by discarding all reference to satisfaction and annoyance, and explaining all learning by the conditioned reflex — along comes Köhler [7] with evidence that the essential thing in learning is not a gradual process, but what he calls "insight." The term is not meant to imply any elevated intellectual grasping of principles, but a typically sudden shaping up of situation and goal-seeking into workable response. An instance is afforded by the behavior of a chimpanzee, left with two pieces of bamboo in his cage and with a banana lying too far outside his cage to be reached by either piece of bamboo alone. After an hour of futile angling with the separate sticks, the chimpanzee accidentally, as it seemed, got the two together into a jointed stick, and immediately used it with success, and retained the trick after this one success. Similar behavior has been observed, experimentally, in young children. There can be no doubt that such learning by insight is a real fact, but we certainly do not have the evidence, as yet, to conclude that all learning is of this type. Nor, on the other hand, have we the evidence to conclude that even the conditioned reflex is altogether free from insight. The Gestalt psychologists may be *fundamentally* right in their theory of learning, or they may simply have added to our collection of well-attested varieties of learning. Here, as in many other lines of psychological work, while we should be inclined to claim important progress during the present century, we have to admit that we are still in the midst of things, and that the progress, to date, consists rather in opening up the problem than in reaching a final

[7] W. Köhler, *The Mentality of Apes* (1925); *Gestalt Psychology* (1929).

solution. For this reason, I am afraid that our showing of progress will be much less impressive than that of other sciences; and yet I cannot but feel that the progress has been genuine and that the prospects for further progress in the near future are remarkably good.

The great contribution of Gestalt psychology is really its stress on perception as a factor in behavior — on seeing as essential to doing. Those psychologists whose aim is to analyze conscious experience have treated perception as affording problems in sensory analysis, without much reference to the part played by perception in action. The behaviorists, in their exclusive emphasis on action, have found little to say of perception. To the Gestalt psychologists, perception and action cannot be separated, and action consists as much in grasping the pattern of the situation as it does in motor activity.

Twenty-five years ago, psychoanalysis was only beginning to be known. For a decade, it had been getting under way, but its career of influence was just beginning. The flourishing of psychoanalysis has certainly been one of the major characteristics of the period. Psychoanalysis represents not an application of existing psychological knowledge to the treatment of nervous disorders, but, quite the contrary, a mode of treatment growing up in the physician's practice, and spreading thence into psychology with a mass of new facts, new outlooks and new theories. Psychology has been subject to pressure from two sides. As a young hopeful in the family of sciences, it has been driven to improve its methods in the effort to become more scientific; and we see the results of this pressure in behaviorism and Gestalt psychology, as well as in many other movements and individual efforts that have not been recorded here. On the other hand, psychology has been urged to prove itself of some value in the life of men, and to show that it, of all subjects, possesses some human interest. Nowhere has the need for psychological understanding been greater than in the problems of personality adjustment — in the neuroses, in the psychoses, in the handling of delinquents and problem children. Many and varied have been the efforts to fathom the psychological problems of personality, and psychoanalysis may be regarded as the most outstanding response to this need, a sign of the times.

The popular interest in psychoanalysis is due largely to the freedom with which Freud and his disciples have handled the problems of sex; and possibly his greatest contribution has lain right here, in making it possible to examine and discuss this important side of life without embarrassment and with some approach to scientific detachment. It is probable, indeed, that Freud overemphasized the rôle of sex in behavior; and psychologists have on the whole found more value in his dynamic conceptions of repression, distortion and sublimation of impulses, and in his increasing insistence, as experience deepened his knowledge of personality difficulties, upon the period of childhood as formative of the personality. His psychology is a study of desires and their conflicts, a study of motivation, doubtless one of the most important, as well as most difficult, topics in our field. In spite of an enormous mass of what seem like unsupported assertions and wild, though brilliant theories, brought into psychology from psychoanalysis, we cannot doubt that our science has been greatly enriched from this source during the past two or three decades. For those of us who are old enough to realize what a short span of time is represented by twenty-five years, it is almost a shock to remember that back in 1904 such terms as repression and sublimation were practically unknown — or such terms as Adler's inferiority complex and compensation — or such as Jung's introvert and extrovert. Certainly the vocabulary of psychology has been greatly expanded during the period — and with the vocabulary, the working conceptions, even if we cannot say so much for the established results.

Twenty-five years ago, the intelligence tests were not in existence, and there were no such terms as "mental age" and "intelligence quotient." Not that there had been no work on tests for individual differences; for Galton, Cattell and others had labored for two decades in devising tests for various performances, and had mapped out some of the important scientific uses of such tests in the study of human variability and its dependence on heredity and environment. The fundamental statistical devices for determining averages, variations and correlations, so extensively applied during the recent decades to the results obtained by tests, were already at hand. But it was not till 1904 that the first serious practical problem demanding the use of tests was put into the hands of psychologists. This was the problem of the retardation of children in school, and of how far this retardation depended upon the incapacity of some children to make satisfactory school progress; and the psychologist into whose hands this problem was placed was Alfred Binet of Paris. He worked at this problem till his death in 1911, and the result of his labors was the intelligence test of the omnibus or varied-sample type, along with ingenious new methods of standardizing and scoring such tests. Many other tests of similar construction have followed, and a tremendous amount of energy on the part of routine workers and also on the part of some of the ablest psychologists of our time has gone into the test field. The tests have been used for placing children in school according to their ability, for educational and vocational advice, for selecting soldiers and officers, and for many similar practical purposes. Educational measurements and trade tests have followed along the lines laid down by the intelligence tests. Not a few psychologists have shaken their heads at what seemed to be an undue diversion of scientific energy into practical channels. But we are beginning to see very important scientific uses of the tests. A test is simply a certain kind of measuring rod, and, just like other measuring rods, it can be used for either practical or theoretical purposes. The problem of intelligence itself is one of the scientific problems which could not be solved until intelligence could be measured. It might seem that the logical development would be first to reach an adequate definition of intelligence, and then to devise ways of measuring it. But the actual sequence of events has been first the measurement of intelligence, and then, with the aid of the measurement, to seek out what intelligence is, whether a simple or a complex function of the organism, whether dependent mostly on speed, or on learning ability, or on a judicious suspension of reaction till the whole pattern of the situation can exert its effect. At the present time, we are just in the midst of this problem.

How far does the superiority of one person to another depend on heredity, and how far on environment, especially early environment? Here is a problem of the first magnitude, both practically and scientifically; and a problem which could scarcely be approached without good measures of intelligence. It is a problem that is just now being attacked with energy and with a clearer view of its difficulties. Special attention may be called to the value of studies of twins, of foster children, and of the development of children generally. When the same adults provide both the heredity and the home environment of children, the influences of heredity and environment are inextricably interwoven. But foster children, adopted in the first year of life, afford an opportunity for disentangling the two factors. Up to the present time, the results obtained are differently interpreted by the environmentalists and the hereditarians — for it appears that on this subject there are for some reason strong emotional biases on one side or the other, making it difficult to weigh the evidence impartially. Some will assure you that the superior potency of heredity, in producing intellectual differences among the individuals of a social group, is demonstrated beyond all cavil; while others are equally sure that what we know of the importance of early conditioning by the social environment makes it perfectly clear that all children of all races are potentially equal. One conclusion is as unjustified as the other, from the evidence at hand. We simply do not know the answer, in this year of grace. Give us another twenty-five years, and we may hope to state a real scientific conclusion.

The child in psychology is at least fifty years old, dating from the work of Darwin and Preyer about 1880; but he has come more and more into his own during recent times. Many conditions of modern life conspire to make the individual child of increasing social importance. Children are becoming a scarcer commodity and must not be wasted; and the adult life into which they are growing is more and more exacting. As the child is important for society, so science is important for the child. Moreover the child is important for science. From the scientific and sympathetic study of the child's development we may hope to solve that difficult problem of heredity and environment. We may hope to discover what the child must learn, and what he has without learning. We may hope to see how he learns, and so penetrate somewhat into the mystery of the learning process. We can note the beginnings of thinking and of creative activity, the concepts which the child first forms of the world about him, and the modification of those concepts with experience. We may hope to unearth the basic demands which the child makes upon his social environment and his modes of adjustment and maladjustment to the family and to groups of his own age. The experimental psychologist and the psychiatrist have begun to combine their efforts upon the problems set by the child. More than that, the sciences that deal with the child's nutrition and physical growth are being brought together into teamwork with the psychological and educational sciences, in the effort to know the child as a whole. Such comprehensive, large-scale enterprises in the study of child development are a thing but of yesterday, but are beginning to bear fruit, and many specific results could be cited, did time permit. It is a pity, also, not to have time for some indication of the great activity in the field of educational psychology, and of the results achieved there.

The relations of psychology to the other sciences have become closer and better defined during these years. The old almost exclusive affiliation with philosophy has broken down. Psychology is so many-sided, and its applications in education, in medicine, in industry and even in law have taken on such prominence as to make it impossible to tie up psychology to any other single discipline. Its status as an independent science is now pretty well recognized. But independence does not mean isolation; it means manifold contacts and coöperations with other groups of scientific workers. It is interesting to note that psychology now has a regular place in both the National Research Council, comprising the natural sciences, and in the Social Science Research Council. Its contacts with the biological sciences on the one side, and with the social sciences on the other, are becoming more and more intimate.

Both physiological psychology and social psychology have made rapid strides during the present century. On the physiological side, we have profited greatly from the studies of physiologists on reflex action, the functions of the brain and the endocrine glands. Nor have psychologists been content merely to receive; by throwing their own interests and methods into the game, they have contributed to the increase of knowledge. By combining the training technique of the animal psychologist with the operative technique of the physiologist, they have thrown some light on the action of the brain at the level of learned behavior, and have apparently reached the result [8] that the brain functions, not in separate segments, but in large patterns of activity spreading over the whole cerebrum — a conclusion more in line, certainly, with the views of the Gestalt

[8] K. S. Lashley, *Brain Mechanisms and Intelligence* (1929).

psychologists than with those of the reflexologists. Studies of
the developing behavior of embryonic animals [9] also lead to
the conclusion that the individual's behavior is always an
integrated total, never a set of disconnected reflexes which
need later to become integrated.

Social psychology has developed along with sociology and
has been cultivated largely by sociologists. The contribution
of the psychologists, naturally enough, has consisted in showing that the individual cannot be treated as a mere pawn in
the hands of society, but must be recognized as having propen-
sities and limitations that are important factors in his own
behavior and so in the behavior of the group in which he participates. McDougall's *Introduction to Social Psychology*, in
1908, marked a new era in the development of this branch, by
his insistence on individual motivation as the basis for group
activity. He traced all motivation to a number of instincts and
primary emotions, and his system had great vogue both in
psychology and in the social sciences, only to encounter severe
criticism with the lapse of time. The instincts have been called
in question, and have been a storm center of debate for the
past decade. Much less stress is laid on them than a few years
ago, as elements of human behavior. In part, this recent shift
of emphasis has come from fuller recognition of the part
played by the environment in conditioning the individual.
Psychology, closely allied both to the biological and to the
social sciences, should be able to see both the inner demands
of the organism and the pressure, or stimulating and directive
influence, of the social environment. Just as at many other
points of the broad front of psychological research and discussion, so here in social psychology, we seem to be on the
verge of new developments and better conceptions. One promising sign of the times is that experimental methods are being
tried out in social psychology.

[9] G. E. Coghill, *Anatomy and the Problem of Behavior* (1929).

The story I have told you seems mostly a story of beginnings. The picture I have sketched, of an enterprise beset with questionings as to what it should undertake and how, reveals a youth among the sciences. To be sure, I have not gone far below the surface, nor indicated the vast amount of painstaking detailed work which has really increased our knowledge of man to a great extent. Our results are neither scanty nor unimportant, even where they are not easy to formulate intelligibly in a few sentences. We really feel that we know our field much better than we did twenty-five years ago. Nor have I told you about the rapid growth of our personnel, sevenfold as large in this country, now as then. As workers in a young science, we feel the confidence of youth. We seem to ourselves to be just well started and are hopeful of important developments in the near future.

EDUCATION

William F. Russell

It was long ago that the invitation was extended to me to participate in this series of lectures portraying the progress of a quarter of a century in a variety of fields of human learning and celebrating the one hundred and seventy-fifth anniversary of the granting of the charter to King's College; and because of the many months intervening between the request and the date of the lecture itself, I was inveigled into accepting a task of extraordinary and surprising difficulty. At first it did not seem hard to compress into a brief space the achievements of twenty-five years in education, but as I entered into the problem I at once became impressed with the impossibility not only of confining the record to the period specified, but also of selecting and emphasizing the matters of greatest importance.

It would be simple, of course, to overwhelm you with columns of figures. By reference to mimeographed tables and by means of lantern slides we could compare conditions of the present with those of the past. Few pupils then, many now; poorly trained teachers then, well trained teachers now; changes in what we teach and how we teach, in textbooks and materials of instruction, in medical inspection, in examinations, tests and measurements, records and reports, in plans of promotion, in school laws, in student government, in extra-curricular activities, in character education, in phychoanalysis and psychiatry, in nursery schools and junior high schools, and in a host of other aspects of education. We then could consider the philosophies, scientific researches, and the social, economic and political changes that have produced these alterations in theory and practice. It would be possible for us to examine with care the course outlines and textbooks used in Teachers College and similar institutions in 1904 and, by contrasting the practices of 1929, to secure a fairly accurate picture of the developments of this period. We could, if time permitted, inventory the whole field of education as has been done in the new edition of the *Encyclopaedia Britannica*, but I fear that the net result of an hour's lecture of this sort would be no more than a jumble of words and figures which would yield only the vague notion that considerable change had taken place in education since the first administration of President Roosevelt.

I think it will be safe for us to admit at the outset that there have been far-reaching changes. We could easily demonstrate this fact if we had time; but rather than tax ourselves with an examination of data complete enough to substantiate this conclusion, let us imagine ourselves outside a wood, into which we occasionally follow an inviting path or trail to a hidden glade. Our return must be rapid so that we may not fail to see the forest for the trees. Let us not stop to examine each part of the forest or to see each tree or bit of underbrush. In fact we may not see the largest and most important trees at all. Our purpose is to make use of a few of the developments that have occurred in this field of education in order that we may have before us the real subject of this paper, which is not these changes that have taken place, but rather whether or not, and to what degree, they constitute progress.

One of the most interesting characteristics of education is the way in which the discovery of a new idea or the elimination of an old belief draws a whole series of alterations and modifications in its wake. Twenty-five years ago much of education was based upon the doctrine of formal discipline. This theory, according to Percy Nunn, was "expressed in popular and epigrammatic form in the statement that a man's education consists in what he retains after he has forgotten everything he learnt at school. School studies have as their aim the development of faculties or powers of the mind, and that development is the real reason for pursuing them. For instance, the Latin verses a boy learns today may all be forgotten soon after he leaves school but (it is held) that the learning has served to strengthen his memory and that is itself sufficient justification; he may have occasion to use the knowledge of chemistry or physics he has acquired, but that does not matter if he has gained from those studies powers of observation and inference which are universally valuable, and the habit of applying the scientific method to the subject of discussion. Similarly, geometry is held to train one's reasoning powers; algebra to develop mental accuracy. The assumption made here is that the strength or training a faculty acquires by being exercised upon a particular kind of material fits it to deal competently with any other kind of material to which it can be applied." It was a convenient doctrine. One did not need to worry about what a pupil studied. Certain subjects, notably mathematics and ancient languages, were deemed peculiarly fitted to discipline the mind. If the teacher but knew his subject and held his pupils strictly to account, all was well with methods of teaching. But the psychologists began to subject this belief to investigation by methods developed in other sciences, with the result that there began gradually to accumulate a weight of evidence tending to cast grave doubt upon this manner of the training of the mind. I do not pretend to say that the evidence is all in. I merely state that most educationists no longer have faith in the doctrine of formal discipline in its extreme form, and what a source of trouble this discovery has been! Thorndike lifted the lid of an educational Pandora's box.

If Latin or mathematics or any other subject could not be justified as an important mental training agency of the school, in and of itself, and if the use of the content of the curriculum itself in daily life was the standard of selection, a host of difficult problems at once presented themselves. What knowledge should the citizen have? What is commonly needed by all? What training should boys have that girls do not need, and vice versa? What special adjustments should be made for city and country, for North and South? The curriculum has changed from a fixed achievement to a source of bewilderment, and students of education are perplexed by the thousands of studies bearing upon this problem today. No longer are there just a few subjects taken by all; and the belief that subjects studied should be those needed in the life of the complex world in which we live today has produced a curriculum as broad as life itself. Formerly we had what might be termed a *table d'hôte* course of study. The waiter brought the soup, vegetables and pie, giving the diner only his choice of roast beef or roast pork, and coffee, tea or milk. The new curriculum is an *à la carte* menu, long and extended, with many dishes marked with a star as ready to serve, but I fear that those whose tastes are strange or exotic receive dishes all too hastily cooked. What shall the student choose? Which courses are best suited to his needs? And in what order? The convenience of the disciplinary theory in the uniform curriculum was completely lost when many new courses were introduced. Here emerged the problems of vocational and educational guidance, and as a result no school system finds its work complete without specialists in these fields; and educational scientists are bending every effort to supply more complete and accurate information.

America has long pursued an educational policy of eliminating from the course of study those subjects upon which there is widespread public controversy. Thus, in the field of religion where there was great disagreement, it was deemed wiser to teach nothing at all than to teach that which might be at variance with the faith of many of the parents. There was not much controversy about Latin or mathematics, or about any subject whose chief aim was to discipline the mind rather than to impart a knowledge of the content itself. The breakdown of the theories of formal discipline has subjected the whole course of study to the difficulties that controversy, propaganda and indoctrination forced upon the school.

The old idea put little emphasis upon the skill of the teacher. The new idea demands that the subject matter and the pupil be treated in a specific way, if mental training be the end. One of the interesting coincidences, if it be a coincidence, in the history of education in the past twenty-five years is the manner in which Dr. Dewey's tremendous contribution in his analysis of the complete act of thought filled the void left by the breakdown of the doctrine of formal discipline. Dr. Dewey developed a new logic. He gave a new insight into how we think, and revealed that the syllogism and the propositions of geometry which we once considered the symbols of thought were not thought at all but rather the vestiges of mummified remains of thought that once had lived. Just as dead typhoid germs injected into the blood stream will prevent typhoid, so there is the implication that the indoctrination of sufficient dead thoughts will prevent thinking. The mere following of prearranged thought tracks will not induce thought. We must learn how to think by thinking, and Dr. Dewey showed us how we think. Thought begins with a difficulty, a something wrong, a problem. This difficulty must challenge the attention. In life no whip forces one to think, no Phi Beta Kappa key entices one on. The challenge lies within the problem and within the person. Once initiated, the thought process continues in the casting about for a possible solution of the difficulty; the bringing to bear of all the experience, information, habits and skill of the individual; the selection of the most promising hypotheses; the testing in the light of practice; and the final conclusion. To the old concept of thought is added a head and a tail, and a new spirit pervades the process. The emphasis goes from the teacher to the pupil, from the classroom out into the world, from the recorded results of previous logic to the continually new process in the mind of the pupil. The startling implication of this analysis is the idea that work in school designed to train the mind must have a specific and unique method and that mental discipline comes neither from hard work in and of itself, nor from some special subject or subjects. It comes only when the emphasis is on the pupil; only when problems arise that are so real as to challenge the pupil; only when the pupil himself thinks the problems through. The pupil — not just the teachers — must see why. The pupil himself must organize the process. His way may be different from that of the expert, but he must do it in his own way. The new discipline is child-centered.

This idea of teaching puts the responsibility upon the teacher. No longer will routine mastery of the subject suffice, nor rules of thumb serve as a guide. Great skill is required and a solid knowledge of the subject, together with good understanding of related subjects and their applications to life. Projects and the new combination survey courses which are the result of the new psychology demand far better trained teachers.

The broad curriculum and the new teacher have in turn forced other educational adaptations. The library assumes new importance. Even such apparently disconnected items as state laws for the certification of teachers, school-building standards and educational finances have been forced to change.

Now the next trail which we shall follow into the forest brings us to a glade surrounded by questionnaires, I.Q.'s, standard deviations, score cards, correlations, tables, tests, surveys, spot maps and scales. These all go together. Not all these educational innovations are the accomplishment of the past twenty-five years, but it is in this period that the most stimulating changes have occurred. Teachers, supervisors and administrators differ from their predecessors of a quarter century ago in the wealth of material that they have at hand to furnish comparison of their work with that of others. Rice collects samples of spelling difficulties in many cities and shows the variations in the results of teaching. Ayres perfects the process and by statistical methods develops standardized tests of spelling ability. Courtis, by collecting the results of thousands of children's efforts in column addition, subtraction and other arithmetical processes, devises standard tests in arithmetic. Thorndike submits hundreds of samples of children's handwriting to judges who rank them in order; then by relying upon the assumption that equally often-noticed differences are equal, he selects samples at equal intervals, thus making a series of illustrations of handwriting progressing from bad to good; and when he has computed a zero point, we have at hand a scale for the measurement of handwriting. Binet and Simon, searching far and wide for a measure of intelligence, found like Tyltil and Mytyl in "The Bluebird" that their goal was at home in the simple and ingenuous questions and answers of the intelligence tests, which now furnish us a guide and an increasingly perfected instrument whereby the pupil may be compared with others of his kind.

In most school subjects standardized tests and scales have been developed. There are score cards to rate buildings and their equipment, teachers and janitors, school citizenship and traits of character. Surveys reveal conditions in schools, cities or countries. Curricula are analyzed, rated, almost weighed and measured. A principal can study his school and subject his unfortunate pupils to a complete testing program. He can sit back in his chair and say, "In comparison with the 76 other schools in this city we rank 7th in arithmetic, 16th in spelling, 31st in school citizenship, 64th in character; our building scores 761; our janitors are 36 per cent efficient; our average I.Q. is 103; we are 11.3 per cent retarded; and so on *ad infinitum.* Our progress from September to February was 7.3 per cent

less effective than it was last year, and behind that of other
schools. Our records and reports are not entered on the
standard form." In other words, a principal has the educational equivalent of the thermometer, stethoscope, microscope,
metabolism tests and scales that assist the doctor in his diagnosis.

A great change has occurred since the time when, as a boy
in the second year of the Horace Mann High School, I
watched the ceremonies of the sesquicentennial celebration at
Columbia University. All these changes are fundamentally the
product of one idea. The old ideal was Mark Hopkins and the
log — the monk and the cell. It was a lonely process. The
teacher was in his classroom, away from the world and apart
from his fellows. Isolation has always been associated with
backwardness. Change comes from seeing the work of others,
from travel, from familiarity with the best that has been
thought, said and done. All these tests and scales, standards
and surveys, serve to break down isolation. A good idea multi-
plies; a bad practice becomes stifled. Robinson Crusoe leaves
his desert isle and goes out into the world, tests his ideas and
practices with those of his fellows, and returns a different man.
So it is with education as affected by this comparative statistical
approach. The result has been change.

The next trail through our educational forest leads to a
glade peopled with the scientists who, so far as their own
subject is concerned, question almost everything, who take
little for granted, who defy convention and the ideas of the
past and seek to follow facts in the hope of finding truth. We
have read the *Microbe Hunters* and *Hunger Fighters*. The
past twenty-five years have witnessed the "Destroyers of Ignorance." We have no time to detail the contributions of these
men in many fields, in adult education, in infant learning, in
group teaching and individual instruction, in the development
of special methods, in the selection of curricula, in the testing

of materials and the like. But for the benefit of those who are not familiar with such developments we might take time to give a rough and brief account of a few discoveries in two or three fundamental fields.

Take the case of spelling. We all know how difficult it is to teach a child to spell correctly. At the same time, we appreciate the importance of correct spelling in American life because, for example, a word wrong in a letter of application will lose the appointment for an otherwise well-qualified applicant. In fact, in this country, education and spelling ability are often popularly confused. Yet if we were at this moment to take a spelling test in the fashion of Mr. Work's admirable radio bridge lessons, we should have difficulty. How many of us could spell the following nine words: intercede, supersede, harass, embarrass, rarefy, vilify, inoculate, innuendo, and pic-nicking?

The educational scientist attacked this problem. The first question was: what words should children be taught to spell? It was obvious that they could not be taught the whole dictionary. Consequently, some selection was necessary. The examination of the old spelling books revealed little general agreement. Some of the larger books contained as many as 15,000 words and some smaller ones, fewer than four or five thousand. Sometimes the large vocabulary failed to contain the words included in the smaller. It is known that every person has three vocabularies: one for speaking, one for reading and one for writing; that one can speak words which he cannot read and can read words which he cannot spell. Obviously the writing vocabulary should form the basis for a selection of words for spelling, and the bulk of writing in the world takes the form of personal correspondence. The analysis of all types of letters by many investigators formed the basis for the spelling vocabulary. Word counts were made in many fields and it was surprising to find the relatively small number of words

that occurred frequently, and the great number that were used
but rarely. Schoolmasters have available today lists of words
arranged in order of frequency of occurrence. These lists form
the basis for the curriculum in spelling.

Not only was it necessary to determine what words to teach,
but it was also important to secure some clue to the order in
which they should be taught. Which should be given in the
second grade, in the third, in the fourth? In an effort to determine this, studies were made to detect the relative difficulty of
the more frequently used words and schoolmasters now know
how frequently a given word is likely to be used and also how
difficult it is to spell.

With the order determined, it remained only to find out how
to teach these words; and all sorts of studies were made to
discover the proper number of words for a lesson; the number
of repetitions; the value of spelling rules, definition, syllabifi-
cation, illustration and many other teaching devices. Suffice it
to say that, despite the fact that the problem has not been
entirely solved, undoubtedly teachers know how to teach children to spell far more effectively than they did a generation
ago.

In arithmetic we find the same ingenious and careful investigation. Take the problem of teaching the child how to add.
We give him a problem and discover that he fails. The old
adages advise "If at first you don't succeed, try, try again!"
"Practice makes perfect." So the old-fashioned teacher would
meet this difficulty by giving more problems in addition. Suppose that we test the child for speed. Can he add quickly? His
parents say "He is slow but sure. The race is not to the swift.
Remember the hare and the tortoise." Modern research points
to the curious fact that undirected practice *does not* make
perfect, that slowness and inaccuracy *do* go hand in hand; and
that within limits the race *is* to the swift. Educational investigators have found out what the golf professional already

knew — that you cannot correct a hook or slice by practice, but that the particular difficulty must first be diagnosed. In golf it may be the grip, stance, swing, wrist, follow-through, eye or what not. So it has been proved that accurate and speedy addition and all other phases of arithmetic require a combination of a variety of skills, each of which must be almost automatic. Proper teaching consists in the diagnosis of the particular difficulties, with drill to follow upon each separate part.

I believe that the most spectacular discovery of the past twenty-five years is to be found in the researches in the teaching of reading. How long have teachers been accustomed to teach little children to read by standing them up, book in hand, orally to pronounce the selection. Scientific investigators knew that the purpose of reading was obviously to enable the reader quickly and accurately to gain meaning from the printed page. Hence, they devised tests to determine what the reader retains of the content of the selection read. These tests were given to good readers and poor, quick readers and slow; and to the amazement of all it was found that some readers, commonly judged as good, caught little of the meaning and, conversely, some readers, deemed poor according to accepted standards, seemed to know what the selection was about. Gradually it became apparent that teachers of reading were training elocutionists. Then it appeared, just as in arithmetic, that speed and comprehension within limits seemed to go hand in hand. Dr. Freeman's careful photography of eye movements gave the explanation. Silent reading exercises were developed to remedy the defects of oral reading, and some of the improvements made by hitherto slow and inaccurate readers were startling. In a sense, here was discovered a "royal road to learning."

These simple illustrations give a clue to the type of change that is coming in education through the application to this

field of the scientific method. Just as in medicine the development of the antitoxin came after scientific instruments of research were developed, so in education our standards, tests,
scales, score cards and other instruments of measurement enable us to diagnose the learning difficulties, and experimenters
and scientists are learning and perfecting the technique necessary for each case.

We have now walked up and down in the fields before this
forest and have entered three glades within, examining briefly
some of the changes that have occurred mostly in the past
twenty-five years. We have seen the ramified results of the
breakdown of the doctrine of formal discipline. We have noted
the changes resulting from the wide application of the comparative method. We have considered a few inadequate illustrations of the new science of education. Change there has been.
Has there been corresponding progress?

This is a question which it is beyond your power or mine to
answer adequately, yet it should always be before us. Certainly
change by itself does not constitute progress. It is even possi-
blue, as I see it, for education to become increasingly efficient
and at the same time degenerate.

There is at present a rapidly changing system of schools in
Soviet Russia. Attendance is increasing, schools are being
built, teachers are being trained. The volume of educational
literature is enormous. Methods are being improved, the curriculum is being built upon the most advanced lines. All agencies of education — the school, the press, the theatre, the
radio, the motion picture, are being combined as a unit to
educate the people. To some this is progress; but if the purpose
of the Russian society be one that I abhor, then the more
efficient the worse. Better if the buildings be cold and poorly
lighted, the equipment inadequate, the attendance officers slack,
the teachers unable to gain their wish. Changes become pro-

gress only when they contribute to the purpose which we consider education to serve.

I hold that education is the means by which the American people may achieve their heart's desire. All over the world for countless generations past men have been bound by the accidents of birth to the station of their fathers. Many a peasant and serf, many a peon and slave, has toiled throughout his life in poverty, squalor and degradation, without hope for the future and with the knowledge that his children will share the same fate. Handicapped in the race of life, deprived of the just fruits of their labor, insecure in person, your ancestors and mine dreamed of a land where these conditions would no longer obtain where happiness and contentment would come to those who labor and where the race of life would be run from an even start and in a free field. Such a place is the United States of America, and our educational system is the chief means toward the realization of this dream. It should open the door of opportunity to all boys and girls; opportunity to earn a living, to enjoy life regardless of accidents of birth and wealth; opportunity to excel, to serve, and to lead. Change in the past twenty-five years can be termed progress to the extent that education has developed more surely to accomplish this purpose; and indeed I believe that this has been the case.

With this standard of progress in mind, it is apparent that the modifications in educational organization and practice consequent upon the breakdown of formal discipline are real progress and not mere change. Formal discipline could not function in a democracy; or, to put it another way, education in an autocracy concealed the weaknesses based upon that theory. With rare exceptions secondary and higher education were confined to the children of the favored classes. These children, as modern researches show, had better native endowment; and since one characteristic of high intelligence is the ability to detect relationships and to apply to new situations, habits, skills, ideas and ideals already acquired, whatever the school did, the graduates would have these traits. Furthermore, most of the children from good homes would already have acquired something of those habits of good expression, proper manners, the sense of human kinship and elements of character which are so valuable in all walks of life. These traits already present in the nervous system and environment of the child would emerge as time passed, regardless of schooling; and it is no wonder that schoolmasters and patrons were reasonably well satisfied with the results which they probably falsely attributed to the subjects of instruction and the discipline of the school. When society asks the school to open its doors to all, and demands that each child be developed to the limit of his possibilities, then the schoolmaster deals not only with Park Avenue and Beacon Hill; he looks to the East Side and the prairies as well. He must keep open the school, teach the subjects, provide the play fields; and he must instil in the pupil those habits of thought which come so easily to the able, and assist him in acquiring good expression, good manners and other elements of culture which, in the favored few, are inborn or gained at home.

The weaknesses of formal discipline under these conditions at once become apparent; and despite the fact that Dr. Briggs and others rail at the result of education today, it is due to the psychologists that we put the blame *not* upon the stupidity and lack of effort of the pupils, which would have been the case under the disciplinary theory, but rather upon the ignorance of principals, teachers and educational scientists. In twenty-five years they have not been able to learn and to investigate sufficiently to readjust completely our system of education that it may do for all what good fortune and the ruling classes did for the few. With the disciplinary theory supreme, the doors of opportunity would be shut, and in time we should have an autocracy with the American equivalent of princes, counts, dukes and barons; our farmers would become peasants and our other workers, slaves. Conversely, we are developing our public school system so that all — rich and poor, able and less favored, urban and rural, intellectual and manual, hale and ill — will have a chance; and to the accomplishment of this purpose, no factor is more important than the new understanding of how the mind works, what must be done to train it, and what the school organization must be to make this accomplishment most sure.

Standards, tests, surveys and other devices resulting from the comparative method have in themselves no intrinsic relation either to progress or to decline. Their sole effect is to intensify the educational effort that was present prior to their introduction. The comparative method merely selects the practices and the procedures existent at the time, weighs them, measures them, ranks them; and by this process enables one to picture the situation in question. There is no new method. There is nothing added. Water cannot rise higher than its source. Consequently, there is no progress intrinsic in the collection of data, in their compilation or in the development of studies, tests and scales.

Progress depends upon what we do with these measures. Our relative rank may give us the clue as to whether to move forward or backward. A general survey shows us which of our practices conform to those of others and which are unique. At no time does this tell us whether we are right or wrong, or on a right or wrong track, but it forces us to question ourselves.

The past twenty-five years have been noted for the wide extension of educational facilities, for the increase in the number of our high schools, and for greatly augmented attendance in the upper grades. We know that a far larger proportion of our children are going into highly technical, vocational and professional education and that all our people are taking increasing advantage of the opportunities that our schools offer. In fact, the American people are demanding these opportunities for their children. This, with reference to the ideal which I set up, is definite progress. In part, this is due to the increasing knowledge of the differences of older education offered elsewhere — both in this land and in foreign countries — which is a result of the use of the comparative method. Education, in the mind of the public, has changed from a vague idea of a school and something mysterious that goes on within it, to a definite series of processes that are known and criticized by all. The public knows far more today than it did in days gone by. The growth of the American school system, the increase in interest, and the general support given by the public are thus, in part, a result of the achievements of the comparative method; and despite the fact there are criticisms of the quality of the work that we do and complaints that no longer do we have the fine, high and scholarly standard that once was set, we must remember that most of our people are glad to accept these opportunities, and in that fact we should take great satisfaction.

In a similar way the results of the application of the scientific method to the problems of learning and teaching in and of themselves do not constitute progress. It is conceivable, although ridiculous, that a scientific investigator might learn how to teach children to lie, to steal or to commit murder. The fact that he discovered how to do these things would in no sense constitute progress or decline. It would merely mean change. The use of his findings in the furtherance of the proper end of education alone would determine progress. The effect of the results of researches in education has been again to make us more sure of what we are doing. We are far more clear as to which children can be improved by further study, which children need special aid, which children are suited to one type or another of occupation. The danger is, as Dr.

Bagley has well pointed out, that our instruments of measurement and other results of scientific investigation may be used quite as well for the hindrance of democracy as for its advancement. Thus, mental tests and comprehensive examination may be used by a college either to encourage those of ability to further effort, which in a democracy is right and proper; or ruthlessly to exclude certain students, leaving behind a sense of despair and a lack of hope which should be condemned.

To conclude, this partial and fragmentary survey of the past twenty-five years shows not only that education has changed in many respects; but also that in so far as it has perfected and extended opportunity to our children, it has achieved progress. We must not delude ourselves that all results of comparative and experimental investigation constitute progress. No doubt many devices, technical methods and administrative procedures which are the result of scholarly endeavor conflict among themselves and many are not harmonious with the ideal for the realization of which our country was founded. The next twenty-five years will give ample opportunity to the statistician, to the bibliographer, to the experimenter and to the scientist; but to test their work and truly to measure progress we shall be compelled, as in all times past, to rely upon wise men — upon our philosophers, who were never more needed than now and who will continue to be needed in the years that lie ahead.

COLLEGE ADMINISTRATION

Herbert E. Hawkes

College Administration, which is the subject of my address, naturally suggests a vision of Presidents and Deans, Treasurers and Secretaries, Directors and Provosts. In seeking an approach to my topic I might begin with a discussion of the development of the function of these and other officers of administration during the last few decades. The difficulty with this manner of approach lies in the fact that no two of these officers have anything like the same duties in different institutions. Perhaps presidents and treasurers come closest to some uniformity. There is, however, no such thing as a standardized dean. There is the dean of this and of that college, but I never have seen any two deans who could exchange places and retain the same duties. There are deans of men whose duties are sometimes pastoral and sometimes statistical. There are deans whose relations are almost entirely with the faculty, others who are virtually assistants to the president. There are deans of diplomatic corps, deans of religious councils, not only professors but deans of shoe polishing. Readers of the morning paper some weeks ago were moved to drop a tear at the demise of the dean of scrub women in one of the great downtown office buildings. It is obvious that we would not get anywhere by discussing the duties of deans.

As a matter of fact the position of dean in the American college is a comparatively recent development. In President Eliot's first report as president of Harvard he states that a dean of the Faculty of Medicine existed, and that a member of the staff of Harvard College had been designated as dean of the college, but that he apparently had only a very nebulous idea of his functions. In one of his other early reports President Eliot outlines the duties of the dean of a college, presumably at Harvard. His statement is purely idealistic, and the functions include those of the present-day dean of students, dean of the faculty, director of admissions, registrar and personnel officers of all kinds. In 1880 a dean of Amherst College was appointed, presumably to assist the president in his duties. Not until 1887 was any member of the staff of Yale College announced as dean in the catalogue. In fact Dean Wright was never formally appointed as dean by faculty or trustee action. His functions were almost entirely pastoral and disciplinary. Not until 1896 was Dean Van Amringe officially designated as Dean of Columbia College. His duties were also pastoral and disciplinary in character. Only when the committee on instruction was organized, and the dean of the college made ex officio chairman of that committee, did educational matters constitute an important feature of his duties. In 1892 the University of Chicago was organized with a full quota of deans for each administrative unit of the university. One may, then, say rightly that the position of dean of a college took on a significant development about twenty-five or more years ago. Since that time the duties attached to the office have increased in scope. In many institutions some of these duties have been delegated to different individuals as they have become clearly differentiated from each other, until at the present time in very few institutions is the position of dean a highly centralized administrative office.

In the face of the haphazard development of the office of dean, it would be difficult to approach the subject of the progress of college administration during the past twenty-five years from the point of view of the growth of the office of dean.

A more hopeful start can be made by an attempt to analyze and to trace the changing emphasis that the American college has placed on the various elements in its problem. When reduced to lowest terms the process of education in school and college comes down to a consideration of three elements: (1) The subject matter; (2) The student; (3) The teacher.

These are the three ingredients, the three primary colors, so to speak, of education. There are also involved the inter-relations between these three elements. A consideration of the relation between subject matter and student would involve the entire technique of instruction and curriculum making. The attitude of the teacher toward subject matter would involve a consideration of the conflict between research and teaching on the part of the faculty. In this brief discussion, however, there is no opportunity to consider the many difficult and technical questions involved in these relations.

In which of these three elements does the center of gravity of collegiate education reside? In the old days subject matter was the prime factor. Topics of required study were believed so to affect the mind as to make it powerful for accomplishment in any field that it might enter. This is no time to discuss so controversial a matter, but the burden of evidence seems to indicate that cause and effect were interchanged in this attitude toward the higher education. It now looks as if a mind which is by natural endowment of such power and quality as to perform with distinction in the old rigid curriculum has the strength to do almost anything. It is not so much the subject that makes the mind, as the mind that grasps the subject. The bombshell that wrecked the rigidly required college course was President Eliot's doctrine of free election of study on the part of the student. Important as this idea was, like all extreme positions it failed to take account of some of the facts in the case.

It is necessary for the American college to accommodate itself both to the strength and to the weakness of our entire school system. We cannot approach our problem as if it were the problem, for example, of the English school system. Young men in the great English schools like Winchester, Rugby and Eton are afforded a breadth of educational experience which is not and cannot be matched in the public high schools in this country. When the well prepared English boy passes to the university he is ready to make the choice implied in President Eliot's plan. Apparently President Eliot assumed that any boy who had been admitted to Harvard *ipso facto* possessed the maturity of judgment and clearness of vision to select his course wisely. This assumption, however, cannot be made for boys in general, a fact that has operated against the complete adoption of President Eliot's program. We must not forget that American colleges must meet the conditions that face them, rather than those which face the older English universities. Since the wide exposure to things intellectual which one finds in some of the English schools is not provided in our schools it follows that the colleges must make up for the lack in the first year or two of the college course. This necessity lies back of the entire shift in attitude that is rapidly taking place regarding the place and function of the required course in a modern college curriculum. This question will be examined more closely a little later. For the moment it is only necessary to remark that the assumption that any particular subject matter is a *sine qua non* in the college curriculum was pretty effectively destroyed by the forces set in motion by President Eliot's radical step.

The second of the three primary educational elements mentioned a few moments ago is the teacher, or the faculty. Not over twenty-five years ago the doctrine was commonly held that the only function of the college that was really important was the provision of positions for professors who might, in as much comfort as their meagre salaries would permit and as much undisturbed quiet as was consistent with their college duties, carry forward studies in their respective fields of scholarship. I recall the repetition *ad nauseam* of a remark attributed to the distinguished Professor Rowland of Johns Hopkins to the effect that he observed that a certain number of students had come to Johns Hopkins expecting to study under him, but that he proposed to neglect them. I frequently noticed in those days that the members of the faculty who were loudest in their opinion that the college existed for the purpose of providing jobs for the professors and that the students were a necessary evil, were often quite sterile in their own scholarly production. I doubt if many members of college faculties would today take the position that I have mentioned. We now have university positions for the scholar whose only interest is in his researches. Furthermore, the whole question of the difference in function between the college and the graduate school is clearer than it was twenty-five years ago.

If neither subject matter nor the faculty is the focus of our system of collegiate education, and if the student is the third and last of the primary elements, the process of exclusion indicates the student as the center of the system.

The same conclusion can be reached in quite a different manner. The college occupies a middle position between the secondary school system on the one side and the professional school or the world of affairs on the other. In the lower school system there is a definite but changing subject matter that must be covered if the student is to enter college. The tremendous changes that have taken place in our system of lower education during the past thirty years have emphasized the necessity of adapting that education to the individual child. This results, or will result when the process is perfected, in finding out the kind of education best adapted to the ability and circumstances of each individual. It will avoid either overeducating or undereducating or miseducating our youth, but will send those on to college who ought to have a higher education, to trade school or commercial school those who will realize their highest usefulness by that kind of education. It goes without saying that we have not yet reached this ideal, but we have been traveling in the right direction and are much nearer the goal than we were twenty-five years ago. The point that I wish to make clear just now is that the lower schools must of necessity devote themselves to a fairly definite subject matter in the case of youth headed for college. Although many a boy comes to college with a clear idea of his future plans, many do not. It is critically important that those who enter college should be known to possess a high level of intelligence, a vital interest in things of the mind, and a reasonably uniform preparation. It is important that they should have the subject matter of the high or secondary school well in hand so that they are in a position to take up collegiate work with only a minimum of discontinuity. But it is one of the fundamental and unescapable responsibilities of the modern college to afford her students as early as possible intellectual contacts and stimuli of a more diagnostic and constructive character than is possible in most schools.

After college the student enters a professional school or takes a job. In either case he is again concerned with a definite subject matter. The medical school and the law school try to admit only those men whose ambitions are clear and who are certain of professional success. Surely any medical school in which the cost of educating each student is over $2000 a year and for which the tuition fee is $500 would have a very feeble conception of the proper trusteeship of funds if it admitted men whom it thought unqualified for the medical profession. For this reason the student body in a professional school is likely to be highly homogeneous, while that in the college, preparing as it does for all kinds of professions and for other walks in life as well, is highly unhomogeneous. Hence the professional school may, nay must, have a curriculum largely prescribed, while the college should not.

We have, then, a picture of the place occupied by the liberal arts college. It is a sort of an assembling and sorting institution — assembling students who present the necessary subject matter for admission and who possess the requisite level of intelligence, giving them an opportunity to discover their personal intellectual bent after adequate exposure to a variety of fields. After this period of exposure and discovery of interest is over the college must afford a solid and broad basis for an intellectual life that will enable the student to develop to his maximum. The college graduate then takes up his work either in a professional school or in the world of affairs in some highly specialized form of endeavor.

This analysis of the place of the college seems to lead to the same result as that arrived at before. While subject matter may be said to occupy the center of the stage for boys preparing for college and for men in professional or graduate schools, the student himself is the most fundamental element in the college. The problem of winnowing the student material that comes from all quarters so that each ambition and each ability and each temperament leaves through the proper exit to its appropriate life work with adequate intellectual and spiritual preparation is the function of the college. In this process of winnowing, a discovery of the exceptional mind ought to result. The very flexibility of the procedure which has been outlined is favorable for the discovery of an intellectual mutation.

We can now approach the topic assigned to this address, College Administration, at least so far as it has to do with the kind of college whose place in our educational system has been described by the foregoing remarks. I would not pretend to say that every college administrator would accept my analysis as applicable to his institution. The fact is that colleges are not standardized either in aim or method. At present they could not and ought not to be so standardized. There are colleges to which an educational idea has not penetrated for twenty-five years. They do not realize that anything much has taken place in collegiate education since the Civil War. Some still operate on the principle that there is something in the long continued study of a closely prescribed and dull course which develops character. True it is that no one without character can doggedly devote himself to subject matter that seems to have nothing to do with him or his interests. But my guess is that such a procedure is a test of character rather than a builder of it. On the other hand, there are colleges that go to other extreme and would almost be willing to give credit toward the degree to a boy who went after the cows and milked them. In what follows I am not speaking of either of these extremes. I am speaking of those colleges that would accept as a rough approximation the statement of the functions of the college outlined a few moments ago. Following that statement, what is to be said about such questions as the following?

What purpose does the required course serve in the curriculum?

How can the college best serve its ablest students?

What responsibility should the college take for the social, the moral, the religious, the athletic, the literary and musical interests of its students?

In what spirit should the college administer moral and academic discipline?

If these questions are answered in terms of College Administration as it was twenty-five years ago, and again in terms of the most enlightened present-day usage, a reasonably clear picture of the spirit of each will be obtained and a definite idea of tendencies which have been in operation will be gained. It goes without saying that many other questions might pertinently be asked. I do not think, however, that the multiplication of questions would modify our conclusions.

What purpose does the required course serve in the curricu-

lum? Unless I am greatly mistaken the reason for the requirement of certain narrowly departmental courses in the college
curriculum of twenty-five to forty years ago rested on two
beliefs: first, that there were certain mental disciplines that
served to toughen the intellectual fibre; and, second, that there
are certain subject matters of which no person who wished
to be known as an educated gentleman should be ignorant.
With the passage of time opinion on each of these questions
has become far from unanimous. In the first place, the old
required courses afforded to the student fully as much practice
in devising means of avoiding a distasteful task as in buckling
down and doing it. It all depended on the kind of character
that a boy brought to the task and the vitality of interest
that the task evoked. It was not contrary to the ethical code of
the time for a student who had money to hire the boy who
wanted more money to write his themes, to predigest his
required courses and to do everything except actually write his
examinations. Even if it were admitted that the discipline of
the required course toughened the fibre of the mind that mas-
tered it, the fact remains that few accomplished the mastery.
Even those who conscientiously did their best in a subject for
which they were ill-prepared or ill-adapted might well have
gained more in a field better suited to their capacity and interest. Is the second traditional reason for the narrowly
departmental required course any more cogent? Is there any
particular subject matter that a given individual must know
in order to be recognized as a cultured gentleman by those who
know one when they see him? This question has been answered
so many times in such a variety of connections that I will
merely state as a consensus of many opinions that apart from
such knowledge of one's native tongue as will enable one to
use it correctly and clearly in speech and in writing, there is
no such specific subject matter.

The purpose which the required course is coming to serve

in the present-day college curriculum depends less upon narrow departmental offering than it has in the past. Perhaps the most accurate and significant survey of intelligent student opinion that has yet been made in an American college is contained in Mr. A. B. Crawford's volume entitled *Incentives to Study*. Mr. Crawford's study makes it clear that in the opinion of the serious and discerning students of Yale College the narrowly departmental required course serves a very barren educational purpose. Apparently students are not stimulated to continue in the departments in which prescribed courses are offered, with the possible exception of English. They regard these required courses as of very slight value or significance, and spend a minimum of time upon them, but strangely enough they find that the marks which they receive in these required courses are as high as those acquired in subjects which are more difficult, more valuable and more attractive.

The function of the required course is increasingly recognized as one of discovery and orientation: of discovery to the student and to his instructors of abilities and intellectual enthusiasms that may possibly have been latent, or at any rate unrecognized; of orientation in placing the various fields of scholarly interest in their proper relation to each other. During the last few years the function of the so-called survey course, which cuts across departmental lines and treats very broad subject matter in natural or physical science, in historical or economic subjects, has been gaining ground with amazing rapidity. Scores of colleges are organizing survey courses, each with its own local conditions regarding staff and character of student body in mind. The function of these required courses is almost always the same, that of opening the windows of the mind for each individual student in the direction from which the light may illuminate his particular intellectual life. Whether the required survey course should involve departmental coöperation, as in the Columbia course in Contemporary Civilization, and the courses in science in Chicago, Rochester and Minnesota, or whether it should involve a number of separate departmental survey courses, is a question for local adjustment. The significant aspect of this development lies in the fact that the college has begun to recognize the fact that its students are individuals, the intellectual appeitite of each one of whom must be discovered and satisfied. The student body cannot be treated as like-minded to the extent that the old rigid curriculum implied. So far, then, as the question of the place and function of the required course is concerned, the whole tendency of the last twenty-five years has been toward an individualization of college instruction.

The second question which I proposed a few moments ago was the following: How can the college best serve its ablest students? Twenty-five years ago so far as I know this question was rarely asked. A scholarly and devoted faculty presented courses many of which were admirably adapted to the intellectual needs of able students. If these men improved the opportunities open to them they received an excellent collegiate education; otherwise not. There was, however, little or no attempt to differentiate between the able student and the incompetent or indifferent one even in the opportunity open to him. During recent years the situation has fundamentally changed. In scores of colleges honors courses of one kind and another are offered to lure the able student to do work commensurate with his ability. This is not the occasion to outline any of these attempts in detail. Suffice it to say that there are almost as many methods of organizing honors work as there are institutions, and almost as many degrees of success as there are methods.

In the larger institutions, where it is practicable to do so, students are sectioned according to ability, determined either by intelligence tests or by previous academic accomplishment. This device undoubtedly serves a good purpose. The recent use of subject-matter tests to insure the placement of each individual student in a grade of work suited to his ability and previous accomplishment is an important contribution to the intelligent care of our ablest students. The increasing flexibility with which rules of attendance are administered for students of serious scholarly ambition is significant in this connection. The development of the comprehensive examination, which cuts across departmental lines and which enables young scholars to devote themselves to a field of study, rather than to a narrow departmental topic, is also important. In answering this question, it is obvious that the whole tendency of the last twenty-five years has been in the direction of an attempt to determine which students have real intellectual power, and to plan work adapted to their individual needs.

I must hasten to the next question. "What responsibility should the college take for the social, the moral, the religious, the athletic, the literary and the musical interests of its students?" Up to the opening years of this century the American college considered its responsibility to its students as entirely discharged by attention to purely intellectual interests. Any boy who devoted himself to any of the activities which I have mentioned did so at his own risk and at his peril. The social, athletic and aesthetic interests of the student were usually considered as running contrary to the objects for which the college stood. Constructive attention to the moral and religious aspect of the student's life was not included in the work of most colleges. To be sure, there were sectarian connections and Young Men's Christian Associations on many campuses, but these were influences from the outside concerning which the college itself took little or no official cognizance. At the present time most colleges recognize the fact that in admitting a boy or a girl the whole individual is involved. College officers are appointed who have at least advisory responsibilities in regard to the social, moral and religious interests of the students. The literary and musical activities are now-a-days closely collaborated with the language departments and with the department of music, so that these extra curriculum activities form a well recognized and effective laboratory for some of the more theoretic work of the various departments. The subject of physical education has developed alongside the intercollegiate athletic interests. Everything is moving slowly but surely toward an assumption of responsibility on the part of the college for the athletic policies of the institution. Although we are at present a long way from a stable adjustment of athletics to the administration of the college, it is increasingly clear that since the college admits the body as well as the mind of the student it must assume the responsibility for the intelligent care of that body. If intercollegiate athletics do not contribute to this end they are doomed to curtailment. Symptoms of this outcome are not far to seek. In many eastern institutions the undergraduate interest in intercollegiate athletics is becoming distinctly dampened. Intercollegiate contests continue to be great spectacles, enjoyed by alumni and by other members of the community. But the kind of undergraduate enthusiasm for these events which was a matter of common knowledge twenty-five years ago is rapidly passing away in many of our eastern institutions. What might be called "athletic hysteria" is moving westward, and in the course of time will pass out into the Pacific Ocean.

In the whole field suggested by the present question the same result noted in the answers to the previous questions is obvious: the tendency of college administration during the past twenty-five years has been to recognize and to provide for all aspects of each individual. The present-day college admits and attempts to educate the whole man, rather than the purely intellectual aspect of an hypothetical average man.

I come to the last question which time will permit me to

discuss in this brief address. In what spirit should the college administer moral and academic discipline?

While the general direction of development of our schemes of study and methods for carrying them out has made a complete turnabout during the past two score years, the usual attitude toward the moral aspects of the higher education has remained in about the same path as of old. It is still something brought to bear on the student from without, rather than a stimulation to his self-development. Though practice varies, I imagine that most officers of college discipline look upon their function as for the most part punitive. The Puritan image of the angry God holding the trembling culprit over the edge of a burning hell, though not vividly in mind, is certainly in the background. The punitive features of college discipline are their highest common factor.

It may be that this attitude was the natural one when the discipline of the family could be counted on for a background of moral maturity more than is possible today. In the happy golden age when fathers and mothers saw to it that their sons grew up with characters based on unchanging laws of conduct it was possible to place any deviation from the code of right living in the category of sin, rather than in that immaturity, and it is very easy to prescribe for sin — in someone else. But I am not very certain as to the dates of this golden age. I only know that it hasn't been so very golden for the past fifty years. Be that as it may, I am convinced that the youth of college age at the present time are as immature morally and as crude socially as they are undeveloped intellectually. If this is true it is a condition, not a theory, that confronts us. If the college is alive to its duty it must recognize the human conditions that actually face it, and deal with them. For when a college admits a student to its membership a double responsibility has been established. On the one hand a responsibility on the part of the youth to do his best and to make the most of the opportunity before him, and also a responsibility on the part of the college to take him as he is, having once declared that he is fit to enter college, and with patience and intelligent care to help him to overcome his weaknesses, whether of mind or body or soul. Of course he has weaknesses. If he were perfect he would not need to go to college at all. And whether he is deficient in one aspect or another does not affect the responsibility of the college to do its best for him.

This means that fixed rules of discipline administered arbitrarily have no place in a college. It means that someone must at all costs determine what is back of a case of cheating or drunkenness or other breach of decent behavior. Not only the factual evidence in the case, but the background and state of mind that lead up to it, must in some way be found out. This takes time and patience and insight, but it is a technique that can be developed and practiced.

It is entirely possible that the penalty, if one call it such, for two offenses that look exactly the same on paper may be quite different on account of the different educative effect that would result in the two individuals concerned.

It goes without saying that sometimes it is discovered that the moral state of a boy is such that he is not a fit member of the college community. His defects may be too serious for the college to hope to remedy. In such a case the boy must be asked to go. We must admit that the college is not adapted for the education of every person, however ignorant or depraved he may be. If all of the facts about the boy's character had been known when the student applied for admission to college he might not have been allowed to enter. That is to say, a mistake might have been made in ever allowing the youth to register at all. Such a boy should be asked to withdraw.

The situation is precisely the same on the scholastic side. The director of admissions uses his best judgment in accepting the credentials of entering students. If he were able to select wisely he would never accept anyone who did not have the preparation and habits of study that insured academic success. The fact that some boys do not make good in their studies and must be asked to withdraw also means that a mistake has been made. To eliminate a large percentage of a class at the end of their first year in college does not necessarily mean high standards. It may mean an improper basis of admission, due either to the unfortunate effect of the laws governing such things, as in the case of some state institutions, or to the incompetence of the system of admission. I do not suppose that any institution would consciously encourage a large number of students to waste a year of their lives for the sake of the tuition fees which more than cover the costs in freshman work.

Discipline should be approached from the angle of moral education of the individual rather than of his punishment. I have met very few boys who were not thankful to have someone point out clearly but sympathetically defects in their character. And when a weakness in character has once been definitely isolated so that the boy can see just what it is and what it implies, he can usually be counted on to make the attempt to strengthen his weak spot. To expel a boy from college as soon as a weak spot in his character has been located, seems to me to indicate either a failure to understand human nature or a blindness to the most solemn responsibility that the college has assumed in admitting him.

One cannot forget, however, that the officer of discipline has a double responsibility. He must keep in mind not only the morals of the individual but the morale of the college community. Many cases have a social bearing and influence as well as a personal importance. After all of the facts in the case have been cleared up, both material and psychological, it may be necessary to say to the youth that if he were the only person in the college it would be right and proper to consider the incident closed, with little or no disciplinary action. But unfortunately the rest of the college must be considered. It would not do to have everyone who knows about the affair assume that that kind of thing can go on with the knowledge and apparent consent of the college authorities. When approached in this way the student never feels that injustice is being done when a penalty is imposed, nor does such an attitude reduce its educative effect on the student. On the contrary it seems to give him a more enlightened sense of social responsibility to feel that to some extent he is his brother's keeper.

We would all agree that self-education is the only real education. The stimulus and opportunity may come from the outside, but the change is on the inside. Likewise the only real kind of discipline is self-discipline. Parents, teachers and deans may point out to the boy his shortcomings and their implications. A penalty may aid in making the point clear. But the penalty for a college boy is not a punishment. It is rather a part of his education, to the end that he may learn to take charge of himself.

How, then, may we sum up the tendencies which have been observed in the administration of our colleges during the last quarter of a century? Just as in the development of our primary and secondary education the recognition and the development of the individual has beome the central feature of our educational system, so in collegiate education the resultant of all the forces that have been at work is expressed in terms of the individualization of our higher education. The whole bewildering development of new type examinations, intelligence tests, personality ratings, so many of which unfortunately fail to hit the mark by so wide a margin, are gradually enabling us to develop a technique for the measurement and understanding of the individual. Methods of instruction have shifted from the purely disciplinary method of question and recitation or lecture to one of discussion and conference. The personal relation between students and faculty has shifted from one of armed neutrality to a coöperative association of friends engaged in a common enterprise. Each individual college is increasingly studying its situation and its possibilities so as to accommodate itself in a more sensitive manner to the service that naturally belongs to it. Although we have far to go in the development of methods and devices for collegiate education, the direction in which these developments must inevitably take place have become clearly indicated during the past few years. If the American college can continue in this direction, if it can possess the wisdom to stimulate and to develop in its students the best that is in human nature, the result will be not a group of isolated and divergent individual interests, but a united and intelligent attack from every side, with every kind of weapon, upon the fortress in which ignorance and intolerance have from time immemorial been entrenched.

LETTERS

Ashley H. Thorndike

What has been the progress of literary scholarship during the past quarter of a century? I have not found the question an easy one to answer. There have been no startling discoveries, no revolutions, such as some of the natural sciences have witnessed. We have not reconceived the universe or expounded it in terms of new indivisibilities. We have not transformed industry or changed the daily living of millions. What advance we have made has been built slowly on old foundations by many workers toiling, in spite of the disruption of the Great War, to construct a better and fuller comprehension of the world's literature. The task is an endless one. The study of letters is forever running a losing race, outstripped both by the enormous speed of the practice of letters and by the acceleration of knowledge of all kinds. In each new generation there is an increase of literature and an increase of learning applicable to the literature of all generations. We can never catch up. Gains have been made unquestionably, but to the individual worker, as to the outsider, they may seem to lie in very specialized undertakings. Have they united in any general change in our knowledge and interest? Can any measure of progress be found for the labors of one generation in this losing race?

It is possible to say at once that this scholarly endeavor has been increasing in quantity. A vast army of workers has been constantly gaining recruits, and its detachments are busy in every civilized country. From Iceland to India, from Japan to South America, men are studying the literature of their own nation and the languages and the literatures of all ages and

places. Scarcely an author remains neglected; the newer recruits are often sadly worried to find employment. In no
country has this activity grown more rapidly than in our own.
More books are being written, more men trained in our
universities, more research pursued, more learned societies
organized, larger funds expended. This study of letters, moreover, has been becoming more diversified. Our scholars are
engaged on a bewildering variety of occupations. One is poring
over the photostats of ancient texts meticulously comparing
their final *e*'s; another in the steam-heated recesses of a great
library is checking page after page of newspaper files, seeking
reference to this play or that book; still another sits in drowsy
comfort surrounded by his students, listening to their reports;
another in a bad temper but with a certain creative exaltation
is penning a contemptuous and annihilating reply to the latest
critic of his theories; still another is composing an interpretation of his favorite author, which he fondly imagines contains
the final words so beautifully expressed that they themselves
are literature. Some are bibliographers, paleographers, an-
tiquarians, linguists; some are historians, biographers, critics,
philosophers. Each specialist may conceal a certain assurance of the superiority of his particular occupation, but
all are workers in the vineyard. The harvest, at least, is
abundant. Much more is known about the literature of the
world than was known twenty-five years ago; this enormous
field has been more thoroughly organized, more carefully
surveyed.

No one, I suppose, would be satisfied with a merely quantitative analysis of literary scholarship, even if that were
possible. Endless labor, unmeasured effort, hosts of students,
whole libraries of new books may or may not indicate any
considerable gain for the human mind or sure promise for
further advance in the future. How are we to distinguish
between pedantry and learning, between mere occupation and

genuine refreshment of the mind? How does all this study aid
in the march of civilization or in the refinement of the human
spirit? What is this literary scholarship? What are its relationships to other studies? Do its achievements offer adequate
returns for its labors? What is it doing? What are its goals?
Whither it is tending?

These are questions which must be kept in view if we are
to arrive at any qualitative estimate of what it has amounted
to in the last twenty-five years. They may serve at least as
starting points for the very casual and cursory remarks which
I have to offer on the subject.

Let us look at some of the well-worn fields where the
laborers have been many, in an effort to form some opinion of
the value of the harvest. Perhaps the oldest and still one of the
main occupations of literary scholarship is the study of the
greatest writers. It sprang into life when a noble civilization
realized its debt to the poems of Homer; it had a renaissance
centuries later when the human mind revealed anew its great-
ness in Dante's *Divine Comedy*. It spread over the modern
world at the call of Shakespeare, Molière, Goethe, of Chaucer,
Cervantes and Milton. It is the peculiar province of literature
to enshrine personality in living words that renew themselves
to each generation, and the literary scholar finds his work
never finished because a great author is never dead. The determination of the text, the preservation of the facts of a life, the
records of an author's immortality as he influences new eras
and persons — such are the most sacred duties that piety can
demand of scholarship. And it is no light service that is required of a vigilant priesthood. False prophets pretend to
worship at the same shrine. Each generation has to correct the
errors and mistakes of the past. In the case of Shakespeare,
we apparently have not yet discovered and eliminated from
documents all of the forgeries perpetrated nearly a century
ago by a once honored scholar. The extent of mankind's

continued interest in these great writers makes the labor of removing errors, broadening knowledge, clearing the shrine, greater year by year. Dr. Tannenbaum's bibliography of Shakespearian studies for the single year 1929 contains eight hundred and eighty items, books or articles, in almost every known language, offering something for the consideration and testing of Shakespearian scholarship.

For Shakespeare, as perhaps for most of the others, the main progress in the twentieth century has been in enlarging and clarifying the historical background; in his case especially that of the drama and theater of his time. How extensive and important this has been may be seen at a glance by a comparison of the first and last editions of the standard biography, that by the late Sir Sidney Lee. The original edition of 1898 had doubled in size seventeen years later because, as the author states, "The new documentary evidence which scholars have lately discovered touching the intricate stage history of Shakespeare's era has proved of special service, and I have also greatly benefitted by the ingenious learning which has been recently brought to bear on vexed questions of Shakespearean bibliography." [1] Continued research in stage history and bibliography would require considerable further enlargement, were a new edition attempted today. Assuredly there is no major author from Homer to Goethe, for whom the last twenty-five years have not provided us with means for a better understanding of his work.

The same may be said of many of the lesser names in modern literature, of Spenser, Dryden, Corneille, Racine, Voltaire, Rousseau, Herder, Lessing, and indeed of most of the more recent writers of rank. We are sometimes accused of spending too much labor on authors of slight interest to the reading public of today. But, if we are mistaken in our evaluations of the books of the past, surely it is best to err on the

[1] Sir Sidney Lee, *A Life of William Shakespeare* (1916 edition), preface.

generous side in deciding what is worth our pains in preserving. Much has been done but much remains to do in the work of securing accurate and reliable texts of what even the greater men have written. Some of them have not yet had careful editing of their complete works, and in other cases difficulties still exist in determining the value of conflicting manuscripts or editions. How varied this task of preparing good texts has been, I may illustrate by citing the accomplishments, within the range of my personal interest, of three distinguished laborers. Sir Israel Gollancz, by an admirable edition of the Caedmon manuscript,[2] has recently added a new distinction to a life devoted to editing of all kinds, including the direction of the Early English Text Society. Mr. W. W. Greg has brought the technic of an expert paleographer and bibliographer to the editing of many documents and plays of the sixteenth century, clearing them of mistaken confusions and forgeries. The late Professor Frank Hubbard in our country carried through the most minute and convincing of the rival texts for two of Shakespeare's plays,[3] which had caused dispute for centuries. These are instances of three quite different kinds of textual labor; many others might be noted in English, and nearly all of them could be paralleled among the publications in the other chief European languages. Through such indefatigable and intelligent toil great progress has been made in rendering the texts and documents of modern literature accurate and available. I scarcely need add that such editing has often led to fresh and significant reinterpretation.

I turn next to another kind of literary study which is less concerned with our duties to the individual author than with the understanding of movements, periods and influences. We may, for example, be interested in the Elizabethan stage

----

[2] Published for the British Academy (1927). Sir Israel Gollancz died in 1930.
[3] *The First Quarto of Hamlet* (1920); *The First Quarto of Romeo and Juliet* (1924).

history because of the light it throws on Shakespeare's life; or we may be interested in it as a part of a literary and cultural development. This latter interest supports the historical method of study, the examination of literature as a part of the history of civilization and thought and as one of the chief records and reflections of their progress. The literature of any period is studied in relation to its environment, the social and political and other cultural conditions which give causes and occasions for creative art, and in connection with its heredity — its inheritance of forms and ideas from preceding literature. This method of study seeks to understand greater and lesser writers alike in terms of their surroundings and it links together the work of this man with that, tracing influences and relationship — until the history of literature becomes mapped out as a series of movements, which may be international in scope. The literature of the Middle Ages, for example, becomes organized and classified and interrelated with all that we know of the life and art of that period.

This historical method of study has been the one chiefly practised in our American universities. It was well established twenty-five years ago, and it has been constantly employed and extended. The focussing of research on a writer or a period or a movement has inevitably led to a quickened interest on the part of readers and students, and they have become eager to partake in or to encourage still more intensive study. I think it would be true to say that literary history has been largely rewritten since the beginning of the century. Few works then considered authoritative would now be thought adequate. Where then a few essays and researches were being undertaken, now we are attempting more and more comprehensive syntheses. The stage history of the Elizabethan period, which I again use for an example, has been filled out by continuous searching of records and analyses of documents, and an enormous amount of material has been accumulated until finally Sir Edmund K. Chambers, the most eminent of many workers in this field, has published four huge volumes [4] devoted to a condensed but exhaustive summary of fifty years' records of the Elizabethan stage. All the work of scholarship has become more and more of a collaboration, whether with one's predecessors or one's students; and the largest enterprises must be organized frankly on that basis. Such is the *Cambridge History of English Literature* and the corresponding *History of American Literature* just completed, both involving collaboration in bibliography, research and criticism. Similarly collaborative are handbooks and encyclopaedias undertaken in Germany since the War.[5] Manifestly there is greater opportunity than ever before for the union of scholars in bringing about some synthetic or at least comprehensive and definitive summation of their labors, and we may look for more of this in the future.

I have already been betrayed into the use of one or two scientific terms, and it cannot be denied that this historical study of literature has been inclined to borrow scientific terms and methods. We need not press hard the biological analogy that gives such literary forms as tragedy and the pastoral an evolution like that of the physical species, and yet we may still seek to find causes and laws of development for literary phenomena. We may not believe in a determinism which takes no regard of the variation and power in personality, and yet we may view literature less as the revelation of individual personalities than as one of the great and continuous undertakings of mankind. Much debate has taken place between those who would find literature determined by outside conditions and those who insist upon it as an affair of personal experience. If we rule out the extreme views on either side, it

[4] *The Elizabethan Stage* (1923).

[5] Oskar Walzel, ed., *Handbuch der Literaturwissenschaft* (1923-) ; Paul Merker and Wolfgang Stammler, eds., *Reallexikon der deutschen Literaturgeschichte* (1925-).

is easy to agree that we have all been greatly interested in origins, developments and relations. We have traced back stories used by Shakespeare or Goethe through centuries of usage, across continents, to their first appearance in the dawn of the race in the highlands of Asia. We follow a form such as comedy or the elegy, noting the ideas and patterns that have clung to it, the imitations made by one era of another, until we lose our way in primitive darkness when there was nobody to lament and nothing to laugh at. We have been especially interested in the beginnings of things. Archaeology and anthropology have meant much to literary as well as to historical study during the quarter-century. It is not quite forty years since the first edition of Sir James Fraser's *Golden Bough*, which gave new impulse to the study of folklore and to speculation on the origins of literary modes in prehistoric times. One of the most important contributions to such study is being carried on in this country by the anthropologists in the effort to record and preserve the rituals and stories — i.e., the literature — of the American Indians. We may safely say that what we have learned from biology and anthropology has not, despite the fears of some, made the study of letters subservient to those sciences, but it has already enlarged the scope of literature and made plainer its relations to other human activities.

Another phase of this quasi-scientific trend in our studies has been the comparative method. Twenty-five years ago a good deal was heard of Comparative Literature, by which was meant the study of the literatures of Western Europe to some degree as a unit. If today less is heard of the rather misleading term, it is because the practice advocated has become commonplace. No one can go far in the study of any national literature without being led to consider the international interplay of forms and ideas. Such study involves far more than the mere tracing of the influence of A on B or the borrowings of Coleridge from the German, although he borrowed a good deal; nor is it aided by such a sweeping generalization as that which describes one period of English literature as dominated by the French. Rather it finds in literature the exchange where national forces in art and thought often meet and barter to their common profit. Indeed, the student of literature is coming to recognize himself as a citizen of the world; and this common interest in letters is a nexus that is binding men into what we hope is a new harmony. We are becoming aware not only of the literary intercourse of Western Europe but of East and West, of the whole world. A Japanese scholar has just completed the translation of Shakespeare;[6] another has begun that of Dante; a scholarly journal in the Imperial University of Tokio displays many languages including Anglo-Saxon; and young scholars in our American universities are turning their minds to the literatures of the East. Although the smaller nations of Europe have been most active, France has of late taken the lead in this international comity. We, despite some notable exceptions, have lagged a little behind, but we have at least had the pleasure of welcoming to this country and profiting from the instruction of a number of French scholars; among them Professors Baldensperger and Hazard, leaders in comparative literature, and Professors Legouis, Feuillerat and Cazamian, masters of the study and interpretation of English literature.

I have spoken of methods historical, scientific and comparative; another approach may without too great ineptness be called the sociological. This takes into account the economic basis of literature, the conditions of publishing, whether the presentation of a manuscript to a patron or the advertising of a novel designed to reach the taste of the million. And it takes into account the social conditions that affect the production and distribution of books, as, for example, the rise in impor-

[6] Prof. Tsubouchi, *The Complete Works of Shakespeare* (Waseda Univ. Press, Tokyo, 1928).

tance during the eighteenth and nineteenth centuries in Western Europe of the middle classes; or the consequent increase of leisure for women who have become the chief readers of certain varieties of books. Moreover, to a certain extent, literature is manifestly a social phenomenon. This poem is the creation of the fancy of an individual possessed by a vision or playing with words; but from another point of view it is the product of a special state of society, of the persons who welcome it and read it. The poet who cannot find a reader and the nation that will not buy books alike remain mute and inglorious. Literature today is what we are reading, what we fill our minds and imaginations with, whether it come from Theocritus or the newspaper. The analysis of society aids in the understanding of its literature, and its literature may illuminate the state of society.

From this point of view the literary history of the United States has had a fresh attraction for our scholars. The phenomena are indeed unique. Literature is transported by emigrants across the ocean and takes a new growth among a pioneer people engaged in settling a continent. Poetry among the Puritans, the novel among the Quakers, the drama on the frontier were not resplendent but they existed and helped to form the culture and the character of our people. The itinerant elocutionist, the lyceum, the circuit-rider who peddled books, the show-boat drifting down the Ohio, McGuffey's famous readers — these are not merely important items for the social historian, they are also means for understanding the very life of literature.

Let me give one other instance in which literature has been employed to delineate the state of society. President Masaryk, of the Czecho-Slovak republic, in his large work on *The Spirit of Russia*,[7] published just before the war, discussed in the first volume the different movements which have stirred the thought

[7] T. G. Masaryk, *Russland und Europe*. 2 Vols. (1913), trans. into English as *The Spirit of Russia* (1919).

of the nation — utilitarianism, socialism, nihilism, etc. — and then devoted the second volume largely to a study of Dostoevsky's novels, as affording a synthesis of the Russian mind.

This may suggest another relationship, that between literature and philosophy. The philosophers have been more successful as makers of literature than as theorizers about it. Plato banished poets from his Republic, but no one doubts that his *Dialogues* are literature. The Utilitarians early in the last century viewed *belle-lettres* as the Scarlet Woman who would seduce humanity from its proper employment in the search of utility, but we count John Stuart Mill as one of the ornaments of Victorian literature. Even today, I note that our educational philosophers are constantly urging that the main aim of college is to teach men to think; they rarely show any interest in what we feel or imagine. But philosophy well knows that the old distinction between thinking and feeling is a dubious one. The two are never separated. If literature appeals more to the emotions than the intellect, it is always bearing its cargo of ideas. As soon as the history of thought is interpreted in any way except as a mechanical system, it is an affair of writing and reading, of ideas made interesting, of excitements to think. Literature is always a means of conveying information, of purveying ideas, leading the march of the mind. How passionately those novels of Dostoevsky convey the confused strivings and lassitudes of the Russian consciousness! How much of the debate between all kind of Tories and Radicals during the last two centuries may be focussed on the interpretation of the writings of Jean Jacques Rousseau! A group of scholars in the United States has been studying anew the complicated symbolism of the *Divine Comedy* as a revealing communication to us of much that we have lost in medieval thought. Another group has been discovering in Milton's theology something very different from conventional doctrine, a new message to us from that portentous debate of the seventeenth century. As to religion, it has always sought literature for its hand-maid, at first as the esoteric rituals of a priestly class, then as the sacred books of revelation, and latterly as the eager evangel of every conceivable faith or hallucination. On the other hand, literature never ceases to concern itself with morals and faith, with the doctrine and mystery of life. Those vast fields of human interest and aspiration which we name philosophy, literature and religion are always closely related and can scarcely be studied separately. I think this century has made some progress in uniting them, nowhere more persuasively than in the books by Mr. Henry Osborn Taylor, which follow the ambitions of the mind through the long centuries from Athens to London.[8]

I turn now to a somewhat different aspect of literature. If at times it is history or philosophy or religion, it is also a fine art, allied to sculpture, painting and music. It has a long tradition of workmanship, it has a special technic, it has created beauty. Poetry has often asserted its divine inspiration, its superiority to other creative arts, the supreme value of its ministrations. Naturally the study of letters is concerned with technic and aesthetics, with the poetic imagination. Against the extremes of positivists and determinists, there arise those who are interested in literature solely as the record of personal experience and who may confine their study to those baffling intangibles, personality and the imagination. The philosophy of Croce has throughout our period proved an incitement to an active discussion of the aesthetics of literature. In Germany a certain school in criticism has followed the ideas of Wilhelm Dilthey, a strong believer in the unique character of personality. Everywhere of late the interpretation of literature has taken note of a changing psychology which views consciousness as less limited, less fixed in its workings, more widely responsive to more variable impulses than in the

[8] H. O. Taylor, *The Classical Heritage of the Middle Ages* (1901); *The Medieval Mind*, 2 Vols. (1911); *Deliverance* (1915); *Thought and Expression in the Sixteenth Century*, 2 Vols. (1920).

old conception. I am not persuaded that much progress has been made in explaining the aesthetic emotions, or in the integration of the methods and effects of the fine arts. Even on the side of technic, such matters as vocabulary, prosody, verse tests, imagery, have received rather less attention than in the preceding twenty-five years. But our age has felt the need of proclaiming anew that literature, whether in a single instance or in its total bulk, exists by itself. It cannot be resolved into science or history or economics or philosophy. Whatever else it may be, it is born as personal experience, and it lives only as a succession of personal experiences. No measuring rods or weights have been found for its dreams and illusions, its insubstantial pageants, the baseless fabrics of its visions. Furthermore, if we have not moved much in aesthetic theory, we have gained in aesthetic information. Here, as elsewhere in letters, additional knowledge has been brought to bear, enlarging our conceptions both of literary creation and appreciation. We have, for example, all been charmed by *The Road to Xanadu* by Professor John L. Lowes, that exploration of the processes of Coleridge's mind in creating *Kubla Khan* and the *Ancient Mariner*.

In my cursory review of some phases of literary research, I must omit others. I have referred only incidentally to certain ancillary sciences such as bibliography and paleography. Handwriting, manuscripts and the printed book engage our attention as well as the *furor poeticus*. I have said nothing about the study of language because that is a subject so large and important that it deserves a place by itself in this series of lectures. Much in linguistic study has indeed no definite connection with literature and needs no comment here. But of course literature rests on language, and scarcely any literary study is possible without linguistic preparation. Certainly we shall not get far in the aesthetics or psychology of literature if we do not first consider language. Even when we are busy over very modern literature and its social or ethical trends, we shall have need of linguistic research. The recent attention which has been paid to the literary history of our own country has been accompanied by a renewed examination of the American speech. The two disciplines have indeed sometimes taken opposite directions and viewed each other with mutual disdain, but a little separation soon brings about a reconciliation. It is to the credit of our universities that they have kept the two together.

I come to still another relationship — that of scholarship and criticism. It is impossible to draw a sharp line between them. To be sure, scholars are often scientists with the will to know and the courage to learn, and they are not going to direct their researches at the beck of any particular program or creed in education, criticism or ethics. But scholars are also philologists, i.e., lovers of literature and learning, and they desire the best that has been thought and said to prevail; they cannot refrain from criticism. Literary scholarship as a whole must go beyond the accumulation of data to synthesis, interpretation, judgment. We have had indeed of late a number of books in which the specialist, having familiarized himself with the body of research so that he can discard some of its scaffolding, undertakes to build an interpretation of an author, a period, a literary type. Moreover, scholarship has been making itself felt in influencing taste, in guiding creative work, in affecting public opinion, very potently in the case of two men who have recently died, William C. Brownell and Stuart Sherman, whose services to good literature were performed in part in a publishing house and on a newspaper. That a university may exercise its scholarship in service to contemporary letters has been shown in the continued success of the *Yale Review*. I might multiply evidences that in our twenty-five years the study of letters in this country has been laying the basis for a vital literary criticism — a free play of discussion and speculation, a debate of formulas and creeds, an intelligent reconsideration of standards and judgments. Moreover, such a criticism must soon find literature opening the way to ethics, politics, art, to every humanistic interest. Literary scholarship should prove one of the supports on which we rest our criticism of life.

One reason why our literary scholarship has not made itself more influential in our current reading is because it has been so much occupied with education. Its criticism has not been mainly exercised in books and periodicals but in our schools and colleges. A hundred years ago a famous essay by Macaulay in the *Edinburgh Review* sent many new readers to Milton. Today his new readers come from our schools. The plays of Molière are not often acted on our stage or mentioned in our magazines, but they are read and enjoyed in our colleges. The planning of courses, the assignment of reading, the lectures and criticism, the textbooks — the entire guidance of our education in letters is in the hands of scholars. Complaints, in fact, are heard that our teachers are too scholarly and, on the other hand, that our scholars have too much teaching, but I do not believe that anyone really wishes to divorce the two occupations. Our scholarship is indeed faced with an almost impossible task, for our national faith in education has led to tremendous demands. We are bound to make our huge democracy not merely literate but literary-minded; we compel every one to read Shakespeare; we insist that literary discrimination begin in childhood and continue until twenty-one; we want everyone to love poetry. The great increase in the amount of schooling given in the modern literatures has been due to an insistent public demand, but it has been mainly under the direction of scholars.

It would take me too far afield to suggest even a few of the many implications and opportunities offered by this union of scholarship and education. I may only say that it is inescapable and its continuance is inevitable. Not America alone but the whole wide world is bound after education and an education in large part from books. Let us think of the unlettered millions of Russia, China, India, South America, and Africa, and then ask ourselves what will literature be in the future? What will the reading public be? When will the scholar cease to be an educator? It is not my part to prophesy but merely to record that in this century if scholarship has not been very influential on current taste or contemporary literature, it has been exercising an ever widening direction on our national education in letters, and has thereby been laying a basis for a criticism of both our literature and our life.

There is one test more which cannot be passed over and must be applied to any field of modern scholarship. Has it produced students? Is it leaving a new generation of young scholars to carry on its enterprises? The progress of twenty-five years cannot be measured solely by books and articles produced but also by the recruits fitted to pursue established methods and to make the most of opportunities indicated. In Europe, when the war took such terrible toll of youth, this vital transmission of scholarship seemed threatened, but the ranks are again closing up and the veterans are again drilling the recruits. In the United States no duty has been more strongly felt in our universities than this of training young scholars; and in our field, where the attractions of literature and of humanistic study have brought a great company of youth to offer their discipleship, this obligation has brought to the older scholars heavy responsibilities. I might recall many who have turned from their own researches to guide the eager though faltering footsteps of their successors. One I cannot refrain from naming, Professor George Lyman Kittredge whose seventieth birthday is soon to renew the homage of his scholastic children and grandchildren who have found discipline and incentive in his vast erudition and his impeccable technic. The new generation of scholars is already proving its worth and giving satisfaction to its sponsors. They are more numerous, better trained than were their predecessors, more united in common aims and helpfulness, not less idealistic and ardent. They have many opportunities opening before them as researchers, teachers, men of letters, critics; they are not likely to hide their light under a bushel.

The progress of literary scholarship in the past twenty-five years — as I see it — has been made through an enlarging view of literature itself. It has been conceived as one of man's noblest monuments and as one of his most incessant occupations, as the record of his doings in this world and of his attempts to escape, as truth and illusion, as beauty and wisdom, as a vision and as an amusement. It has been revealed not under one but under a dozen conceptions; it has been approached not by one method but by many. Its study has become more diversified and more linked with other subjects — with history, sociology, philosophy. We are all specialists working in narrow fields with due regard to thoroughness and accuracy, but also we are specialists working toward a synthesis of knowledge and a criticism of the ways of man. Of his works literature is peculiarly human and many-sided, perhaps especially serviceable as a means to interpreting his abasements and exaltations, his deeds and dreams, his wanderings through ages and movements under the direction of varying impulses. It seems likely always to excite our curiosity and inquiry. At all events this generation is leaving to the next alluring possibilities of contributing something through the study of letters to our understanding of whatever is human in this universe.

CLASSICAL STUDIES

Frank Gardner Moore

It was long a reproach to the majority of classical scholars
that their range of interest tended to narrow itself to a certain
period and to a choice selection of authors. Indeed, the very
term "classical" seemed to justify such concentration upon the
high lights. When a Latinist had acquired more than a bowing
acquaintance with writers of post-classical times, other than
commentators or grammarians, he usually felt it incumbent
upon him to offer as apology the fact that he occasionally
lighted upon a passage useful in supporting or refuting some
current view of the text or interpretation of a disputed *locus*
in Vergil or Horace.

To specialize in the works of late writers was reserved for
those of a theological bent, or of a lexicographical turn of
mind, for example, the Harvard recluse, Professor Sophocles.
When a German scholar a generation ago deliberately abandoned the classic Greek field for the Byzantine, he found it
necessary to defend such an unaccountable choice in a memorable preface:

If a natural scientist should declare that he would occupy himself only
with the lion and eagle, the oak and the rose, with pearls and precious
stones, but not with objects that are repulsive or ugly, as the spider, or
burdock, or sulphuric acid, he would cause an outburst of merriment. In
philology such epicures are the rule, who find it beneath their dignity
to devote their precious powers to anything but the majestic eagle and the
perfumed rose; and we have not yet learned to smile at these dignitaries.

With such shafts did Krumbacher, the first historian of
Byzantine literature, think it wise in 1891 to defend himself in
advance. That later on, when edition followed edition, he

could omit these sentences, is a true index of the altered feeling toward a field of study at last properly recognized as worthy of lifelong cultivation, and now promoted by journals both in Germany and France and publications in Italy. One observes also that the same German collection of invaluable works of reference for every department of classical study — that veritable library known as Iwan Müller for short — not content with what Krumbacher had done for medieval Greek, added in 1911, two years after his death, a history of medieval Latin literature by Manitius. No longer does *Altertumswissenschaft* presume to draw a sharp line at some supposed limit of classical antiquity. Conspicuous examples of unlimited interest, marked versatility and extraordinary influence we have had in these decades, and still have, in the person of men of such different types as Wilamowitz, Shorey, Norden and Gilbert Murray.

The breaking down of old barriers was already in progress forty years ago, and may be exemplified still earlier by Mommsen, whose old age brought him down to 1903, a year before our quarter century began. As Greek scholars have carried their studies beyond the first eleven centuries of Greek literature, an overflowing millennium which may be called classic, to a second period of equal length reaching down to the fall of Constantinople — so Latin scholarship with no thought of apology or defence carries on through the entire Middle Age into the Renaissance. And even in this country we have seen a striking revival of medieval studies in the last decade under the leadership of a few of our most enterprising classicists, notably Professor Rand, of Harvard. In 1925 they founded a Mediaeval Academy, with a journal of its own, the *Speculum*. They have also invaded the land of the undergraduate by editing attractive books of selections, so that college courses in Latin literature of the Middle Ages are now practicable.

This whole movement is most promising, not least because it publicly demonstrates the vitality and longevity of a language which only the most thoughtless will be able to call dead.

The extent to which the medieval field is being cultivated by Greek and Latin scholars may be shown by the bare mention of three large collections now in the making; a *corpus* of the philosophers of the Middle Ages; another of Latin literature medieval and Renaissance; another of the glossaries of that period, directed by an English Plautine scholar, Lindsay, under the auspices of the British Academy. If a medieval chronicle, as that of Geoffrey of Monmouth, is to be edited with expert collation of many manuscripts, quite as a matter of course the task will be assigned by preference to a classical scholar, in Geoffrey's case to one of our recent Columbia doctors.

Nor do our Latinists set any limit at the close of the Middle Ages. The Latin of the Renaissance also has its diligent students, results of whose labors may be seen in the monumental edition of Erasmus' Letters by an English scholar, Mr. P. S. Allen; also in such a series of scholarly editions of Renaissance works as those for which we are indebted to Professor Mustard, of Johns Hopkins, including the eclogues of Sannazaro, those of Baptista Mantuanus, and more recently the *De Curialium Miseriis* of Pope Pius II (Aeneas Silvius Piccolomini). When our classicists now spend a winter in Rome no one is greatly surprised if the outcome is some contribution to the history of the Revival of Learning. Of unbounded interest in the Rome of any and every age we have in our ranks no more notable example than Professor Showerman in his *Eternal Rome*. Thus the old hedges no longer divide. To take one more example, when the Regius Professor of Greek at the University of Cambridge, Professor D. S. Robertson, recently published an excellent *Handbook of Greek and Roman Architecture* we had one more proof of the fact that devotion to pure philology and love of an ancient art are not mutually exclusive passions. What a Roman archaeologist is now doing for Greek lexicography, we shall see in another context.

The fences which once seemed to separate the Orient from the classical field are likewise giving way, as it becomes increasingly evident that East and West were intimately bound together. There in particular, archaeology and philology walk hand in hand, where the interpretation of cults and religious practices requires a kind of collaboration hitherto rare. And to name one other meeting place of East and West, New Turkey attracted our attention the other day, when we were told that Kemal was being urged to make provision at the ultra-modern Angora for a new museum to contain the recently excavated Hittite antiquities. Thus inscriptions in a very ancient language upon which the philologists, many of them classicists, are at work, with some prospect of proving that it is an Indo-European speech, will be stored in that ancient Ancyra, whose Temple of Rome and Augustus preserves bilingually the most famous document in Roman history, the Acts of Augustus. It will remain for the new régime to uncover something worth while to represent those Gallic invaders of the third century B.C., the Galatians.

Prehistoric researches would take us too far afield, but they have shown their important bearing upon any study of the Greeks before Greece, of the Italian stocks before there could be an Italy. Historical work in general in the Graeco-Roman field has been very productive in our period. And it is noteworthy that some of the most eminent historians have commanded the amplest resources, archaeological, philological and economic, to furnish their evidence. Examples would be Camille Jullian, whose *Histoire de la Gaule*, in which exact science is matched by rare literary art, has won him the honors of the French Academy; Michael Rostovtzeff, of old St. Petersburg, Wisconsin and Yale, for whom, as for our Tenney

Frank, economic history has had its special attraction; and then Eduard Meyer, Pais and Piganiol.

Meanwhile the Etruscan question remains a mystery, in spite of the labors of many specialists. A brilliant and versatile scholar, George Hempl of Stanford University, announced in 1908 that he had succeeded in reading about fifty inscriptions in the Etruscan language, finding it an Italic dialect to be grouped with Latin and Faliscan. But his results have not met with acceptance, and while most Italian scholars prefer to believe that the Etruscan civilization was native to the soil, the pendulum tends to swing again toward the ancient explanation that Lydia was the motherland of the Etruscans.

Grammatical study has not languished, even if its output seems less since the war than in the years which preceded. Gildersleeve's *Syntax of Classical Greek* was completed in 1911, and he himself continued to be a power and an inspiration in his unique eminence till his death at a great age in 1924. Bennett's *Syntax of Early Latin* was finished in 1914, but he was cut down in his prime in 1921. In Europe, as well as among us, philology in the narrowest sense has flourished, and alongside of the names we have just mentioned, or those of Hale and Morris, as eminent representatives of historical grammar, we may name those of Brugmann, Stolz, Schmalz, Delbrück, of Sonnenschein, the English grammarian who has died recently, or Meillet, the distinguished French scholar who is to be our guest the coming semester.

A tendency away from grammar in the direction of style is to be noted in the comparatively new field of rhythmical prose, largely under the influence of Zielinski, whose chief work on the cadences in Cicero's oratory appeared precisely in our year of 1904, and whose work has been carried on by many others, particularly by De Groot in Holland, with a wider range and a safer restraint. That style, if it cannot be reduced to a science, may be studied in a scientific spirit, was pointed out by Professor Morris fourteen years ago to a gathering of the clan at Princeton.

For one characteristic product of classical scholarship we may here spare little more than a sentence: that is, the learned edition with ample comment in which the results of wide-ranging studies in many fields are made available for the interpretation of a single text. Such are Kirby Smith's remarkable edition of Tibullus; that of Cicero's *de Divinatione* by Dr. Pease, now President of Amherst; and most recently the great edition of Ovid's *Fasti* in five volumes by Sir James Frazer (1929), a mine of information on every subject connected with folklore and religion.

The study of ancient religions has continued to flourish through our whole period, with much fresh light from new sources archaeological and epigraphic. Here again spade and book have been inseparable. But with the merest reference to this immense subject we must close our very hasty survey of the general field of classical study — a field from which most of the old landmarks have disappeared in an era of unlimited expansion.

Within the last quarter of a century, classical studies have had a very notable accession of material, large in amount and infinitely varied in content, from the dry soil of Egypt, especially from the sand-drifted towns and necropolises on the edge of the desert, above the reach of the annual inundation.

It is now a little more than a hundred and fifty years since the first papyrus — a single roll — from beneath the sands of Egypt reached Europe (1778). Purchased by a skeptical merchant who watched the Arabs burn with delight some fifty others which he had declined to buy, it was the forerunner of others which became known in no great numbers in the first half of the nineteenth century. Fifty years ago the great finds in the Fayum were beginning to be made, with the result that dealers in antiquities undertook excavations for the purpose. A decade later it was discovered that mummy cases were often made of old papyri glued together. These could be detached and deciphered, as could the long rolls of the same material which were sometimes used for mummy wrappings.

The first systematic excavations for papyri under expert direction were in 1895-96 (Hogarth, Grenfell and Hunt). In the next year important discoveries at Oxyrhynchus marked the real beginning of an epoch. These were soon followed by similar excavations by the Germans and the French (Wilcken and Schaefer, Jouguet and Lefebvre, respectively).

A newborn science was rapidly reaching maturity with the beginning of the new century, and has been exceedingly active ever since, except for the interruption caused by the war. Papyrology, as it is called, has attracted an increasing number of our scholars, and can never in the future be neglected. Like other sciences worthy of the name it is a school of patience and precision. The masses of damaged papers and dismembered books from the tombs and dumps of Egypt must be handled with the utmost care, so fragile are they, unless protected by glass plates or otherwise. They can be read with accuracy only by those who have acquired a thorough familiarity with all the different types of handwriting practised at different dates. To understand and interpret the business papers, contracts, leases, receipts, etc., calls for thorough knowledge of the Greek of the period involved, as also of law and commercial usage, not to mention economic conditions. Official documents require even more of expert acquaintance with history and administration, as well as skill in grasping the situation and in making plausible suggestions for the conjectural restoration of words lost or illegible.

Fortunately for the advancement of knowledge, as for the training of specialists in a new department, the papyri have not been concentrated in a few great collections on Egyptian soil, or even in the most historic libraries in Europe. Masses of specimens have been sold to museums and libraries widely scattered on both sides of the Atlantic, including a number of our university libraries, as Harvard, Cornell, Michigan, and others. Our own university library came into possession of about 525 fragments in 1923, and to that collection others have been added from time to time. These are to be duly protected by shatter-proof glass, and are in process of publication at the hands of Professors Westermann, Keyes and Kraemer.

Certainly the "scrap of paper" receives a new significance when we realize that out of an immense number of such scattered scraps we have secured very substantial additions to our knowledge of law and government, of trade and transportation, of agriculture and of daily life in one of the most interesting countries of the ancient world through a period of a thousand years. In particular the interpretation of our classical historians and other prose writers enters upon a new phase, now that Egypt furnishes the means of correcting and supplementing, and may be said to take the pen in hand herself to add many illuminating footnotes, destructive or otherwise, to our current commentaries. And while this applies chiefly to the affairs of the East, the whole subject of Roman provincial administration is likely to be set in a somewhat different light if discoveries continue. How much Rome was indebted to the Hellenistic monarchies whose institutions she inherited, we are beginning to realize. No history either of the world of Alexander and his successors or of the Roman *orbis terrarum* can now be written without first mastering the new and abundant materials from Egypt.

Of those that bear upon private life none are more valuable than the letters written by average persons, whose unstudied pens would never have ensured preservation in Greece or Italy. Many of these have a strangely familiar sound. When we read a father's unpolished letter to his student son, urging him to stick to his books, and adding that he is sending money, we somehow feel at home. Elsewhere the correspondence of ordinary careless mortals has perished, and with it much precious information about the social life of the time, the joys and sorrows of the masses. Into that long-deplored dearth there comes now a wealth of the commonplace, establishing for us a very direct and personal contact with men, women and children of average mould. Thus we may venture upon a synthesis, and produce a mosaic picture of human life as it was lived by millions in Egypt, Hellenistic, Roman, and Byzantine. And with some corrections of detail for other regions we shall have a panorama of life in the Hellenistic and Roman world, far more realistic, far more trustworthy than anything we have had before.

If we turn from the field of history, political, economic and social, to that of literature and studies, we find that the papyri, in spite of their rags and tatters, have yielded many treasures of the highest importance and thus have given a fresh stimulus to classical studies.

To speak first of the rags and tatters, even insignificant fragments in their aggregate, as they tend variously to supplement each other, enable us to draw important inferences as to the popularity of this or that Greek author at different times, and as to the condition of his text in a period which antedates the oldest previously known manuscripts — those parchment codices which are treasured in the most famous libraries, and positively venerated in those rare examples which go back as far as the fourth or fifth century, whereas the papyrus fragments range from the third century B.C. to the sixth century after Christ.

Of course one asks: "Do the oldest parchments of the Vatican, the Laurentian, and other sanctuaries of classical scholarship bear the test of direct comparison with the papyri, in some cases older by six or seven hundred years? Were Iliad and Odyssey substantially the same as we have them now in print?" We find in fact that Homer's text was much less settled in the third century B.C., when even the number of verses shows variations; that in the next century it had become more fixed, thanks to the labors of the Alexandrian scholars. And as he was the universal schoolbook, it is not surprising that the later papyri show in the main a standard text in substantial agreement with our best parchments. Thus we are sure that the Homer read and reread by Vergil and Horace was our Homer, with only minor divergences in the text.

An interesting example of such a minor discrepancy recently came to light here in our own library. Odysseus, in the seventeenth book of the Odyssey (354f.), is praying to Zeus for blessings on the head of Telemachus. But the dependent accusative and infinitive — obvious enough in its meaning even to human hearers of the prayer — lacks a governing verb. And the commentators, less benign than the father of gods and men, positively insist upon our supplying an imperative δός, "grant." But just where that monosyllable might stand all previously known manuscripts have μοί, "to me." And here comes a Columbia papyrus of twenty-four verses, recently published by Professor Keyes in the *American Journal of Philology*, showing exactly that imperative in place of the pronoun. Thus a variant reading, especially if it be absolutely new, offers food for not a little reflection, even if we are inclined to assume that a copyist following dictation of a reader unconsciously substituted a word implied for one not needed. Or did some schoolmaster, weary of repeating the same comment every year, think perhaps to save trouble, and at the same time silence future scholiasts, by boldly changing two letters?

As with Homer, so in the case of such writers as Plato and Thucydides the Egyptian fragments have proved that the text of these authors was essentially the same then as now. They show also that careless copies of Greek authors were often in the book-market at the same time with more correct texts, so that a purchaser must have needed to exercise discrimination or to call in an adviser. Corruptions were, of course, creeping in, as fresh blunders were made in copying or old errors were made worse. But a study of the different styles of writing will enable us to discover what letters or combinations of letters were likely to be confused by copyists. Thus we are now in a better position to explain the corruptions in the more complete manuscripts of a later period.

Other debts of scholarship to the papyri are these: that where our manuscripts of tragedies and comedies have confused or failed to indicate the speakers in a dialogue, the papyrus fragment sometimes saves the day by its double point, indicating a change of speakers, or by adding the names of those speakers; and further that in lyrical passages of the drama and in the lyric poets the new fragments have better preserved the metre, so often distorted in the later manuscripts.

As to the form of books we learn much from Egypt, as that the papyrus rolls differed very much in length, and refused to be standardized, as modern theory has been prone to assume. And the more completely we realize the conditions under which books were written the sounder will be our judgments of the authors. Thus a regular, logically ordered plan for a philosophical work or a history would seem all the more necessary when a reader would need to depend more upon memory and could not readily turn back to earlier chapters or look ahead. But these very mechanical difficulties of rolling and unrolling would tempt the average reader to an easy-going habit of mind. And the writer of voluminous works composed at top speed would be inclined to take advantage of the improbability that a reader would take the trouble to ferret out inconsistencies of plan or argument where any comparison was quite laborious.

Not all ancient books, however, had the form of a roll. The book form familiar to the modern world, and which we had thought almost confined to works written on parchment, is now represented by many Egyptian examples on paper, commonly showing from four to six leaves doubled and placed one within the other, thus forming what we should call a signature.

Of schoolbooks we may make only the briefest mention. Not a few of them have been found in a fragmentary state, including pages out of vocabularies to Homer and Vergil, and from commentaries and vocabularies for Demosthenes.

In pure literature the papyri brought to light in the last twenty-five years have given us back one lost writer of the first order, the foremost writer of the Attic New Comedy, Menander; part of a satyr-drama, the *Ichneutae*, by Sophocles; part of a fourth-century history of Greece, the *Hellenica*, possibly by Ephorus or Theopompus; and many important fragments of works, hitherto all but unknown, by the greatest of the Alexandrian poets, Callimachus. Latin literature is scantily represented, but mention may be made of three fragments out of as many orations of Cicero, all discovered within six months of each other; also of fragments of Vergil (*Aeneid* IV) and Sallust (*Catiline*); and part of an epitome of Livy covering the years 150-137 B.C.

In 1905, while excavating in a city anciently named Aphroditopolis, a French scholar, Gustave Lefebvre, came upon a large earthen jar filled with upwards of 150 rolls of papyrus, consisting of records, wills and contracts, of the age of Justinian and his successor. To protect these documents of the sixth century an old book, already in pieces, had been placed in the top of the jar, so that numerous leaves had fallen to the ground. The book was a copy of the comedies of Menander. Two years later the discoverer published at Cairo the first edition of these plays so far as they were represented in his fragments. Later editors have incorporated such other fragments of the poet as were previously known from quotations in Greek writers, such as Plutarch and Athenaeus; also from other papyrus fragments discovered before 1905 or since, and from three parchment fragments from the convent on Mt. Sinai. Thus, as the beginning of our period saw the discovery in the City of Aphrodite, so its end is marked by Jensen's scholarly edition of Menander up-to-date, appearing in Berlin, 1929, as the first of a new classical series.

From one play, the *Epitrepontes*, or *The Arbitrants*, we have about six hundred lines, and four hundred and fifty from the *Periceiromene*, literally latinized as *Circumtonsa*, and aptly translated *The Rape of the Ringlets*. Thus we have enough of these two plays, in spite of serious losses, to give us a good idea of the action and of the dramatic methods of Menander, especially of his lifelike drawing of characters in their very human mixture of good and bad in the same person, regardless of the popular demand for villains utterly black, devoid of any redeeming traits. If we are unable as yet quite to accept Julius Caesar's evaluation, which, if literally taken, would make the Athenian worth two of the African Terence, we are at least able to understand the high praises of Menander's lifelikeness, his invention, his style, his characterization, his treatment of emotions. These were the qualities which justified Quintilian in citing him as a model eminently serviceable to the would-be orator; the master, in fact, points out that Menander was an orator himself in the half-dozen plays he mentions by name, including our *Epitrepontes*.

It is instructive to study in an extant scene of this play the speeches of the shepherd and the charcoal-burner as examples of a type which we should not at first expect to find praised without reservation by the great Spanish master. These peasants speak absolutely in character in terse and homely vein, but with abundance of natural rhetoric and no lack of familiarity with the ways and the lingo of Attic litigants. The highly trained rhetorical art of the poet has effectually concealed itself from inattentive spectator and hasty reader. But the foremost teacher of studied oratory, who certainly was not writing for the improvement of charcoal burners and other rustics, finds in this scene and others in our poet what after all constitutes the sum and substance of his teaching — *cuncta quae praecipimus*.

On the whole one must admit that the partly recovered Menander has made an impression less deep than might have been anticipated. The thrill may perhaps come when some still happier discovery shall give us a complete comedy. Then we shall better judge of his fidelity to life, as expressed not only in the famous saying of a librarian of Alexandria, Aristophanes of Byzantium, but also in the words of the astronomer poet Manilius, *qui vitae ostendit vitam*, and in the judgment of Aulus Gellius, who describes him as drawing *de vita hominum media*.

Such was the foremost writer of Attic New Comedy, till so recently the mere shadow of a great name. The friend of Epicurus and favored of fortune, though Athens had within his lifetime lost her independence, Menander could not be prevailed upon by Ptolemy Philadelphus to remove to Alexandria.

Of Callimachus, the court poet of that Macedonian monarch, and librarian of the famous library, the papyri, as we have already seen, have given us numerous fragments, naturally enough in view of his high position and great popularity. But here we must take time only to mention the most recent of these literary finds — that of some twenty lines of a celebrated poem of Callimachus, hitherto known only in the translation of Catullus, that *Coma Berenices* which with all

its learned artificiality is least like the Catullus whom we love.
Now, within a year, we recover in large part a passage from
the middle of the original elegy, and the tattered papyrus
shows how closely the Roman poet rendered the Alexandrian.
Editors rejoice that one hitherto hopeless corruption in the
fifty-fourth line of the Latin version is now removed. The
ales equus, the "winged steed" of this verse is now seen to be,
not the ostrich, accepted by some of the best critics of the
nineteenth century, but poetic painting of the west wind. Thus
a torn leaf of ancient paper has just corrected a fairly respectable error, and Greek poet and Roman translator must no
longer be accused of assuming that an ostrich could fly even in
poetry.

From a much later period also, as much as six centuries after
Callimachus, Egypt is giving us fragments of true poetry
from writers who have been mere names. Thus we now find
the poet in a picturesque adventurer who in the sixth century
left his birthplace, Panopolis in Upper Egypt, and though a
pagan, won his way at Athens and then even in court circles at
Constantinople. Finally this Pamprepios supported a usurper
and a revolting general with whom he shared defeat, flight and
siege in a fortress of Isauria. An intriguer to the last, and
put to death there as a traitor to his old chief and his upstart
emperor, he now appears to have been a writer of verse,
including an epyllion on the seasons in imitation of the prolific
Nonnos, his fellow-townsman, and of earlier Alexandrian
models.

We must not leave the papyri without mentioning the very
extensive polyglot literature which this new branch of learning has created. It has been necessary to publish the documents
as rapidly as possible — hence the great series sponsored by
governments, libraries, museums and societies, in several different countries. There is, of course, an *Archiv* to announce
discoveries and otherwise to serve the cause. And a special

lexicon has been provided by an eminent German specialist, Preisigke, who was a high official of the German Post, not a mere professor. Other noted papyrologists have smoothed the way for ambitious youth by producing bulky manuals with select texts. A special grammar goes without saying, and many volumes of studies based upon the new material have appeared, while impressive works of reference endeavor to make the newly acquired knowledge serve the purposes of scholars in very different fields.

Time would fail us to mention in any detail the important increase of our sources through the unearthing of valuable inscriptions, to be added to the immense collections already existing. Some, to be sure, confirm rather than extend our knowledge, but are otherwise of great interest, for example the fragments of one more copy of the *Res gestae* of Augustus, discovered under English and American auspices at Antioch in Pisidia a few years ago. More significant are several inscriptions brought to light at Cyrene some eight years since by the Italians. One of these shows this prosperous city in the rôle of an almoner on a Near East scale at a time when Greek lands suffered from a dearth of food for several years (329-326 B.C.). Reckoned in modern terms these donations of wheat by Cyrene to a list of forty-two cities or ethnic groups amounted to a million and a third of bushels. Another inscription in eighty-eight lines gives us a large part of the constitution of Cyrene under the Ptolemies. Still another Greek inscription at Cyrene contains five edicts of Augustus between 7 and 4 B.C. These throw new light on the relation of the first *princeps* to the senate in his government of provinces that were in name senatorial.

From papyri we turn to a not less surprising discovery, that of parchment fragments in unexpected quarters. A stone jar hermetically sealed, discovered at Avroman in Kurdistan in 1915, contained deeds of sale in Greek on parchment, dating from the second century B.C. Unfortunately there is only a faint hope that other jars closed in so exceptional a manner will some day give us literary treasures.

Far more promising is the recent discovery of parchment fragments preserved simply in a deep bed of sand. The scene of these finds was a deserted city on the right bank of the Euphrates, about 125 miles east of Palmyra, with which it had the closest commercial relations, both being on the route of caravans bringing to the Mediterranean countries the precious wares of India from the navigable Euphrates, or even from the lower waters of the Tigris, to which came the ships, availing themselves of this much shorter course than that by way of the Red Sea. Of this city, called Doura (or Dura)-Europos, there are extensive remains of walls and towers, a citadel and temples, almost completely buried by the sands blown eastward from the Syrian desert or westward from the waterless steppes of southern Mesopotamia. It was at first a fortified outpost of Hellenism, built in a strong position to command the river by Seleucus, Alexander's general and one of his successors. At the height of his power Seleucus reigned from the Aegean to the Indus, and it was his aim to hellenize the vast regions of the East. In a tower of the citadel of this Macedonian city by the Euphrates French soldiers of the Army of the Levant, excavating in 1922-1923, discovered a number of parchment fragments, some of which had apparently been blown thither from the archives of the town and were preserved from complete destruction by the masses of sand. Thus we have part of a record in Greek, dating from about 195 B.C., of a sale subject to repurchase of land with its fruit trees and gardens and farm buildings where now there are only sand dunes. Documentary evidence that the region was extensively irrigated was not needed, but this confirmation happens to be the oldest known parchment, earlier in date than the supposed invention of that material at Pergamon, to which it owes its name.

Another Greek fragment which cannot be precisely dated is from a law book and deals with intestate succession. The official language of the Roman army is represented by one fragment of a list showing what soldiers of the garrison were present, detached, promoted or honorably discharged at that date.

At the same spot, along with well-preserved shoes, palm-fibre sandals, etc., were found remains of wooden shields of the twentieth cohort of archers of Palmyra, a mounted force, showing the lessons Rome had learned from Parthia. These shields had been covered with leather, and one of the archers had his adorned with a blue oval, evidently the Black Sea, with its ships and boats, separated by an elliptical white line from the red border of the shield. In the small part preserved this shows an itinerary suggestive of the Tabula Peutingerana, that famous Roman road map of the thirteenth century, but copied from a much older original. The stages of a long march around the western and northwestern shores of the Euxine are indicated. The extant names begin with the city which we know as Varna, in Bulgaria. Tomi, the place of Ovid's exile, is mentioned; and so the march continues as far as the Crimea, whence the cohort had evidently taken ship across to Trapezus (Trebizond), on the southeastern coast. Thence a long march is briefly indicated — 300 miles to Artaxata, in Armenia. The names are given in Greek, though the Danube appears also in its Latin form spelt with Greek letters. It seems clear that the decorator of the shield had copied from a military map of the first half of the third century after Christ, with the distances in Roman miles. No doubt this border contained in its lost portion (perhaps nine-tenths) many other geographical names, to remind the owner and his comrades of their long marches in other lands. So the sands of the desert have yielded a unique document out of a period in which southern Russia with its Greek cities was still defended by Roman arms, before the first invasion of the Goths (238 A.D.).

These discoveries give strong ground for the hope voiced by M. Cumont, director of the first excavations, that what has been done for Egypt by papyrology will some day be done for the Greek Orient by a science as yet in embryo — the science of pergamenology. Of course everything will depend upon the number of parchments which can be recovered. And, as in Egypt, the finds may not be limited to documents commercial or official. In that region too the schoolboy had his Homer and other poets, and the wind may have lodged discarded leaves of his textbooks in some corners where they may be safely buried under the sand drifts.

Nor must we pass over the paintings of Dura, a whole series of frescoes which adorned the walls of a temple to the gods of Palmyra. They represent religious ceremonies, offerings to the divinities by the worshippers, in part the donors of the decorative paintings, together with their families, very suggestive of Renaissance altar pieces immortalizing those who paid the painter. The oldest of these murals date from the age of Vespasian, thus antedating contacts with the Roman world. Their inspiration is from Palmyra, whose artists probably labored here in person, as in their own city they had taught pupils from Dura. The art then is not that of the West, but one in which Syrian influences are combined with the Hellenistic. And in these stately scenes, with a certain solemn stiffness, but rich in coloring and in every way impressive, we are reading a previously unknown chapter in the art history of the Near East, a necessary introduction to that which we call Byzantine. These paintings were first uncovered by our American Egyptologist, Professor Breasted, in 1920, when a belligerent situation at the end of the British occupation allowed him but a single day for his work, including color photography. Since then irreparable damage has been done by exposure and the superstitious vandalism of the Bedouin.

Fortunately the excavations begun thus auspiciously on the bank of the Euphrates were resumed in 1928 by Yale University in coöperation with the French Academy of Inscriptions and Letters. They are still in progress, with every prospect of systematic prosecution for some years to come. Already valuable results are being obtained, especially in inscriptions, under the direction of M. Pillet, not without the counsel and assistance of Cumont, Rostovtzeff and others. A preliminary report of the work of the first season appeared in 1929.

Of archaeological work in general and its results in our twenty-five years it will be impossible to speak here, except in the briefest compass. The interruption of the war and unfavorable conditions thereafter seriously retarded progress, but there has been a partial compensation in increased activity in the last few years, particularly in Italy, where evocation of the past is in the creed of Fascism. Renewed excavations at Pompeii have led to the far more difficult, but more promising, undertaking at Herculaneum. Much work has been done at the port of Ostia, where some buildings of three stories and many inscriptions have been uncovered. In Rome itself the Forum of Augustus and that of Trajan have been more thoroughly excavated. Adjoining the latter a semicircular street of shops has been brought to light, and on a higher level a most interesting vaulted arcade with three stories of shops, on the slope of the Quirinal. In the Campus Martius the Theatre of Marcellus is being freed from its sordid encumbrances, and demolition and excavation combine to reveal ancient temples and porticoes. Further north, near the site of Pompey's Theatre, an excavated block, with four temples of the third and second centuries B.C., now compels a busy quarter to remember Republican Rome. As for the topography of the city and the Campagna, this garden plot has been intensively cultivated by such men as Hülsen, Boni, Lanciani, Tomassetti, Ashby and Platner, the joint production of the last two being the admirable *Topographical Dictionary of Ancient Rome*, 1929.

In Greek lands much had been accomplished before the war, especially in Crete, and at such sites as Ephesus, Miletus, Didyma, Delos, Antioch in Pisidia, Pergamon, Samos, Delphi. For us a special interest attaches to the excavations at Sardis, Olynthus and Corinth, directed respectively by Professors Butler of Princeton, Robinson of Johns Hopkins, and our former colleague Dr. Shear, to whom falls the conduct of the great work now beginning in the Agora of Athens.

In North Africa archaeology and history join hands both on French and Italian soil, with notable results, as in Gsell's eight volume *Histoire de l'Afrique du Nord* (1914-), not yet finished. Italian activity has been chiefly in the Tripolitana, and especially at Leptis Magna, birthplace of Septimius Severus, who lavishly adorned the city with a splendid basilica and other buildings, among them baths better preserved than any of the *thermae* at Rome, and almost entirely in massive *opus quadratum*.

Our quarter century in classical learning has been particularly marked by enterprises on an imposing scale, in which a large number of scholars have contributed their services and the results of their researches. Many others who would gladly have been drafted for such undertakings have found themselves absorbed in what may be called works of general promotion, such as the conduct of organizations national or local which must not be allowed to lapse, and the editing of important journals, such as the *American Journal of Philology, Classical Philology*, the *Classical Review*, the *Classical Weekly*, to name only a few English and American examples. These together with the annual volumes of collected contributions may represent for us the steady output of our classical scholars, while not a few have labored to raise the standard of textbooks, and still others have compiled *Jahresberichte*, or bibliographies, such as that of Marouzeau.

For the most imposing of the great enterprises the limitations of our period restrict us to a mere report of slow progress. This is the *Thesaurus Linguae Latinae*, under the patronage of German and Austrian academies. The immense material had been previously gathered and so far digested that the first two volumes had appeared in the years 1900-1906. Two more were completed by 1912. The fifth and sixth, interrupted by war and financial difficulties, have reached completion only within the past two years. The letter *G* is still incomplete, from which we may calculate that quite three-fifths of the work are still to be awaited.

A similar *Thesaurus Linguae Graecae* was projected by Sir Richard Jebb in 1904 — a still more monumental undertaking, since Greek literature bulks about ten times as large as Latin. The project was considered for several years, and weighed against the counterproposal of Diels, that separate dictionaries for epic, lyric, tragedy, etc., should be issued — a series of no less than ten huge lexicons. The whole plan was finally abandoned about 1910.

Meantime the revision of Liddell and Scott had been proposed in 1903, and in 1925 the first instalment of this much-used lexicon appeared under the editorship of Mr. H. Stuart Jones, well known in a totally different field as a Roman archaeologist and former director of the British School in Rome. Up to 1929 four parts have appeared, about three-eighths of the whole. And for the fields which this work has been obliged to ignore, namely the Greek of the Church Fathers and that of medieval and modern times, provision is being made by a special lexicon of Patristic and Byzantine Greek under English auspices, and by another in the hands of the Greeks. It should be added that the most cogent reason for the revision of Greek dictionaries of the ancient period is the considerable stock of new words and new uses for which we are indebted to the papyri.

One of the most enduring as well as one of the most useful monuments of Latin scholarship of our time will probably be the huge lexicon of medieval Latin, to cover some six centuries from about 500 A.D. This is to be no mere revision of Du Cange, whose voluminous work, several times revised, has been the standard from the seventeenth century to our day. The new lexicon will be international in more than one sense, first as an enterprise carried on by scholars of many countries under the direction of the Union Académique Internationale, and second as limiting itself to the period in which Latin was itself truly international, as the parent trunk from which grew all the different national branches. And while the vast collections of material are being made by volunteer workers in almost every country, preliminary studies and contributions appear in the *Bulletin Du Cange*, edited by a noted French Latinist, M. Henri Goelzer.

Another type of enterprise in recent years takes the form of a great series of carefully edited texts with a translation (usually a new one) on the opposite page. That such series of large scope are now in progress is a sign of the times, and one which may easily be misinterpreted. For an outsider, impressed by the yards and yards of shelving occupied by the "Loeb Classical Library" or the corresponding French series of the Association Guillaume Budé, might find in all this array something suggestive of a state funeral with international participation — the final obsequies of the classics after their slow demise. It will no doubt be argued that with text and an up-to-date translation paired with each other page by page we have the ultimate tribute to the great departed, while tasteful introductions in effect pronounce a *laudatio funebris* over one after another of these ancient worthies. But this is to assume that there can ever be a definitive translation, a fallacy against which we have had the vigorous protest of Gamaliel Bradford. It is also to assume that these spectres, if for argument's sake we may call them such, can ever be laid.

To the collections of texts with translations named a moment ago many of the best known scholars in England, France and America have contributed. Imitating their example, a group of Spanish scholars is producing a similar series at Barcelona under the patronage of a local foundation and the language, it is interesting to note, is the local Catalan.

Addressed to an audience of specialists is the notable English series of translations of the works of Aristotle. And many other translations of classical writers have appeared in recent years from the University Presses of Oxford and Cambridge. Germany too has not been idle in this matter of fresh translations.

Of Latin versions from the English we may commend as refreshment for the tired student the clever Horatian renderings by the late Alfred Godley, of Oxford, of a series of English odes written by Rudyard Kipling and Charles Graves in imitation of Horace. The amusement of the reader is heightened by the fact that the little work boldly appeared as a fifth book of Horace's Odes, with absurd critical notes at the foot of the page and a mock-pedantic Latin preface. Thus may staid philology for the moment step down from her lofty *cathedra* and don the cap and bells with real distinction.

In this country a group of Latinists have been enlisted in a cause which at first sight might seem to lie beyond the bounds of their province — that of International Law as represented by the first great works on that subject, ranging from the fourteenth to the eighteenth century and including such celebrities as Hugo Grotius and Pufendorf, the whole making an entire series of the "Classics of International Law," published by the Carnegie Endowment for International Peace.

The systematic presentation of classical civilization as a whole and in its relation to modern life has been a dominant note in these two decades and a half. A great German series, "Die Kultur der Gegenwart," presented the classical elements in a series of works by eminent specialists, Wilamowitz, Norden and others just twenty-five years ago. In 1908-1909 Mahaffy, who represented perhaps better than any other English-speaking scholar the increasing interest in the Hellenistic period and the bonds of union between Greece and Rome, delivered his Lowell Lectures on *What Have the Greeks Done for Modern Civilization?* In this spirit scores of scholars have combined in different surveys of our ancient heritage from every angle. The result appears in a whole class of works meant for the cultivated non-professional reader. Not a few classicists of different nationalities have made large contributions, if they have not directed the entire enterprise. These series treat of the civilization of Greece, or that of the Graeco-Roman world, as the larger part of the inheritance handed down to us moderns.

The German series of this type bears the title "Das Erbe der Alten," and covers a wide range of subject, including the influence of certain celebrated writers upon later ages. One editor of this series has been the Polish scholar, Zielinski, whose delightful *Cicero im Wandel der Jahrhunderte* (1897) had given a special stimulus to books of that character.

From England come *The Legacy of Greece, The Legacy of Rome*, continued in *The Legacy of the Middle Ages* — works of collaboration to which distinguished specialists have contributed each a chapter, the authors ranging from Gilbert Murray and the Gloomy Dean to Mackail and Dr. Bradley.

American in plan and direction, but with a few English contributors, is the series "Our Debt to Greece and Rome," conducted by Professor Hadzsits, of the University of Pennsylvania — a collection of fifty small and readable volumes on a good part of the subjects which make up our immense inheritance from the classic civilization, including studies of a few great writers and their influence upon successive ages.

In contrast with these numerous evidences of collaboration on an extensive scale for the benefit of the general reader, we must not fail to speak of special tools produced single-handed for scholar and student. These include concordances, indices, and the special lexicons, none of which takes a higher rank than the *Lexicon Plautinum* of our own Professor Lodge.

We have all too hurriedly scanned the greatly enlarged horizon of the studies which we still call classical. We have lingered perhaps too long by the Nile and the Euphrates, with the excuse, if excuse be needed, that our period has indeed proved an age of discovery. We have glanced at some of our notable enterprises in pure scholarship or reinterpretation. Already their collective value is immense. Best of all, they prove vitality and the power of these studies to inspire the devotion of many men who are perfectly willing to be misjudged by the outside world, and by many even of their own colleagues, as votaries of a cult of the past, so long as they are themselves inwardly conscious of an unfailing, lifelong inspiration which they derive from the many-sided classic civilization, but most of all from what still lives and will live on and on in the great masters of two perennial literatures.

In conclusion I can pay no higher tribute to these twin branches of learning, whose very age is in some quarters felt to be a serious detraction, than by applying to them both the chance remark of a scientific colleague who recently, upon hearing that Latin was my occupation, exclaimed "That's marvelous; it never grows old!"

ARCHITECTURE

William A. Boring

Architecture is a creation of man, working in harmony with the laws of structure as revealed by nature. Architecture is the art of expressing in building that convincing truth and beauty that appeals to the finer senses of man, and this perfection of expression lifts the structure of usefulness into the realm of the fine arts. It involves that apparent fitness of a building to its purpose which is instantly convincing to the beholder, and it impresses him with a peculiar beauty expressed in form, color and texture, harmonious with the natural responses we feel in our contact with all things designed by nature to surround us, to maintain us, to give us the wish to live, and by seeing, hearing, feeling, consciously to be a part of the cosmus.

Architecture is the mother of the fine arts. It was conceived and erected first for the convenience of man, and then by reason of his yearning for beauty it was made beautiful. In making it beautiful he put into it the qualities of his soul, he expressed his faith, his religion, his government, and his manner of life and thus he made it a record of all his greatest achievements. The nations of the past are today judged by the remains of their architecture; as the archaeologist interprets the remains of past civilizations we can visualize their buildings, which tell the story of how they lived and how they built. We can reconstruct them in the same way that the paleontologist can reconstruct a prehistoric animal by the study of its few scattered bones. A portion of marble from a Roman temple tells us who was emperor when the building was constructed, as we examine a stone found in the excavation in Greence we recognize the date and monument of which it was a part.

Every fragment from the ruins of a classic temple expresses beauty. The building as a whole was beautiful, as was every part which was correctly designed for its particular place in the structure.

Architecture brings to its use science, and all of the arts — science properly to determine the necessary action and reaction for stability and carrying on the functions of the building, and art to bring these qualities into harmony with the natural laws of beauty. Thus is established an equipoise which holds the assemblage within proper bounds. It shows that action is counterbalanced with the inertia of mass or by reaction of structural members the lines of which are instantly apparent. It shows that the life lines of the building are in harmony with the laws of nature. Mass, line, symmetry, proportion and color are established, and these determine the character and truth of the structure. But a finer beauty is usually desired than could be shown by the simplicity of the main functional lines. Embellishment and the perfection of texture round out the building, as a beautiful thought is finer when told in beautiful language. These achievements are not possible by the architect alone. He must have the coöperation and sympathy of those for whom he builds, and he must enter into their thoughts and they into his in such a way that they will be really in part creators of the building. It is not possible to build a beautiful building without adjusting the functions in a certain degree so that resultant beauty of form is possible. Each problem is in itself a creation of the architect, working with the necessities laid down by the projectors of the building, but those who control the functions of the building must conform in their demands to those things which are reasonable and are possible to make the structure beautiful. It is not possible to design a beautiful building on absolutely rigid requirements set down by those who have no knowledge of what will be the resulting form of their combination of areas. It is a notable fact that when people lay out technically what they think is their absolute requirement, giving no thought to the architectural form, the resulting building develops into an ugly shape. There must be coöperation, give and take; there must be leadership by the architect, and assistance by those who are in control of the necessities of the building. The architect can plan better technical buildings under the guidance of technicians than the technicians themselves can possibly lay out. The architect must be resourceful, patient, tactful and industrious. The client must be insistent upon having his technical requirements met, but he should not say in what form they should be met and he should be in sympathy with the architect's idea and believe in his guidance.

The keynote of fine architecture is good proportion. Good proportion is a subtle and miraculous quality. It corresponds in the art of architecture to harmony in color, harmony in music and the beauty of rhythm in poetry. Proportion is that correct adjustment of spaces and line which in its perfection exemplifies the ideals of the Greeks expressed by that truest principle of good taste — "nothing too much." This observation applies to every kind of a building which man can erect. Proportion is as necessary in the skyscraper as it is in the art gallery. It is a quality which the architect has in true proportion to his ability to create a good building. Although a building may have power, height, strength, gaiety and variety, if it is lacking that subtle charm of good proportion it is not entirely successful. Proportion is not the result of theories nor rules. It is a delicate sense as fine in feeling as that which makes a beautiful form in sculpture, a masterpiece of painting or a great opera. The natural expressions which we see about us in daily life, in form, in color, in motion, are in themselves a harmony with each other which is instinctively felt by the sympathetic soul.

If building in form, texture and color is out of tune with nature she attempts to bring it into harmony if left to her own

devices. The erosive action of the elements will soften the outlines by frost and heat, rain will tone and blend the color, and
growing things will embrace to make it harmonious with its
surroundings. It is said that nature abhors a vacuum, but she
seems to hate ugliness even more from the prompt action she
takes to remove it.

The first requirement of a building is that it should serve its
purpose. It should be convenient in arrangement, the proper
size and adaptability for whatever goes on inside of its walls.
After that quality has been perfectly determined, it must be
arranged for solidity so that it will be a sound building and will
continue to serve its purpose. These two things must be accomplished before any building can be considered successful. In doing these things, however, the architect makes his
building as beautiful as he can. Some kinds of buildings are
more easily made beautiful than others, but each building must
have its peculiar quality of beauty and it is the architects duty
to see that the convenience and solidity are also expressed in
beauty of line, mass, color and detail. Such a work of art re-
sembles in its attributes a work of art in any other field. The
terms even with which we describe it are related to the same
things in music, in art, in poetry and dancing.

Architecture is studied and represented in its conception and
development by drawings. The architect must learn to draw so
easily and naturally that it will be as instinctive as it would be to
write a word, as instinctive to express oneself in drawing as in
speech. A student of today is more proficient in drawing than
one of twenty-five years ago. It is to be remembered, however,
that beautiful drawings alone will not make beautiful architecture. A beautiful sketch will show an idea, an inspiration.
However, to have that inspiration realized in a building requires deep, thoughtful study and great care in analysis. It is to
be remembered that a drawing is a flat sheet of paper, while a
building is solid substance in three dimensions, and can be seen

from every angle. Therefore the building, in order to look well, must be studied in a way which a drawing of two dimensions will not reveal.

A beautiful architectural drawing is a work of art in itself. The building which it represents is another and different work of art, far more difficult to realize. After the practicing architect has conceived the design of the building in a general way he must have collaborators who will help him to analyze and to develop all the different parts. It is the architect's duty then to bring all of his drawings and designs to work together as a complete whole. We at the school are criticized often for insisting upon differential and integral calculus as a course in the study of architecture. Our position is defended upon the theory that the quality of the mind which can differentiate correctly, then integrate correctly — as is necessary in the analysis and drawing out of a large complex plan of a group of buildings, or bringing the different smaller parts of the building into one grand whole — requires the same grasp of mind and process of thought found necessary for the solution of problems with the calculus. An architect must know mathematics, he must know drawing, and he must have good taste. There are parents we have met who think that their sons draw pretty well, but not enough to be a painter, they are pretty good at mathematics but not enough to be an engineer, and they conclude that he therefore would make a very good architect. How little they see the truth! As a matter of fact it is the architect who directs the energies of both the engineer and the painter on his building, and who has to have a thorough grasp of both mathematics and drawing. The architect is essentially a planner for convenience and beauty, while the engineer is a highly scientific planner for convenience and economy, without regard to the form of his structure.

The course of instruction in architecture at Columbia follows along a very carefully laid out program for all of these different things. We do not, however, pretend that a man is a practicing architect the moment he leaves the school. He should then practice under a preceptor as do doctors and lawyers before he assumes the responsibility of taking full charge of a building. Although at school he will have been trained in all of the processes, he needs a certain amount of actual practice on his own responsibility under the guidance of a preceptor in order to become thoroughly reliable. It takes a long time for an architect to arrive at his best. He will have many failures, and many regrets. He will be glad to have an opportunity to tear down his building and build it over. He is unfortunately not like the doctor who can bury his failure. It stares him and the world in the face so long as it stands! On the other hand, he has the joy, if his work is a success, of having created beauty, and of having something which will give him pleasure the rest of his life. Architecture is a joyous profession although it treads a thorny path. I advise no one to launch upon the study who is not willing to work hard and long for success and who has not enough of love for it to work without great money reward.

We are building rapidly, and we destroy rapidly. The increasing wealth makes us act like the man in the Bible who pulled down his barns to build greater. It is probable that our buildings of today may be destroyed and replaced by others, and only the printed descriptions be available for conveying accurate ideas of what now exists. Our perfection in the graphic arts will preserve the essential ideas in the architecture of the day, where no remains are left when the future archaeologists dig up Manhattan.

The teaching of architecture in a university is eminently consistent and proper. The university stands for integrity of purpose, sound priniples, orderly thinking, an impulse to create, a love of the beautiful, and good taste. These attributes so essential in architecture, are the guiding principles of all fine academic study and in a greater or lesser degree indicate the quality of orderly instruction which leads to the highest attainments in learning and in art. One difference between the work in architecture and that in many other subjects studied in the university, is that the student is always cognizant of progress and the effect of his creation as he goes along in his course. There is an ideal, a guiding impulse, which seems to lead one on to achievement in the finer things without his even knowing clearly the way. While the technical equipment in the earlier days of our school was not highly developed as it now is, the scholarship and refinement which adorned the men who went from Columbia in those years stamped them with the hall mark of good taste. Their achievements in architecture have been guided by this scholarship, and they make a glorious picture to record.

The study of architecture is the study of creation. Instruction in architecture has the advantage of placing before the student a clear conception of what is the aim and end of his studies. Each activity leading to his final attainments in the school is arranged in a sequence and of an importance which he understands and for which he works with enthusiasm. He has a passion for creation which is more or less exemplified in all of the work which he does during the course. He can see what the end is of all the instruction given to him and his attainment as he goes along is evident to all who watch. The competitions which are arranged in the student work automatically range the students in their respective degrees of efficiency. The student in all his professional study goes through the process of competition which will be his method of placing his ideas before the world when he gets into practice, and his ideas are exhibited to the public graphically in a manner which all can understand. The creation and presentation of a design is as personal to the student as his facial appearance and expression. It is possible to recognize his personality in his drawing and design, and the individual methods of expression, are so different and personal that they can be read by one who is acquainted with the student almost as easily as his handwriting and his signature. This personality is encouraged in design. Each student is expected to attain the high standard of an academic ideal with his personality dominating the ideas and beauty of the design. Academic architecture without personality behind it and showing through it is dead art. This personality does not require extraordinary expression of architecture. It is not necessarily indicated by a wide diversion from the normal, but it does require a certain expression of soul which, in an academic performance, is necessary to make a fine quality of product.

The architect must have the quality of leadership among men, and his mind must be trained more or less in the habits of thought of those men who are going to control things in the world. The architects of Egypt, of Greece, of Rome, of the Gothic and Renaissance periods were men who were sought by the kings and courts. They were men who understood the culture of their time and crystallized the greatest expressions of these respective cultures in the architecture which they have left us in every age.

Academic instruction in architecture in this country is of comparatively recent date. Since we inherit no traditions in the schooling of young architects, it follows that a great deal of experimentation has taken place. At the present time the methods of instruction are pretty well standardized in all of the schools; that is to say, the instruction is standardized so far as the catalogue portrays it. The actual teaching of the art of architecture goes back a little farther. It is not what the announcement says in its description which determines the excellence of a school, but it is the quality of the man who is giving the inspiration to the student. The catalogue of one of the newest and most primitive schools has about the same description of courses we find in the announcement of Columbia, but the young men who finish at such a school have not that real quality which properly accompanies the title of architect. This is in no wise different from the same relative traditions between academic subjects on the frontier and those at Harvard University, for instance. The quality of the architect will reflect largely the quality of the men who have the guidance of his instruction.

The study of architecture is long and arduous, but it is always a pleasure. There is no restriction upon any time that is spent upon exercises in the school, but you will notice if you pass the campus at eleven o'clock at night that the last lights on the campus are in the drafting room which is brilliantly lighted for the men who are eager to work up to that hour. The students seem to take pleasure in their work. I am convinced that an unhappy man can not make a good design. While he might be miserable in some ways he is happy in the joys of creation. A student in architecture can perceive from the beginning what he is aiming at and every process toward that goal is an agreeable process and is cheerfully accomplished.

In four short years a man cannot learn the art of architecture. He can learn the past by the study of the masterpieces. He can learn to draw, to study, to analyze, and to follow the methods of design. He can go forward from this stage of development if he has good taste and sound ideals. He must go on with the advancing march of his time and build for the requirements of society to accord with the necessity of the changing conditions in social progress. His situation is similar to that of the student in literature who goes on from his studies in letters, ever growing, to blossom out in poetry. What has been attained during the past twenty-five years, and the influence of the Columbia School of Architecture in this progress is impressive. These are the fruits of scholarship, ideals and character.

The founder of the School of Architecture, whose memory is revered and recorded in the Ware Professorship in Architecture, established the school on an idea of scholarship, and good taste, and the growth of the school has flowered out from this well-founded root. It conforms to the ideal of higher learning in Columbia University, marching toward better attainment hand in hand with philosophy, science, law and medicine.

Formerly there was established a combination course between Columbia college and the School of Architecture whereby a student in his first two years could take some studies in architecture. This has been abandoned because Dean Hawkes has stated that if he ever lets a man go over to the School of Architecture to work he cannot get him back again. The boys do love this work, even if all of them will not turn out to be practicing architects. Great architects are born not made. They must have some genius born in them in order to make great creators of architecture. There are only a few more good architects in proportion to the students than there are good poets who come from the courses in the study of English. Any intelligent man can be trained up to the point where he can construct sound buildings, but only those who have something of an endowment can instinctively create beauty. At the school we can develop such creative ability as the student has, but if he has no inherent quality for it, study will not make him a great creator of beauty.

At the university we are trying to hold to the idea of beauty in building and while we insist upon excellent construction and the knowledge thereof, we do not place that as the higher quality of a building. There was a time when a two years special course was considered sufficient to educate an architect. That time has gone by. We now at Columbia demand that a man have two years of academic training before entering the school, and four years of technical training in architecture.

We prefer to have them have even more time. Many of them come to us from colleges where they have received a degree and they build four years of architecture on that preparation. One more year is even better and that gives them the degree of Master of Science in Architecture. We even have candidates for the Doctor of Philosophy in Architecture at this time.

Architecture is not a verbal art. Words cannot accurately describe the work of architecture. A written description of a monument is a reflection of the effect it produced upon the writer. The interior of Notre Dame has been described as the result of the architect being inspired when walking through a grove of overarching trees. This is pure fancy — the architect produced that building by evolution from early crude attempts through ages of progress.

Architecture must be seen to be realized and comprehended; it is an art of form and substance which is in three dimensions of solid material constructed to perform a perfectly useful function, and it is beautiful or not beautiful according to the perceptions of those for whom and by whom it is created. Written history is only comparatively truthful, depending on the people who write it. The buildings of any culture are absolutely truthful because they show what was in the world at that time. They show the conveniences of the people in their daily life, in their religion, in their laws, their beliefs in immortality, and even their efforts to attain an immortality. Twenty-five years ago our ideas of construction were based upon those which have come down to us from the glorious past. The requirements of society today are entirely different so far as the conduct of business and mechanical affairs are concerned. Formerly the hand of man was evident on every piece of material in the building; today it is the machine which puts its stamp upon the building. From the beginning of a structure, the machine takes charge. The steam shovel, huge truck, long-armed derrick, the pattering riveter, the compressed-air stone chisel, and the mortar-mixing machines largely confine the workman's activity on a building to that of guiding intelligence for the machines which do the work. It is not now the craftsman who builds the building but the manipulator of mechanical devices and the machine has left its mark on the building. It has given us large buildings, tall buildings, buildings faultless in engineering lines as laid out by the engineer, but it has robbed us of a good deal of that personal element which formerly went into the appearance of a building because the hand of man fashioned it, and what the hand of man fashions he understands. It is, however, necessary for us to accept these conditions and for the architect to utilize the machines by the requirements of his designs.

The machine can do with great accuracy whatever is demanded of it. It is therefore for the architect to devise now a method of harmonizing the mechanical processes with those things of beauty to which men will be sensitive. This new idea of huge units as compared with the former buildings is not easy to harmonize with our daily lives as we have been accustomed to live. We will have to change somewhat and the buildings will eventually come a bit deeper into the ken of the man in the street.

The competition for magnitude, for height, for novelty, will after a while change to things which are more human and more understandable. They will become so because of that insatiable yearning of man for beauty and our architects are those who will eventually bring harmony out of this well founded mechanical method of building which seems to accurately respond to the demands of the public today. There is little to be desired so far as convenience, safety and sanitation are concerned in our modern building. What they lack is soul, soul which can be put in by the architect in response to a demand by the people.

The skyscraper is the only important new invention in

architecture in the last century. It is the result of several influences: the necessity for men to get together within a limited
area; the advantage of men congregating in a certain geographical area for the concentration of business; the economy
of putting much floor space over a given ground area; the
new methods now used for indirect administration — these are
the things that brought it into the field. Going high into the
air, which appeals to the imagination of men, and the ambition
of building to excel others in the same field by going higher in
the air and thus advertising greater power are byproducts of
the process. Now that we know how to build them, tall buildings are built simply to be tall. They appeal to the imagination.
The skyscraper breaks all precedent about the line considered
beautiful. The question is, are we going to accept this new
creation as a blessing or are we going to consider it deplorable
in its effect upon style and upon the beauty of our city. The
social and economic result is that it is bringing too many people
together in the street for the width of the street, and by a
system of construction is practically excluding the recognized
ideas of beauty in detail and in proportion. I do not say that
it reverses true principles of good design. Good design should
be made to incorporate every kind of building that society
demands. When, however, the dimensions exceed anything
which the human imagination has ever conceived before, it is
not easy for us to adjust ourselves to them. Now the invention
and perfection of the skyscraper is not the work of one man,
it is an outgrowth of needs of society and the attempts to solve
them in a beautiful way. While the schools of architecture
cannot claim credit for the creation of this new architectural
idea, they have had a part in it and it would not have been
possible without their contribution to its development. Among
the leaders of this type of building and construction the men
from Columbia are eminent.

Illustrations of such buildings by Columbia men show that

an ideal of beauty has been striven for. They try to solve the actual problem in a scientific manner and at the same time impart to the buildings a character of beauty and an appearance of being "natural" buildings as nearly as this new type of architecture can be said to express that idea to us in our present state of acquaintance with it. The skyscraper has proven itself to be a scientific solution of the problem of housing commercial activities together in the most satisfactory way. It must be accepted because of that fact and it is useless to discount it because it is out of scale with the other buildings which surround it. We must so place it and so handle it that it will be a success rather than a hindrance to life. In order to accept it we must first address our minds to the ideas of size and height which put every adjoining building out of scale. The generally accepted expression of building is that of masonry. It now appears that we are now to have some of our tall buildings express on the exterior only metal and glass. At least that is the idea of the designers of the latest and largest building projected in New York, a building which stands so high alongside of its neighbors and is so different in its exterior appearance that it will have to be accepted as a friendly giant, like an elephant grazing with a flock of sheep.

Improvements in the methods of structure must keep pace with the demands of business and the habits of the life of the day. While formerly buildings were made mostly of masonry with only the forces of gravity to counteract, these forces of gravitation are not now the major problem. Steel as a building material removes the limit of height and width of span. Elevators make great height convenient while formerly it caused much physical effort. Mechanical control of communication, electricity, distribution of heat and of its control, mechanical aid in the operation of building a structure and the superior facilities we now have for fabricating the different parts of the building in different places and bringing it together quickly on its site, have changed the methods of construction. Formerly, after the designs were made, the material was brought to the site and there fashioned into the different structural parts which were erected by the hand of man. Today all of the parts of building are previously arranged at some distant point, brought to the building and quickly placed together. This involves very careful preparation of actual working drawings for every part of the building. The architect must visualize his building from diagrams which are to be used by the workmen in preparing the materials. His success stands or falls by what he produces in his office as the guiding drawings for the workmen. Each part of the building is fashioned by a different trade but all these parts come together to make a complete whole. The architect must determine what must be in the building and then proceed from small sketches and ideas to the development of a picture which will accurately tell what the building will look like. When this has been accomplished it is then necessary to analyze this picture and make working drawings which will reproduce the picture in steel and masonry. These working drawings are given to the different people who prepare the material and each of the parts must fit accurately when they come to the building.

I recite all this rather tiresome detail in order to impress you with the necessity for clear thinking, clear visualization and very accurate designing on the part of the architect. This cannot be accomplished without fine training and the sensitive knowledge of the qualities of design. This highly technical process for the construction of building has made us forget somewhat the importance of beauty in the design. The public seems to be more impressed with the succesful scientific solution of building than they are with the fine qualities of architecture, and naturally so when faced with the gigantic steel frame the like of which the world has never seen.

All this constitutes an insistent challenge to the schools

that train the future architect. The teacher must know not only the past but the present and, indeed, see beyond it, and he must communicate his vision as well as his technique. There are those who are held by the fascination of study and the guidance of youth in the pursuit of architecture. They have a singular and very precious talent. Fortunately the list is long and impressive. For us in this room it is a satisfying circumstance that the majority of great schools of architecture in the United States have at the head Columbia men. We may be pardoned their enumeration: Carnegie Institute of Technology, Columbia University, the University of Florida, the Georgia School of Technology, Howard University, the University of Manitoba, the Massachusetts Institute of Technology, Princeton University, Rice Institute, Yale University. Until recently the Ohio State University had such leadership. Columbia in the past twenty-five years has contributed to architecture that which is greater than the bone and sinew of architecture — better scholarship and an ideal.

BIOLOGY

Edmund B. Wilson

To attempt an hour's survey of biological progress during the past quarter century is an undertaking that requires some courage. Modern biology has reached out in so many labyrinthine and far-flung lines of advance, has split up into so great a number of component biological sciences, that we hardly know where to mark out its limits. Long ago those sciences pushed across the frontiers of human life and affairs in the splendid conquests of experimental medicine, which touch so closely our health and happiness. Our very personality and conduct are inseparably bound up with that wonderful physiological balance that is maintained by the nervous system and by the chemical equilibrium of the blood and tissues. The origin and rise of mankind is but a particular incident in the course of organic evolution. Man's brain and all that it has created are products of that process.

Bacteriology, protozoology, pathology and experimental medicine obviously belong in the domain of biology. Psychology and anthropology can not be separated from it. Researches on the endocrine glands during the past three decades even raise the question whether we can shut out the meddlesome activities of the biologist from archaeology, sociology, history, politics, literature, art and ethics. But I will not press this question. The biologist does not really intend to lay claim to the earth. If at times he seems too grasping it is because of a haunting consciousness that beneath every manifestation of life lie the same basic phenomena, the same fundamental activities of protoplasm.

The era that opened with the twentieth century has been

one of remarkable achievement in biology. It has been a time of rapidly changing points of view, of new problems, new methods, new and fundamental discoveries. It has been a time of searching critical analysis, of remarkably effective popular exposition of the technical results of discovery. So crowded with all this has been the past quarter century that one hardly knows where to begin with its review. At best I can offer no more than a fleeting glimpse of a few outstanding aspects of progress. As a matter of convenience the subject will here be considered under three heads, namely: (1) evolution and heredity; (2) individual development; (3) the organism as it exists here and now; but I will not adhere too closely to the strict letter of this grouping.

I

During the latter half of the nineteenth century researches on evolution were largely engaged in amassing fresh proofs of the theory, in the examination of special problems and difficulties, and in efforts to trace out the course that evolution has followed in bygone ages. Progress along these lines has since been continued by many memorable discoveries, some of which have aroused world wide interest because of the new light that they have thrown on the origin and evolution of primitive man. Among other important results these discoveries have made it almost certain that man must have emerged as such more than a million years ago and not later than the Tertiary period. Towards the turn of the century, however, the center of interest had begun to shift from the historical problems of descent towards the even more momentous ones involved in the causes and conditions of evolution. It was this shift, I suppose, that was responsible for an impression at one time that biologists had begun to lose faith in evolution; but this was due to a complete misunderstanding. The evidence for evolution is overwhelming. No competent biologist now doubts its reality. His uncertainty relates solely to the question how evolution has been brought about and by what agencies its course determined. With problems of this type twentieth-century biology has been actively engaged.

Darwin recognized several causes of evolution of which the most important were natural selection, sexual selection, the isolating effects of natural barriers, and the so-called inheritance of acquired characters (or, to speak more accurately, of acquired bodily changes), including the direct and supposedly hereditary effects of use and disuse, food, climate and the like. To these supposed causes later writers added several others, including hybridization, the process of sudden mutation or saltation as urged by De Vries, and the so-called orthogenesis or evolution along determinate lines, as advocated by Naegeli and by Eimer. During the past quarter century these various attempts to explain evolution have been subjected to a continuous fire of criticism and reëxamination which in some respects has materially altered our view of the problem. Some of the Darwinian causes, such as the inheritance of acquired bodily changes, have thus been in large degree discredited or remain the subject of controversy. Others, like sexual selection, occupy a subordinate position. Still others, such as isolation, appear rather as limiting or conditioning factors; while orthogenesis still occupies at best a doubtful place. From all this, it would seem that natural selection appears at present as the only major cause of evolution which, up to a certain point, is accepted by the whole body of working biologists.

Among the various causes just enumerated a position of outstanding importance is occupied by natural selection and the inheritance of acquired characters; for these alone have attempted to offer, each in its own way, a partial explanation of organic adaptations. As to natural selection, its truth is so obvious as to be almost a truism. It is evident that organisms vary; that only those fitted to live can survive; that those best fitted have the best chance of living long enough to transmit their superior fitness to their offspring. Whether such a process can offer an adequate explanation of evolution is another and very different question. Some of the most baffling difficulties that puzzled Darwin have been cleared away by modern researches on variation and heredity. We now see that Darwin's view of the problem was obscured by a failure to distinguish between two widely different kinds of variation now generally known respectively as fluctuating variations and mutations. Fluctuating variations are temporary and shifting effects produced by varying external conditions, such as food, climate and the like; and experiment has proved that many of these, to say the least, are not heritable, though they may seem to be inherited because of the continuing influence of the environment in successive generations. Such non-hereditary variations, obviously, can have played little or no part in progressive evolution. Mutations, on the other hand, are definite, stable and strongly hereditary changes; and a large body of evidence indicates that they do not arise in the body at all but in the germ-cells that the body carries, as was urged by Weismann fifty years ago. A good example of this evidence is offered by the recent discovery that definite hereditary mutations may in some cases be called forth by the application of radium or X-rays to the parents; but the effects do not appear in the animals thus treated but *only in their offspring*, i.e., in the products of their germ-cells.

Researches along these lines have also led to important changes in our conception of mutations. By DeVries and his predecessors mutations were regarded as comparatively large changes, or saltations; but more recent researches have shown that variations of this type are often very small, so as to be indistinguishable by the eye from fluctuating variations. In such cases it is only by exact and long continued breeding experiments that the two types can be distinguished with certainty. Though this distinction was in some degree known to earlier observers, its first precise experimental proof was accomplished in 1909 by Johannsen, who thus cleared the way for all later researches on selection and opened a new era in the development of Darwin's theory. If these results seem to deprive selection of half its working supplies we may console ourselves with the reflection that half a good loaf is better than a whole one of dubious quality.

Inseparable from the foregoing, evidently, is the long disputed question of the inheritance of acquired bodily and mental changes.[1] Most of us, perhaps, would like to believe that what we acquire individually in body or mind by effort, training and experience might be handed on by heredity to those who come after us — though such a prospect, it must be said, would not be an unmixed blessing. Apparently, however, neither our hopes nor our fears in this respect have much prospect of realization. Each generation must learn anew its ABC's, its multiplication table and its ten commandments. The same is often true, certainly, of our acquired physical traits, such as the traditional strong right arm of the blacksmith, the piano player's carefully acquired dexterity of hand, or the mutilations that have been practised for centuries in social or religious rites. A vast number of careful experiments have fortified this conclusion. Most of the evidence indicates unequivocally that in sexual reproduction acquired bodily traits produce no perceptible effect upon the offspring. New supposed cases to the contrary, it is true, are periodically reported; but most of these have turned out to be false alarms or have received the Scotch verdict of not proven. Such a case is the recent one of Pavlov's famous mice that learned to come to dinner at the sound of a

---

[1] This phrase is preferable to the earlier one "inheritance of acquired characters," since it specifically denotes changes produced in the body itself in contradistinction to those that arise in the germ-cells which the body carries. It is hardly necessary to remark that all existing characters must originally have somehow been acquired.

bell. That eminent physiologist believed at first that these mice transmitted the trick by heredity to their offspring in steadily increasing degree in successive generations. The evidence proved however to be entirely inconclusive, as Pavlov himself has recently admitted, and these unlucky mice seem now to have retired into well deserved obscurity. It now remains to be seen whether a better record may be made by Professor MacDougal's clever rats which learned to find their way out of a maze and are reported to have done so with increasing skill in successive generations.

I have no wish to ridicule experiments of this type, still less to dogmatize concerning an issue that is one of the most momentous with which natural science has to deal. Nevertheless it is my own opinion that up to the present time not one well confirmed or convincing case of the transmission of acquired bodily or mental traits has yet been recorded — certainly none that can not be explained as effects produced by agencies that act directly on the germ-cells as well as on the body. If this opinion be well founded we would seem to be thrown back upon natural selection as the main, if not the only, known explanation of organic adaptations. This conclusion is not in any manner inconsistent with the existence of many useless characters that have in themselves no discoverable adaptive value. It does not exclude the important effects of isolation by physical barriers, as shown by many facts of geographical distribution, such as the conditions in the Galapagos archipelago or in the mountain valleys of Tahiti. Even if orthogenesis be a reality, even were the inheritance of acquired characters to be established, we still should not escape the dominating importance of natural selection as the main known cause by which the course of organic evolution has been shaped.

I must frankly confess to a certain dissatisfaction with this situation. Natural selection would seem to be a casual, hit-or-

miss series of lucky accidents, one that has been happily characterized as "evolution by higgledy-piggledy." In this respect,
however, the biologist is not, so far as I can see, in much worse
case than the modern physicist with his Heisenbergian principle of indeterminacy in the sub-atomic world. In any case
I am not yet quite ready to admit that higgledy-piggledy can
provide an adequate explanation of organic adaptations, above
all, of the wonderful powers of self-adjustment, self-repair and
self-protection that are coextensive with the phenomena of
life. We still know too little about the causes of evolution to
commit ourselves to such a conclusion. Who is ready to say we
have yet completed the list of those causes? Here indeed we
are still out of our depth. The living world has been countless
millions of years in the making. We shall not so easily lay bare
the secrets of the process in a few generations of men.

II

The egg and its development are at once the delight and
the despair of the biologist — his delight because the phenomena of life are here displayed in so direct and dramatic
a fashion, his despair because so many of those phenomena are
still far beyond his comprehension. It has often been said that
man's brain is the greatest marvel of nature. I venture to
think, however, that the egg is an even greater marvel; for
it can make a man, brain and all, while man is totally incapable
of making an egg. The problems that center in development
have never been more eagerly or resourcefully attacked by
experiment than during the last three decades. In some directions many highly interesting discoveries have resulted, in
others we still find ourselves wandering in the wilderness.

Development involves two major problems, namely, the
basis of its determination, and the mechanism of its accomplishment. The first of these, obviously, is a problem of heredity;
for it is by heredity that the characteristic mode of develop-

ment of each species is determined. The second problem is one of embryology, for it is by development that the hereditary potencies concealed within the egg are brought to realization. Researches on the first of these problems have brought forth some of the most remarkable discoveries of our time. The second problem, on the other hand, has thus far been approached in only the most crude and superficial manner.

The way for twentieth-century researches on the mechanism of determination and heredity was first opened in the seventies of the last century by parallel researches on heredity and on the microscopical structure of cells. Their more recent point of departure was given in 1900 by the dramatic rediscovery of Mendel's almost forgotten laws of heredity, and by microscopical discoveries which culminated almost at the same moment in the work of Boveri and of Sutton. Those discoveries, and the ones that ensued, demonstrated that the primary determination of heredity is somehow accomplished by the nucleus of the fertilized egg, in particular by those bodies known as chromosomes from which that nucleus and its products are built up. The chromosomes are received by the egg in equal numbers from both parents. Their products are distributed in equal numbers by cell-division to all the cells of the offspring. They share among them the determination of heredity in such a manner that each chromosome is in some unknown way responsible for a particular group of traits. During the life-cycle that begins with the egg and ends with the production of eggs for the next generation the chromosomes undergo a series of manoeuvers that run exactly parallel to a corresponding series of manoeuvers on the part of the hereditary traits — the two fit each other, indeed, like hand and glove.

Without entering into technical detail the nature of this parallellism may be roughly indicated by an analogy. The chromosomes may be likened to cards in a pack, the hereditary endowment, to the pack as a whole. The cards may be shuffled again and again to produce always varying arrangements but without destroying the integrity of the pack as a whole. To employ a more adequate figure, the chromosomes are like threads of different colors which in each generation may be woven together to form a fabric of definite pattern, then unraveled and rewoven, again and again in successive generations, always producing the same general type of design, but with endless variations in the details of the picture. All this fits precisely with what we are familiar with in the patterns of hereditary traits shown in related groups of individuals, whether within single families, in related families, or in successive generations. All becomes clear if we assume that the chromosomes are somehow actual bearers of hereditary traits, or rather of things that are responsible for the development of those traits. That this assumption corresponds with the truth is demonstrated by correlated experiments of the most varied nature on heredity, on embryological development, and on the microscopical structure of cells. The resulting discoveries are, I believe, among the most interesting in the whole history of biology. They offer a precise and detailed explanation of numerous phenomena of heredity that were formerly mysterious, for instance, the two fundamental laws of Mendel, the heredity of sex, of color-blindness, or of "criss-cross" heredity in which sons are like their mothers and daughters like their fathers. They have transformed our knowledge of heredity, have created the modern science of genetics, and have at least opened the way to a rational science of eugenics for the improvement of our race. And incidentally they have produced strong evidence against orthogenesis and the inheritance of acquired characters.

When we turn from the determination of development to its mechanism we find many highly interesting discoveries of fact, but are also confronted by some of the most enigmatical of biological phenomena. Superficially regarded, development looks very simple. We see that the egg is a single cell; that it divides into many cells that build up the body of the embryo; that these cells are transformed into the elements of the tissues. We see the embryo gradually being moulded into its characteristic form. It all looks perfectly easy. The egg goes through its characteristic performance with an air of complete assurance, exactly as if it were a skilled workman. And yet, from the standpoint of precise physico-chemical analysis, not one of these operations is known to us in more than the most superficial and rudimentary manner. In the hope of arriving at a better understanding we have subjected the unfortunate egg to every kind of experimental insult. Elaborate instruments have been devised by which the egg may be vivisected under the microscope. It has been cut in two, pulled apart, shaken to pieces, exposed to heat, cold, electricity, radium, X-ray; treated with drugs and poisons, deformed by mechanical pressure, its insides turned topsy-turvy by whirling at high speed on the centrifuge machine. Nothing could be more interesting than the behavior of the egg as it undergoes all this maltreatment. It can have had no preparation in previous experience for such a series of ordeals. Nevertheless it struggles with uncanny dexterity to shake off its tormentors. Often it perishes in the attempt or achieves no more than an abortive or monstrous development; but there are grand moments when every obstacle is surmounted and the egg fulfills its normal destiny.

Through all this our knowledge of development has been enriched during the past three decades by a multitude of discoveries. We have learned that the normal process of fertilization may be superseded by chemical, physical or even mechanical agents, a discovery which at the time produced in some circles the illusory impression that life had been artificially created in the laboratory, or that at least a long step towards such an achievement had been taken. We have

learned that pieces of an egg may be fertilized and produce
perfect dwarf embryos; that one egg may thus be caused to
produce twins or double monsters; that two separate eggs
may fuse together and produce a single giant embryo. We
have witnessed a thousand such displays of jugglery, and here
and there we get some dim notion of how the trick is done.
Thus far, however, the egg easily has the best of the game,
leaving us with only the vaguest notions concerning the
apparatus by which its prodigious feats are accomplished. To
the embryologist the most interesting and baffling of those
feats are displayed in the so-called phenomena of "localization," that is to say, the bringing forth of the parts of the
embryo in a specific order of space and time. It is astounding
to watch the operations by which the egg, like the artist that
it is, proceeds to block out the embryo in the rough and then,
step by step, to add the finer details. The technique is not
always the same. In some species, for instance in worms and
snails, the egg works by bold and swift strokes which quickly
fix the general design. In others the process is more leisurely
and tentative, so that for a considerable time the design
remains capable of readjustment and alteration, as has recently been shown in a beautiful manner by the experiments
of Spemann and his followers on the eggs of salamanders.

It is precisely in respect to this capacity for design, combined with seeming freedom of action, that our understanding
of development remains today most rudimentary — here,
indeed, we are brought face to face with the fundamental
secret of life, as I shall presently try to indicate. It is not
surprising that there are embryologists such as Driesch,
physiologists such as Haldane or von Üxküll, and philosophers
like Bergson, who have insisted that some of the most characteristic of these phenomena lie outside the range of the
physico-chemical laws that rule the non-living world. If a
veteran embryologist may be permitted to speak personally

and confidentially, he will frankly confess that there are unguarded moments when he all but succumbs to the lure of these beguiling writers. When, however, he throws off the spell and regains the use of his scientific faculties he puts on sackcloth and ashes and returns to his scalpel and microscope; for of such is the kingdom of scientific discovery.

III

We have just now caught a glimpse of the central problem of biology, namely, that of the unity and individuality of the organism. When we turn to the organism as we find it here and now we set foot on a road that in the end will lead to the same problem. In the mean time it is well not to forget that an adequate view of the existing organism is only possible when we keep in view the historical background of evolutionary and embryological development that lies behind it.

In the field now before us we are confronted with so vast a wealth of material that I must confine myself mainly to generalities. Biological progress in this direction during the past quarter century offers two outstanding features. What first comes to mind is its splendid service to human life. What the world owes to the advances of experimental medicine and surgery is not to be expressed in words. When we consider the victories over human suffering that are every day being won by advances in bacteriology and protozoology, in serum therapy, in warfare on the insect-borne diseases, in the advancing refinements of modern surgery, in the progress of sanitary science — when we consider all this we are ready to acknowledge that man has built no temples more splendid than our medical schools, hospitals and institutions for medical research. Less spectacular, but of far-reaching importance for the public welfare, are the achievements of applied botany and zoology in the conservation of our national resources by warfare on the plant and animal enemies of our food supplies and forests, and by the protection and dissemination of our good friends among the birds, insects and other useful animals. The new discoveries in heredity are steadily at work for the improvement of our cultivated plants and animals, while the agricultural schools and experiment stations, now at work in every state in the Union, may well merit a place on the same roll of honor with our institutions for medical research.

The second conspicuous feature of recent biological advance has been the steady drift towards experimental and quantitative methods and the always closer alliance of biology with physico-chemical science. Physiology, alone among the older biological sciences, has always been an experimental science. The striking thing since 1900 has been the rapid spread of experimental methods through every other branch of biology where such methods are practicable, and in consequence the steadily increasing importance in biological research of biochemistry, physical chemistry, colloid chemistry, biophysics and general physiology. The results have been so diversified and far flung as to forbid more than the briefest mention here.

Numerous discoveries have advanced our knowledge of the chemical basis of living organisms and the chemical control of their activities by the enzymes, hormones, inorganic salts and many other soluble substances carried by the blood and lymph; of the chemical basis of heredity and specificity as shown in the composition of the proteins and other organic substances; of the problems of nutrition as affected by discovery of the vitamines; of the chemical defenses of body of which modern discoveries in immunity and serology are making such remarkable use. Far-reaching results have come from new investigations on the structure and activities of the nervous system with especial reference to reflex actions, forced movements, tropisms, habits, instincts and social life in lower animals. All this has had a profound influence on comparative psychology and its twin brother, behaviorism; and it has at least threatened to invade the field of sociology.

Another far-flung chapter in twentieth-century biology relates to new discoveries concerning the structure and activities of cells, in health and in disease. Many of the facts thus revealed are too technical for review here, for instance, those relating to the problems of nervous action, secretion, growth, cell-division, differentiation, tumor-formation, development, sex-determination and heredity. Reference has earlier been made to the new art of micro-dissection or micro-surgery by which living cells can be experimented with directly and individually, under high powers of the microscope, and which is bringing forth highly interesting results. An important place in cell-research during the quarter-century has been taken by the new science of protozoölogy, which deals with organisms consisting of a single cell. Such organisms are of almost infinite variety, and some of them display the phenomena of life in their simplest known form. Their microscopical and experimental study, including pure cultures that have in some cases been carried on continuously through thousands of generations, have illuminated many important problems of general biology, such as growth, variation, heredity, sex and vitality; while in another direction, working in affiliation with bacteriology, they have contributed important discoveries relating to the causation and spread of infectious diseases. In this general field belong also interesting researches on the so-called filterable viruses some of which are almost certainly organisms too small to be visible by even the highest powers of the microscope, while others show characters which have suggested that they may belong to a borderland between living organisms and nonliving matter.

Closely akin to all this has been the development during the quarter century of the so-called tissue-culture by which the

living cells of higher animals, isolated from their fellows, may
be maintained in active life and multiplication in pure cultures
outside the body. Such cultures, like those of the one-celled
organisms, may sometimes be carried on with undiminished
vitality for long periods of time, even for months or years.
This method has been succesfully applied not alone to isolated
tissue-cells but also to embryonic cells, the differentiation of
which may thus be followed step by step under the microscope.
Such researches open wonderful possibilities for future exact
research, for instance, in the case of tumor cells, which can
now be successfully grown *in vitro* by this method for considerable periods of time. The same is true of whole embryos of
higher animals after removal from the maternal body at an
early period of development. Discoveries of this type (including the physico-chemical fertilization of the egg mentioned on
a preceding page) need only a little good will to lend verisimili-
tude to an entertaining fantasy by J. B. S. Haldane (in
Daedalus) which pictures the future production of a race of
supermen by strictly laboratory methods.

From all this wealth of special discovery I turn away,
finally, in order to glance at more general questions; in particular I shall try to indicate briefly the attitude of the twentieth-
century biologist with respect to the fundamental problems
involved in the nature of life. The difficulties involved in this
problem are so formidable that it is essential to avoid every
possibility of misunderstanding. If in trying to accomplish this
I adopt a seemingly flippant way of speaking it is with a wholly
serious purpose. In man, at least, life appears to us in two
totally different aspects — and we are led by analogy, backed
by the theory of evolution, to suspect that the same duality of
aspect may somehow or other exist also in lower organisms,
however simple. Someone whose name I have forgotten has
expressed this duality with incomparable terseness in the
famous couplet:

> Life is a fitful spasm,
> Made up of love and protoplasm.

For our present purpose, however, I will be more specific. The aim of the biologist may more readily be made clear by referring to the two aspects of life in question as Dr. Jekyll and Mr. Hyde. Jekyll is the invisible, conscious man, who feels and thinks, loves and hates, who has a sense of ethical and artistic values, and whose insatiable curiosity about the world in which he lives has created modern science. Hyde, the inseparable comrade of Jekyll, is the visible protoplasmic man, who appears as a conglomeration of cells organized to form a prodigiously complicated physico-chemical machine. It is no part of my present purpose to consider the nature of the partnership between Jekyll and Hyde. That problem must be left to our good friends the philosophers and the psychologists. Some of them, I have heard, think of Jekyll and Hyde as only two names for the same man. A behaviorist has even suggested that when Jekyll thinks he is conscious he is only aware somehow of certain muscular movements that are going on inside of Hyde. From all such puzzles, however, we turn away, leaving Jekyll entirely out of the picture, not that he is of no interest to us — far from it — but because we are incompetent to deal with him. The biologist as such is occupied only with the protoplasmic living system that he can see, handle, dissect and subject to experiment. His attack, admittedly, is directed against only one side of the great problem, but the difficulties there encountered are quite enough to tax all the resources of his science.

Now protoplasm, the fundamental living basis of the body, is an exceedingly complex colloidal material — enormously complex physically and chemically, most of all complex, perhaps, in its infinitely varied activities. So long as the organism lives those activities are in a continual state of change. They offer a picture always shifting, like that in a kaleidoscope, yet

one which in some astounding fashion holds fast always to the
same general design. In the words of the admirable Gallic
saying, the more it changes the more it is the same thing. That
a thing so plastic, so delicate, so perishable can maintain its
organic identity through all the vicissitudes of life is a stupendous fact. The marvel grows when we ponder the fact that
living things are endowed with an almost miraculous power
of adjustment to changed conditions, of self-repair after
injury, and above all of reproducing themselves, generation
after generation, with microscopic exactness, through thousands or millions of years. So vast and intricate is the problem
here presented to us that the physiologist has as yet only begun
the attack upon its outermost defenses. Enormous advances, it
is true, have been made in the investigation of particular activities of the living system; but the basic problem of life, as so
many eminent biologists have insisted, lies at a deeper level.
This problem relates to the process by which the multitudinous
and ever shifting activities of life are integrated, coördinated
and organized to form an harmonious and self-adjusting
whole.

I am not here referring directly to the visible apparatus of
coördination displayed in the machine-like construction of the
body in higher organisms, including the telegraphic apparatus
of the nervous system. These things belong to a larger problem.
For one thing, the operation of this visible apparatus is conditioned at every point by a great variety of chemical substances, carried by the blood-stream, which exert a profound
influence on the operation of the protoplasmic machine, the
brain and nerves included. For another thing, even more important, the problem must in the last analysis be carried down
to the activities of the individual cells of which the whole body
is built; and these are themselves complex living systems in
each of which the same problem of integration and organization is repeated on a small scale. This fact is brought home to

us, above all else, by the egg, a single cell that displays the *ne plus ultra* of organized and purpose-like activity, yet shows no trace of any preformed apparatus from which we might foresee its astonishing performance.

It is only when all this is taken into account that the tremendous difficulties of the general problem are fully realized. In spite of all this, there are numerous well known facts that encourage us to proceed with its investigation. With few exceptions physiologists are now agreed that whatever else protoplasmic systems may be they are undoubtedly physico-chemical systems, which apparently do not in any manner violate the fundamental laws to which the non-living world conforms. The living system can create neither new energy nor new life. It can only make use of previously existing free energy. It can only produce new living systems by handing on to its offspring a portion of its own living substance.

There is no evidence [I quote from the distinguished English physiologist A. V. Hill] that momentum and kinetic energy, that chemical transformations, that surface forces, that electrical and magnetic phenomena, occur in the living body in any manner or degree that differs from that appearing in the more readily investigated non-living world. . . . Nor will many dispute the application to the living world of the principles of the conservation of energy and of mass. . . . There is no evidence of a precise or definite character which suggests that the living cell can escape from the second law [of thermodynamics].

To continue with a quotation from Professor Morgan: "Is it not sufficient to approach such systems with the expectation, perchance, of explaining their reactions as a result of the chemical properties and arrangements of highly complex organic materials bound together in a quasi-stable system?"

The foregoing two quotations give, I think, a fair indication of the working attitude of physiologists generally; but there are some notable exceptions. Prominent among these is the position of Professor J. S. Haldane, one of the leaders of English physiology. I quote from his recent highly interesting

book *The Sciences and Philosophy*, as follows: "We are forced
to the conclusion that in the phenomena of life we are in the
presence of what can not be interpreted physically, but implies
a fundamental conception different from those of physical
science. . . . The widely spread popular belief that the physical
and chemical structure of a living organism accounts for its
specific behavior is baseless." [2] Again: "Biology must be regarded as a science which is differentiated from the physical
sciences owing to its fundamental axioms being different from
those of the physical sciences. . . . That the application of
accurate physical and chemical investigation to life has been
leading towards a physico-chemical conception of life is a
ridiculous travesty of scientific history." [3]

It would be unfair to cite one or two isolated passages as an
adequate statement of Professor Haldane's views; they have
behind them a background of distinguished physiological research and philosophical analysis. It is evident, too, that the
physico-chemical analysis of vital activities still remains incomplete in every direction; that no perceptible approach has yet
been made towards the artificial production of life. But when
all this has fully been admitted it must be said that the outlook
indicated by the passages just cited (and others of similar
implication) is remote from that of most working physiologists
today — here indeed we are standing at a parting of the ways.
The advances of modern biology have been so swift and fruitful that investigators as a body are at present more preoccupied
with the pursuit of research than with the philosophical implications of its results. For the time being, at least, they find it
profitable to assume that the integrating and organizing activities of living systems are fundamentally analogous to the
equilibration automatically accomplished in non-living systems;
and that, accordingly, living systems may fruitfully be ap-

[2] Page 13.
[3] Pages 182-183.

proached along the lines marked out fifty years ago by Willard
Gibbs in his famous investigations on the equilibrium of heterogeneous systems in general. Some of the most remarkable discoveries of the twentieth century have in fact resulted from
investigations on the chemical equilibrium (to which reference has earlier been made) that is automatically maintained in the blood and between the blood and the tissues. The
most familiar of these discoveries relate to the hormones, those
soluble "chemical messengers" produced by the endocrine
glands and other structures, which so powerfully affect the
balance of our bodily activities and structures, and of our
instincts, emotions and types of personality. It is in this direction that biology may justly be said to have some legitimate
concern with those broader human activities, such as history,
literature or ethics, which at first sight may seem so remote
from any contact with our science.

The time has not yet come to venture any prediction as to
how far physico-chemical researches along these lines may
carry us; thus far they have accomplished little more than to
open a great field for future exploration. The man of science
is not a prophet; he must go where the facts lead him. I venture to think, however, that a final solution of the great problem lies beyond the most remote horizon of our present knowledge. And it is well to remember that science does not look to
a solution of the ultimate problems of nature. We strive only
to push forwards the boundaries of knowledge. We know that
sooner or later our advances will be turned aside by an im-
passable barrier. In the mean time the great game that science
plays is worth while for its own sake. The rewards that it
brings are beyond all price.

MEDICINE

William Darrach

Many advances have been made in the field of medicine in the last quarter of a century. It is difficult to select wisely and to present concisely the most outstanding examples.[1] In medical education noticeable changes have occurred both in medical schools and in methods of teaching. Many of the poorer schools have gone out of existence. Most of the others have improved greatly. The need for financial assistance has been recognized in a most generous manner and large sums have been given for buildings, for endowment and for research. Hospitals have recognized their opportunities and their obligations and have opened their doors to teaching and to laboratory investigation to a far greater degree than formerly. With added endowments, men have been found who had the qualifications, training and desire to devote more and more of their time and energy to their university work. This was seen first in the fundamental departments and later developed in the clinical departments. Today in many of the medical schools a large proportion of the teaching staff devote as much of their time to their university duties as do their colleagues in other parts of the university.

Twenty-five years ago the majority of the teaching schedule was taken up with lectures, though anatomy, physiology and chemistry offered a good deal of laboratory work, and pathology and bacteriology some. Today the laboratory work has increased a good deal. In the clinical departments most of the teaching is now done at the bedside or in the dispensary in

---

[1] Grateful acknowledgment is made for the aid received from my associates in the College of Physicians and Surgeons.

small groups and the student spends a large portion of his time in personal contact with the patient. He learns by doing.

The boundary lines between the different medical sciences have become less easily recognized. The different groups are working together on common problems and they are using each other's methods. Pathologists and bacteriologists are not only using chemical and physiological technique but chemists and physicists are working in bacteriological and medical laboratories.

New methods of investigation have been discovered. Living tissue is now grown outside of the body and watched under the microscope. Embryos are operated on at early stages and portions transplanted to new positions. Future eyes and arms are moved about or even borrowed from other forms, and allowed to grow to adult stages. Harrison of Yale stands out as a leader in this work. Through a wider application of animal experimentation many new methods of attack have been developed. As a whole, there has been a change from the study of static conditions to those more dynamic in character.

The living body is better understood today. Owing to new staining methods developed by Cajal and Hortega, the architecture of the nervous system is becoming clearer. The blood cells are better understood, where they come from and where they go as well as what they do. Far more is known of the function of the ductless glands and knowledge of their function has been applied to their use in regulating abnormal states. This had developed to a degree which has warranted the application of the term endocrinology to their study and use.

Certain hormones have been isolated, identified and even synthesized. These are complex, organic chemical substances, the presence of which in invisibly small amounts, can be responsible for profound physiological action. The most famous of these, insulin from a portion of the pancreas, brought out by Banting and Best, is responsible for sugar metabolism.

By its use, diabetes has been robbed of much of its terror. Thyroxin, isolated from the thyroid gland was identified by Kendall and has recently been synthesized by Harington in England. The rôle of the parathyroids in calcium metabolism has been determined and an active principle of this gland obtained, which is being administered with success clinically.

The active principle of the adrenal medulla has been determined chemically and reproduced artificially. Two highly puri-- fied and physiologically different extracts of the posterior lobe of the pituitary gland have been prepared. The several clinical syndromes caused by disorders of the pituitary-hypothalamic complex have been reproduced experimentally. This makes it possible not only to determine the site of injury or disease responsible for these symptoms, but also to prepare crude extracts of the anterior pituitary lobe which cure experimentally certain of these disorders. Extracts of the ovaries have been prepared which have made possible the analysis of the rôle of these secretions in the female sexual cycle, in implantation and in the nutrition of the foetus. The functioning of the male and female sex glands has been shown to be dependent upon, and controlled by, the anterior pituitary lobe, work which has resulted in the discovery of an early and accurate diagnosis of pregnancy by physiological tests of the urine. Important advances also have been made in our knowledge of the interrelationships of the different endocrine glands.

There have been great advances in the chemistry of the body, especially the physical chemistry of respiration — not only of the blood but the tissues as well. Graham Lusk has not only simplified basal metabolism but made it applicable to medical practice. There is better knowledge of the intermediate metabolism, just how fats, carbohydrates and proteins are used. Dakin's work on the oxidation of amino acids has been of note. Microchemical methods in blood analysis have not only been widely applied but have been of great clinical value.

It is now possible to determine almost exactly the proportion of various contents of the blood in very small amounts. This makes it possible to recognize smaller departures from normal conditions than is possible from examination of the urine, and at an earlier time.

Physics has also made its contributions to medicine. By electrical methods the condition of the heart and its actions can be graphically shown. The development of the electrocardiograph by Einthoven and the more general use of an apparatus to accurately measure blood pressure have been of great assistance to the finger and ear of the physician.

The refinements in X-ray production and use have been of vital importance. There is almost no part of the body where X-ray examination will not be of help in making a diagnosis. At first, fractures and diseases of bone were shown, owing to the greater density of this tissue. By injection of various substances the hollow viscera were then outlined, barium and bismuth in the stomach and intestines, various fluids first into the bladder and then into the ureter and up to the kidney, and later through the air passages into the lung. Air is now being injected into the cavities of the brain to show distortions of these spaces. By injecting into the blood a long-named drug [2] which is excreted into the gall bladder this organ also can be outlined. By these means not only can form be shown but function as well. Under the fluoroscope, or by films at different times, a barium meal can be followed on its course for days. By looking at two films, taken at a little different angle, with a stereoscope, a three-dimension picture can be visualized.

The X-ray has also proved of great therapeutic value and with radium has joined the ranks of curative agents at our disposal. That radiant energy has some effect on cancer is well proven. Many superficial tumors have been dispelled, some of

.[2] Tetraiodophenolphthalein.

them never to recur; others have been decreased or delayed; in many the pain has been more or less controlled. In many other conditions radiant energy has proved of considerable curative value. There is also a tragic side to this story. As with so many new agents, before their dangers are understood, much harm can result, and many of the pioneers in this field have died, victims of cancer caused by the very means they were using to try and cure this condition in others. The methods of protection and the regulation of dosage came too late for them.

Other electrical methods are more highly developed than they were twenty-five years ago and more efficiently used, such as the high-frequency current, the mercury arc, the quartz lamp, diathermy and the ultra-violet and infra-red rays. Sunlight is better understood and more widely and wisely used. By combining suitable tubes, mirrors and electric lights, apparatus has been devised by which various portions of the body can be directly inspected. The ear, eye, nasal passages, trachea and bronchi, lower intestine, urethra and bladder are not only open to view but also to direct attack. Many safety pins and other foreign bodies have been removed in this way from the windpipe and even from its extensions into the lungs.

Among the most spectacular discoveries in nutrition are the vitamins. After some clever guesses by others, Hopkins in 1906 showed experimental evidence that food, to have all the essentials for growth, must contain something more than proteins, fats, carbohydrates and mineral substances. In 1912 he published details of his studies, which, together with the work of Osborne and Mendel, McCallum and Davis, Fink, Sherman, McCollum, Shibley, Park, and others, enlarged the science of nutrition by the advent of vitamins. It is now known that scurvy, beriberi, xerophthalmia, rickets, and possibly pellagra, are due to deficiencies in diet of one or more of these substances. In addition to the vitamins, the better appreciation of the specific properties, the physiological action and the bio-chemistry of the various food substances has made the science of nutrition much more exact. This has vitally changed infant feeding and replaced former attempts at merely imitating breast milk.

Marked progress has been made in the study of those minute forms of life which are the sources of so many human ills. New classes of organisms have been brought to light. The filterable viruses — substances small enough to escape the modern microscope and to pass through Berkenfeldt filters — are now considered to be the causative agents of fifty or more human, animal, plant, insect and bacterial diseases. The more important items in this work have been the transmission of poliomyelitis (infantile paralysis) to monkeys by Land-steiner and Popper in 1909; the description of inclusion bodies in rabies by Negri in 1905; the transmission of experimental herpes to rabbits by Gruter in 1920 and the description of the bacteriophage by Twort in 1915. The latter are minute, invisi-ble, filterable substances arising in cultures of bacteria, which have the property of attacking these bacteria more or less specifically. Whether they are living organisms or ferment-like bodies is not known.

The causative living agents of several infectious diseases have been discovered and in most cases grown in culture out-side the body. The most important of these are the spirochaete or treponema pallidum, the cause of syphilis (Schaudinn in 1915); the bacillus of whooping cough (Bordet and Gengou in 1906); the pasteurella tularensis (McCoy, 1911), shown to be the cause of tularemia in man and rabbits (Francis); spiro-chaeta partenuis, the cause of yaws (Castellani, 1905), Leish-mania tropica and braziliensis — or oriental sore and espundia (Laveran, Nattan-Larrier, 1912, and Vianna, 1911); many fungi have been found to be behind certain skin diseases.

More intimate knowledge of many of the previously known

organisms has been acquired. It is now recognized that various immunilogical types exist within a given bacterial species, as Dopter showed for the meningococcus in 1909, Neufeld for the pneumococcus in 1910, and Van Ermenghen for the bacillus botulinus in 1912. Viruses have been grown in tissue culture by Steinhardt and Lambert, 1913. Not only are these minute organisms being studied from the standpoint of their appearance and life history, their products, their effect on animals and man; but they are now being attacked chemically. The chemical make up of the bacteria, their poisons and the various substances built up by the body to resist them, is being brought to light. Obermeyer and Pick, Lansteiner, Avery and Heidelberger have contributed richly to this field.

As a result of these studies new methods of diagnosis of disease or man's susceptibility to disease have been established, as the Wasserman reaction in syphilis, 1906; the local tuber-culin reactions of Calmette and von Pirquet, 1907, the Schick test for susceptibility to diphtheria, 1913, and the Dick test for susceptibility to scarlet fever, 1923.

In the treatment of disease, the advance has been marked as well. The old list of drugs has been greatly reduced. Much of the chaff has been separated from the wheat, leaving only those drugs whose therapeutic value can be demonstrated. Their administration has been simplified and made less un-pleasant and more direct. By intravenous injection a more rapid effect is gained when necessary than by waiting for it to be absorbed from the digestive tract or from the tissues. Many new agents have been created, not from the vegetable world as formerly, but in the chemical or bacteriological laboratory. The organic chemist has prepared synthetically many antisep-tics, anaesthetics and narcotics. By extracting the esters from chalmoogra oil, leprosy has been controlled.

Cerebrospinal meningitis is now treated by a specific serum, thanks to Wasserman, Jochmann, Flexner and Jobling; poliomyelitis, by serum obtained from patients who have recovered from the acute stage of the disease; scarlet fever, by anti-toxin; diphtheria prevented by toxin-antitoxin. The direct transfusion of blood from a healthy individual to one in dire need has progressed from a spectacular operation by an artist of rare skill to an every day occurrence. A little over twenty years ago Carrel sutured the artery of a prominent surgeon to his newborn son who was dying from hemorrhage. Within a few years that same boy will, as part of his routine duties as an interne, telephone for a professional donor of blood and then, quietly transfer fifty or five hundred cubic centimeters of blood to a patient under his charge. It is still often a life-saving measure, but it is also used as a tonic and one patient may receive a dozen or more transfusions. Not only are drugs and blood thrown directly into the veins today, but food and drink are given that way. Water, with a proper amount of salt, and glucose solution are daily used in considerable amounts, not only to sustain the patient but also to regulate the interchange between the tissues and the blood stream.

Syphilis provides a most striking illustration of many of the advances which have been enumerated. Twenty-five years ago, it was suspected because of its primary lesion, the hard chancre, and diagnosis was confirmed when a rash appeared a few weeks later. These may not have been noticed and the condition not suspected for months, when the later conditions appeared scattered all over the body. Perhaps years later the more severe destructive conditions appeared or the late nerve changes of locomotor ataxia or general paresis. Mercury and iodide of potash were the best hope of cure. This treatment had to be continued for two years or more. In 1903 Schaudinn and Hoffman discovered the cause, and two years later Wasserman established a pretty definite diagnostic test. In 1909, after countless experiments, Ehrlich elaborated salvarsan, an arsenic compound which controlled the disease after a few intravenous injections. Both the diagnostic reaction and the application of the cure were applied to the central nervous system by Swift and Ellis and later Fordyce, from 1912 to 1920. In 1918 Wagner and von Jauregg discovered that one of the late results, general paresis of the insane, could be greatly helped by inoculation with the parasite of malaria. As a result of these many new methods the diagnosis has been made more definite and the treatment more rapid and sure. The late evidences which formerly filled our clinics are becoming more and more rare. With the knowledge at our disposal today, syphilis could be made as rare as yellow fever. The causes of many of the diseases of the skin have been discovered and their treatment rendered more efficacious. Many of these conditions have been found to yield to X-ray, radium, and various electrical and other physical methods.

In the clinical branches of medicine much of the progress has been founded on the advances in knowledge made in the medical sciences which have been enumerated. This intimate association between the investigative side of medicine and its practical application to the patient has been greatly fostered by the fact that so many hospitals have realized the advantage to their patients of ward and out-patient teaching of medicine. In the various special fields only a few examples can be given to illustrate the progress that has been made.

In internal medicine perhaps the most striking example is typhoid fever. In 1904 approximately one-half of the medical wards of some hospitals were occupied by typhoid fever patients during the summer months. Today it has become a rare disease. This change is due to better control of water and milk supply and preventive inoculation. The lives of diabetic patients are being indefinitely prolonged by diet and insulin. Bright's disease is recognized earlier and better controlled. The effect of liver diet has revolutionized the treatment of the anemias. The infectious diseases are better controlled and the mortality greatly decreased.

In surgery anaesthesia has been made safer and far less unpleasant by new anaesthetics, new methods and new control. Local and spinal anaesthesia have become safer, simpler and more effective. The prevention of infection of operative wounds has been developed greatly by better methods of sterilization of the materials, the use of rubber gloves and protection of the operating teams. Diagnostic methods are far more exact. The patient is more carefully prepared for his operative experience and many dangers avoided. Earlier and more exact diagnosis and earlier operation have greatly reduced the dangers of operations. New fields have been opened up and old ones broadened. The surgery of the chest and of the brain have developed to an astounding degree. The two great advances in the treatment of fractures have been the recognition that fractures are emergencies and need immediate attention and the method of traction and suspension, where a steady pull on the broken bone is maintained until union has taken place. In the surgery of the bladder, kidneys and prostate, we see the same progress. By means of the cystoscope, the X-ray and functional tests of the kidney, exact diognoses are now possible that were not dreamt of twenty-five years ago. Through this, and perfection of operative technique, the mortality has been markedly decreased.

In otolaryngology the diseased tonsil is now removed instead of its top taken off. Infections of the accessory sinuses are far better understood and more safely and surely treated. Earlier diagnosis and treatment of middle ear inflammations has greatly reduced the danger of mastoid infection. When this does occur, it is much more safely handled.

The advances in treatment of diseases of the eye are due largely to better methods of examination and to the perfection of the operative treatment, especially of glaucoma, cataract and the plastic repair of deformities of the eyelids.

In orthopedics surgical methods are replacing the brace and plaster of Paris. In one hospital more braces were used twenty-five years ago for five thousand patients than are now used for thirty thousand. By operative methods stability can be given to the bony framework itself instead of depending on braces. Paralyzed muscles can often be compensated for by transplanting others to take over their function.

In obstetrics the pregnant woman has learned to report earlier for medical care. The complications are better understood, earlier recognized and the dangers often avoided. Caesarian section has been perfected and its mortality greatly reduced. By treating the syphilitic mother, the child is often born free from that disease.

The diseases of childhood have been markedly cut down. The diarrhœal diseases have been reduced greatly by better milk control and wiser feeding. The infectious diseases, especially dipphtheria and scarlet fever, have lost much of their terror. It has been said that the practice of pediatrics has become largely a matter of educating the mothers. More and more it deals with the management of all types of physical and temperamental abnormalities occurring in the stage of rapid growth and development.

Progress in the field of psychiatry has perhaps been more marked than in almost any other. Twenty-five years ago there were two main problems: first, to decide whether an individual was insane or not; and secondly, if he were, to provide a place where he could be protected from society and society protected from him and his acts. Today, although this second problem is even greater than ever, because of the numbers of these pitiable people, the main problem is to recognize the early symptoms of mental disorder, to ascertain the causes and to reëstablish normal adjustments. The tremendous growth of the mental hygiene movement is most hopeful for the future. Unfortunately, it seems that the early history of the X-ray is being repeated in this field. Methods of investigation and of treatment are being used recklessly before their dangers are thoroughly understood. Psychiatry is leaving its former isolated position and infiltrating all other branches of medicine and being welcomed with open arms by practitioners in those other fields who have recognized that their patients are only too often mentally as well as physically ill and require treatment for both conditions. In neurology a much more exact and detailed understanding of the anatomy and physiology of the nervous system has led to better knowledge of its abnormalities and means of restoring them to normal.

Much study and experiment has been expended all over the world during the last twenty-five years on the problem of cancer. Certain facts have been established. It was shown that malignant tumors can be produced in animals by experimental means, that certain chicken tumors are filterable and that tumor cells grown on artificial media develop certain characteristics which serve to differentiate them from similar cultures of normal cells; that a sensitivity to tumor growth is inheritable; that malignant tumors can be destroyed by radiation, but that these effects are independent of the wave length but do depend on time and intensity; that massage can distribute cancer particles throughout the body and so hasten metastases; that benign tumors can be transplanted; that tumors can be caused by application of tar and by other methods; that a single type of irritant may produce several different types of tumor.

More and more attention is being paid to the prevention of disease. The public is much wiser today regarding hygienic living and applies its wisdom. Fresh air, exercise, sunlight, clothing, diet, temperance in eating, drinking and working are better understood and made use of.

In matters of public health it is interesting to note that practically all the national health organizations have developed during this period. These agencies are in the fields of tuberculosis, social hygiene, mental hygiene, child health, cancer control and heart disease. Other important changes are: the success of compulsory commercial pasteurization of milk and the elevation of the standards of milk collection, handling and transportation, which have had a great effect on the reduction of the spread of such diseases as typhoid fever, septic sore throat, diphtheria, scarlet fever and enteritis of infancy; the protection of most of the large municipal water supplies by chlorination has been responsible for the reduction of the incidence of typhoid fever; widespread adoption of active artificial immunization against diphtheria in infancy and early childhood and the application of the Schick test to determine individual immunity or susceptibility; provision of medical supervision of the health of school children almost universally, and the extension of this to children of the pre-school age; establishment of public health services for rural communities on as thorough a basis as those of cities; the spread of public health nursing as a medico-social agency indispensable for the application of preventive medicine in the home; use of medical services in industry as a means of recognizing and preventing the health hazards of occupied persons; progress in the control of yellow fever by the advances in knowledge of endemic centers, the life history of the vector mosquito and specific serum reactions.

The relation of dentistry to medicine has changed. More and more the professions realize the importance of dental conditions as related to general disease and the influence of dental hygiene in prevention and cure of various bodily ills. Coöperation of the two branches is increasing in teaching, practice and research.

The relation of the patient to the physician has altered. In earlier days the medical man was apt to talk down to his patient and by the use of long terms to impress him with his superiority. Today it is more a question of the two working together. The physician attempts to explain to his patient what it is that is wrong. He is much franker and feels less ashamed to say he does not know, than our grandfathers were. Because of this the patient has more confidence and behaves accordingly.

During the past quarter century new facts have been discovered in medicine by the group of investigators, many of them have been applied to the prevention and cure or alleviation of human ills by the practicing physicians. But of even greater importance, this knowledge has been spread abroad so that the general public today has a far better understanding of the possibilities of preventive medicine and has become more truly a partner in the all important business of maintaining the health of the community.

CHEMISTRY

Henry C. Sherman

One way of expressing the present trend in science is to say that physics becomes more mathematical, chemistry more physical, biology and geology more chemical.

This is not due to a shifting of boundaries; it is because all science is becoming more exact. It is also true that the volume of scientific knowledge is growing at an enormous rate; but when we speak of the recent development of science as essentially *quantitative*, this word does not stand for bulkiness but for exactness, refinement and precision.

And this has made the sciences more helpful to each other. For example in a recent publication of the Carnegie Institution of Washington it is said:

Hitherto it has been usual to consider the subject of geology as a descriptive science; in the Geophysical Laboratory it is treated as an exact science. The reasons why it is now possible to approach geological problems from the quantitative standpoint are not to be found in any profound change of views of geologists but rather in the remarkable development of physics and chemistry during the past two generations.

Chemistry during the past quarter century has grown with such unprecedented rapidity that to attempt to list its achievements would result in a mere catalogue. Hence we must here speak less of specific events and more of general trends.

The two great trends are: an ever increasing exactness; and a broadening toward, and interpenetration with, the neighboring sciences. The twofold result is simultaneous growth both in breadth of view and in depth of insight.

Today we shall consider first the progress of those branches of chemistry which are traditionally its more exclusive responsibility (chemical synthesis and analysis) : then, the broadening of chemistry, toward physics on the one hand and biology on the other, with resulting advances in our understanding of the structure of matter and of the processes of life.

Synthetic chemistry appeals with special cogency both to the philosophical and to the popular mind. Berthelot wrote:

Chemistry creates its object. This creative faculty, comparable to that of art itself, distinguishes it essentially from the natural and historical sciences. These sciences do not control their objects. Thus they are often condemned to an eternal impotence in the search for truth of which they must content themselves with possessing some few and often uncertain fragments. On the contrary, the experimental sciences have the power to realize their conjectures. . . . What they dream of, that they can manifest in actuality. . . . Chemistry possesses this creative faculty in a more eminent degree than the other sciences.

Twenty-five years ago many workers were already busy, realizing their conjectures and converting their dreams into actualities, in the laboratories of synthetic chemistry. Over 100,000 substances, most of them never before known, had then been synthesized; and during the past quarter century at least another 100,000 have been added.

The numbers just given refer to new substances in the sense of actual chemical individuals, chiefly what we call synthetic organic compounds. But only chemists use the word compounds in this restricted sense. In the ordinary sense of the word, the compounds newly created include, along with these chemical individuals, an untold multiplication of what the chemist would distinguish as mixtures, blends, alloys, etc., but which to the world at large are just as significantly new products as are the chemically individual substances.

Thus synthetic chemistry presents the world of today with a countless wealth and variety of things which were previously entirely unknown, well justifying the effective popular use made by Dr. Slosson of the phrase *creative chemistry*.

And not only thus, for there has also been accomplished, by

chemical synthesis, the cheap production of things which previously were obtained from nature, but in such small quantities and at such great cost as formerly to restrict their enjoyment to the few. Thus as Dr. Slosson liked to point out, it is through this aspect of chemical advance, "that every working girl can now wear Royal Purple."

Nor should the triumphs of synthetic chemistry be thought of simply in terms of those things which most insistently obtrude themselves: such as the multiplication of phenomenally explosive and ingeniously toxic compounds during the war, and the present vast expansion of the armamentum of substances designed to bombard the senses of sight and smell; for, through the same general type of research activity, there are now being produced a wide range of new synthetic drugs which greatly extend the scope of chemo-therapy and sharpen the precision with which disease germs can be killed or controlled, even within the patient and without injury to the tissues of the human body itself.

And our indebtedness to synthetic chemistry extends far afield from such substances as have just been cited. As a few of the innumerable other new contributions, we may mention: fibres and fabrics; paints and plastics; insulators and alloys, which in addition to their direct popular use have made possible many new industrial developments; and, perhaps above all, the economic synthesis of ammonia as a means of fixing atmospheric nitrogen for human uses.

In this last, chemistry furnishes the outstanding example of the present-day version of the beating of swords into plowshares; for, since the war, cannon barrels have been converted into high-pressure reaction apparatus for use in making ammonium salts to increase the productiveness of the farmer's fields.

By increasing the productivity of the soil, and by guiding the utilization of farm products, both as food and in industry, chemistry is rendering so great a service to the cause of food supply that we may well afford to be not only patient but good-naturedly skeptical in regard to the economically profitable artificial production of our staple foodstuffs. Many drugs, dyes and perfumes are already being made more economically in the factory than they can be grown on the farm, and we may confidently expect to see many additions to these categories. But all these are things which play but a minor part in the physiological economy of the organisms which produce them. When, on the other hand, we turn to such things as the sugars, the scientific triumphs of synthetic chemistry are still conspicuous; but the economic relationships are quite different. For sugar is something that the growing plant produces in large quantity as a prime factor in its own economy. So while it is one of the scientific advances of recent years that cane sugar has been synthesized in the laboratory, we do not expect, in any future which we can now foresee, that the chemist will be able to make it artificially as cheaply as the farmer can produce it by raising sugar cane or sugar beets with chemistry at the service of his agriculture.

But synthetic chemistry does not exist for economic reasons alone. As "a man's life consisteth not in the abundance of the things which he possesseth" so synthetic chemistry looks beyond the mere multiplication of *things*, and interests itself also in the light which it can throw upon the molecular structures of the carbon compounds and the mechanisms of their reactions, and thence into some of the most complex and far-reaching problems of the interrelations of environment and life.

Analytical chemistry also has shown during the past quarter century a most noteworthy growth and development in what was already an efficient body of learning and professional practice. Here especially does chemistry come to the fore in that development of the quantitative (in the sense of exact) point of view which we have seen to be so characteristic of the science of today. This line of advance involves the interweaving of abstract theory and the most highly skilled experimentation. Its spirit may be indicated by brief quotations from two excellent recent textbooks, on qualitative and quantitative analysis, respectively.

Regarding present-day qualitative analysis we read: "A purely qualitative analysis is impossible: the question, present or absent, can never be answered. The methods of qualitative analysis determine whether the amount of a given constituent present is greater or less than the least quantity which the test can detect, and the result means nothing unless something is known about the delicacy of the test. This is quantitative. . . ." And the textbook of quantitative analysis sets forth as its special aim, ". . . to apply the principles of physical chemistry to the theory of quantitative analysis in the same detailed and thorough manner [as in] the teaching of qualitative analysis and of general chemistry as well." And the success with which this ideal has been pursued in recent years has on the one hand greatly advanced the theoretical value of analytical chemistry, and, on the other, has led to such developments in precision that quantitative analysis has not only become a more exact and potent factor in practical affairs but has also furnished the chief facts and experimental methods with which the theoretical or physical chemist works. Thus just as, in a sense, all chemistry is physical chemistry, so with equal justice it may be said that analytical chemistry makes possible the development of chemistry as a whole.

This higher development of analytical chemistry has both induced, and been supported by, a constantly growing recognition of the fact that economy and efficiency in the use of nearly all material things — whether they be the natural resources taken from the mines, the forests and the sea; or the products of farms or of factories — depend upon a knowledge of what chemical elements or substances these things contain, and in what quantities or proportions. And this knowledge must always depend upon chemical analysis; whether the particular thing in hand is analyzed, or its composition and properties are deduced from analyses of similar things.

Hence large corporations now commonly have their own chemical laboratories for the analysis and control of their supplies, their processes, and their products; trade organizations often undertake similar services for their members; the interests of producers and consumers are in some fields now coördinated and safeguarded through governmental control made possible by chemical analysis; and it is gratifying to note that quite recently, and first of all in our own city, the independent practitioners of analytical and consulting chemistry have formed a voluntary association for the primary purpose of standardizing and further advancing the efficiency, the precision and the professional ideals of work in this field.

Largely as an outgrowth of its analytical development, chemistry has during the past quarter century come into constantly increasing requisition in the service of the advancement of learning through professions other than chemistry itself. The services of chemistry to medicine we may leave for Dean Darrach to discuss.

The dean of engineering in one of our great state universities has recently said that chemistry is to engineering what blood is to the body. In many such universities, systematic permanently organized, publicly supported chemical research has, during the past quarter century, been greatly expanded under the agricultural auspices where it had usually been begun, and has now also been established in connection with engineering and in many cases in still other fields. Naturally the research chemist, under whatever auspices he works, will bring to bear upon his problems the widest range of chemical knowledge which he is able to acquire; but the origination of the far-reaching programs of chemical research just mentioned should be credited primarily to the confidence inspired by the services of analytical chemists.

So also, it was largely because the chemical analysis of foods and the chemical control of the food industries was beginning to command the necessary confidence, that Congress was able to agree upon the very advanced and comprehensive "pure food law" of June 30, 1906. When it is remembered that the mass of the people must spend about half of their total earnings for food, the renaissance of business ethics and of public good will in this homely but vastly important phase of the economic life of our country would in itself make the past quarter century noteworthy for the service rendered by chemistry to human welfare.

Analytical chemistry is, in fact, now helping to set standards for the development of all the exact sciences. Chemical analysis is the one side, as physical measurement is the other, of the foundation upon which has been built during the past quarter century the now extremely far-reaching work of our National Bureau of Standards and of the corresponding institutions in other countries.

Findlay has well said: "On the science of chemistry, indeed, more than on any other branch of organized knowledge, depends the material well-being and comfort of man. But the end and aim of chemistry is not merely material. Chemistry offers its contribution also to the deeper interests of the human mind."

So analytical chemistry has found time, notwithstanding its manifold mundane duties, to develop the use of the spectroscope and to turn it upon the sun and stars, with the result (among others) of finding that not only the whole of our own solar system but other worlds, in all stages of their making and aging, are composed of the same chemical elements which we find on and in our own earth and its atmosphere.

The broadening of chemistry toward physics has been so

fruitful of theoretical advance that it is not uncommon to hear the term *physical* used as almost synonymous with *theoretical* chemistry. In this phase of our science the advances of the past quarter century have brought what, from the standpoint of this attempt at brief summary, may perhaps best be characterized as a literally indescribable embarrassment of riches!

Perhaps the most outstanding trends of recent theoretical advance have been in the better understanding of the structure of matter, the thermodynamics of chemical changes, and the extension of statistical methods in the interpretation of chemical phenomena.

To cite but a few of the more specific lines of advance, we may mention: the noteworthy progress in development of the relationships of atoms, molecules and quanta; atomic structure, atomic number, with the clearing up of the anomalies of the periodic table of atomic weights and the explanation of fractional weights in terms of isotopes; the discovery of chemical elements through research guided by these new conceptions (notably hafnium in Europe and illinium in America); the experimental transmutation of certain elements; the very recent discovery of the multiple nature of hydrogen; new developments in kinetic theory; X-ray analysis of crystal structure with its great broadening of our conceptions of molecules; valence; oxidation-reduction theory; hydrogen-ion activity; theories of solutions; conductance; radiation; photochemistry and spectral analysis; the work with radicles as chemical entities coördinate with molecules and ions; surface tension and surface film phenomena, the study of which has resulted in the formulation, in 1916-1921, of Langmuir's Theory of Heterogeneous Reaction Velocity, which, with its broad and deep significance in research and highly practical value to the industry which supported the work, well illustrates the wisdom of industrial support of research of the most fundamental character; colloid chemistry; the new thermochemistry, so strikingly more significant and successful than that of fifty to sixty years ago — but time forbids the further extension of this triumphal procession.

Nernst's Heat Theorem enunciated in 1906 has proven so serviceable as now to be called the Third Law of Thermodynamics, and is playing an important part both in the theoretical development of our science through correlation with kinetic theory and statistical mechanics, and in such industrial developments as the economic synthesis of methanol.

Interlocking with many of the studies above mentioned and interesting as an introduction to the study of the structure of matter, because it deals with particles of the order of magnitude only next smaller than those which we can see with a good microscope, is *colloid chemistry*. A quarter century ago the chemistry of colloids was beginning to be actively discussed; but it was, in the figure of speech of its English investigator, Hardy, "a sort of Alsatia in which difficult states of matter could find refuge from a too exacting inquiry." But through the researches of recent years the characteristics of colloid-chemical behavior are step by step being satisfactorily explained in terms of true chemical principles.

Inasmuch as the hardest rock and the softest soil, the turbidity of river or stream and the brilliance of the sunset, are all exemplifications of colloid behavior, and as the tissues of all known living things are chiefly composed of colloidal material, colloid chemistry is prominently involved in our understanding both of inorganic and of living nature. Thus the recent recognition of the possession of fundamental chemical properties by colloidal matter and the development of rigid quantitative description of colloidal behavior have contributed to rapid advances in certain aspects of the biological sciences.

Passing to the problems of the behavior of what we may perhaps call simpler chemical entities, as they exist in their solutions, we enter a domain one field of which had already been actively cultivated for some years before the beginning of the period here under review. Arrhenius had published, and Ostwald had driven home to the consciousness of all chemists, the now familiar ionization theory as picturing the condition of acids, bases and salts in solution and the mechanism of most of their reactions.

Certain facts were not entirely consistent with the scheme of interpretation propounded by Arrhenius and expounded by Ostwald; but these seem now to have found satisfactory explanation in the supplementary theory of Debye and Hückel, together with the amplifications and clarifications which this latter theory has received through the researches of both European and American chemists.

Highly significant also are recent advances in knowledge of the forces holding atoms in compounds; while the developments of the past quarter century in the study of the structure of the atoms themselves are, needless to say, of the very highest significance and of the most fundamental character. Because of the extent to which the work of physicists and the use of methods belonging primarily to the physical laboratory have contributed to its development, the discussion of atomic structure may here properly be left to the lecture on physics.

The concept of atomic number has marked a very great advance in clarity over the previous views of the periodic classification of the elements. As early as 1897, Rydberg had suggested that an improved basis for correlation of properties is obtainable by writing down the elements in order of increasing atomic weight and assigning a whole number to each element in this order: hydrogen 1, helium 2, lithium 3, beryllium 4, boron 5, carbon 6, and so on. These were called the atomic numbers; but this general concept was first freed from the anomalies of the atomic-weight table and became a potent factor in the interpretation of atomic structure in 1914 when Moseley published his X-ray work upon the elements, which promptly won recognition as an epoch-making contribution to chemical insight and achievement. Killed in action at Gallipoli in his twenty-eighth year, Moseley leaves, in his work upon atomic number, an accomplishment which alone would suffice to make the past quarter century an outstanding period in the history of science. For the formulation of relationships made possible by this conception of the atoms, throws important light upon the interpretation both of cosmic evolution, and of the chemical aspects of the development of life.

The years here under review have also seen the first authenticated cases of transmutation of chemical elements by human agency. In any period less fertile of great achievements in physico-chemical research, this might well have been regarded as a truly epoch-making event. But jostled as it has been by so many other great discoveries of the past quarter-century, it has settled into a matter-of-fact paragraph in the textbook of general chemistry and probably not all of the students who learn it today realize that here within their own lifetime has been done what the chemists of an earlier era sought in vain to accomplish through hundreds upon hundreds of years, and what our more recent predecessors had come to regard as absurdly impossible because inconsistent with the nineteenth-century theory of the atom as an indivisible unit. How different the newer conceptions of the atom!

Again, we are here concerned with general trends rather than specific theories or findings, for under the limits of time of this lecture we must content ourselves with a summary statement of the general effect of these advances upon our point of view.

It may, then, be said that the quantum theory, taken with any theory of atomic structure which one may prefer, pushes us from the physical side, as does the mutation theory of evolution from the biological, with such cogency as to compel us at last to break away from the time-old belief that Nature doesn't make jumps; and, what is more important, we now definitely reject the assumptions of strict causality and of a rigidly mechanical determinism which have dominated too much both of scientific thinking strictly so called and of the more general thinking of the recent era which has been strongly influenced by, if not deeply versed in, science.

The breaking away of scientific thinking from these assumptions, the general trend to the statistical point of view in science, the replacement of attempts at rigid yes-or-no answers by the really more accurate statements in terms of probability: this is certainly one of the most significant features of the past quarter century of scientific advance. And it is all the more significant in that it characterizes a period of steadily advancing standards of exactness in scientific research.

This point has, of course, been made familiar through many recent writings; but, lest it be thought a popularization, let us read a few sentences from the latest Presidential Address before the American Chemical Society — that of our distinguished alumnus, Dr. Irving Langmuir. In speaking of the application of quantum mechanics in chemistry he says:

Atomic processes seem to be governed fundamentally by the law of probability. It has no meaning to ask when will a particular radium atom disintegrate, for no operation is conceivable by which such an event could be predicted. The same is true of every individual quantum process. We have no guarantee whatever that the expulsion of an α-particle from an atom of radium has any immediate cause. [Likewise] the formation of nuclei in supercooled liquids, etc., must be essentially quantum phenomena in which no cause can be assigned for the formation of the individual nucleus. By varying the conditions we may alter the probability that a nucleus will appear at a given point, but in no absolute sense can we ever make a nucleus form through a direct cause.

Plainly this point of view, to which we are brought by recent research in the structure of matter, suggests interesting parallels in the *chemistry of life*. Some writers would have us believe that our mental reactions are rigidly determined by our internal secretions; but if a Langmuir can speak only of probabilities regarding the reactions occurring in such relatively simple systems as those to which he has here referred, can anyone properly attempt to speak with greater certainty as to how the still unknown substances in the brain cells will react under conditions enormously more complicated and less clearly defined? Undoubtedly it is largely through the chemical mechanisms of the body that heredity and environment work, but it is equally true that education (physical, mental and moral) can, as in Langmuir's illustration, "alter the probability that a nucleus will appear at a given point." (But we cannot, in one lecture, attempt to sketch the character of chemistry, and the chemistry of character, too!)

The chemistry of the internal secretions is an important field of research, fruitful although beset with difficulties which appear unique. One does not recall any other field in which research is so embarrassed by the distortions resulting from the excessive enthusiasms of some of its friends, and by outsiders' attempts at commercialization in forms varying from the old-fashioned patent medicine to the modern problem novel. Yet soundly scientific work goes quietly and steadily forward; and the past quarter century has seen the complete chemical identification of some of the active substances of these secretions and great advances in our knowledge of several of the others.

Chemistry is also throwing light upon life processes through the study of the nutritional reactions of the organism as a whole. In a sense this is an outgrowth of analytical chemistry, for in many laboratories it began with experiments in the feeding of animals in order to learn something more about food values than was revealed by food analysis *in vitro*.

Once chemistry had fairly begun (about twenty years ago) to broaden thus toward physiology as it had already broadened toward physics, there soon followed in rapid succession the discovery of a group of substances which, while absolutely essential, had previously been entirely unknown. They do not all belong together chemically; but as time has not yet sufficed for the complete chemical identification of any of them, they are tentatively grouped together as the vitamins. But the discovery of the vitamins has been only the beginning of this new chapter in chemistry.

The immediate significance of this discovery was to permit the formulation of a scientifically sound conception of what substances must be supplied from without to meet the needs of the life processes, or, in other words, to define in chemical terms the adequate in nutrition; but chemical research has promptly pressed forward, from the qualitative definition of the adequate, towards the quantitative determination of the optimal. From one point of view, this is but an example of the general tendency of twentieth century science to develop its quantitative aspects — to hold itself rigorously and scrupulously to the task of becoming a more and more exact science. But from another point of view, this pursuit of the quantitative ideal of the optimal in the present-day chemistry of nutrition is yielding results of very special interest. For it is showing that chemistry can not only coöperate effectively with biology and medicine in the preservation of young lives but that chemistry can also do, what many biologists and medical men have been inclined to regard as beyond the powers of science, namely, so improve the normal life-process as to induce a well-marked positive extension of the average *adult* life span; and, what is perhaps more significant, to prolong the prime of life in even greater ratio, growth and development being enhanced and senility deferred in the same individuals.

Let us end, as we began, with the reflection that modern chemistry does not stand or work alone. Occupying, as it does, a central position in the general body of scientific knowledge, its advances should be viewed in the light of those of the surrounding sciences, and in such philosophical perspective as may be.

By most students of science, evolution is now conceived as a much-more-than-biological process, beginning perhaps in the shaping of a system of chemical elements of the highest imaginable fitness for the life processes which later appeared, and finally, in man, passing (whether by innumerable small steps or by the mightiest of mutations) from the biological to the social and spiritual evolution of the race as a whole. In the majority of human lives, more time is needed for altruistic than for egocentric development; and in showing the way to a longer lease of healthier life, the research of this quarter-century has advanced our understanding of the world in which we live and at the same time enlarged our opportunity both for the attainment of a higher and more abundant life and for the increasingly more effective handing on of human progress, through education and social inheritance.

Finally, it should be said that the advances which we have sought to summarize, gratifying as they are in what has been accomplished, are also full of promise for further development, in the steady growth of chemistry into ever greater prominence and potency, in the practical affairs of the world, and in the interpretation of the universe.

PHYSICS

George B. Pegram

In an hour's discourse to sketch in any coherent and illuminating manner the advance through the past twenty-five years in any one of the major divisions of science necessitates a restriction to some single aspect of this advance. In physics this is particularly necessary, for so far as can now be judged no similar period of years has been more fruitful in this subject.

The strides that have been made in applied physics, that now so quickly becomes technical or engineering practice, represent great advances in knowledge. In any general treatment the story of these should form a large chapter, for between new discoveries and their applications to economic use there is usually a great amount of human effort; often there is genius, an Edison or a Pupin. In these recent years applied physics has brought into our daily life such marvels of illumination, of communication by wire and broadcast, of reproduction of sound and images, of the clairvoyant X-rays, of machines that guide great ships more truly than the magnetic needle and the most skilled steersman, and of many other kinds, that they transcend all the imaginings of the ancient romancers and dull our own wonder by their frequency. The most astounding thing that could happen in the next twenty-five years would be to have no new marvel of applied physics come into common daily use. Advances in applied physics come not only in the wake of signal new discoveries but also through the deeper cultivation of such well-established fields of physics as those of the mechanics of rigid and elastic solids, plastic solids, liquids and gases, the electric and magnetic properties of old and new materials, optics, acoustics, heat and radiation; all these fields have been fertile through the period we are reviewing.

Accomplishments in applied physics have been greatly accelerated by the development, almost entirely within the last twenty-five years, of organized research for industrial ends by groups of men of the finest scientific training, and that is another important new chapter in the story of physics which however cannot be followed out here.

It seems most appropriate for the purposes of this survey to restrict our attention to those advances in our experimental and theoretical knowledge that have characterized the foremost salients of discovery in physics in this period. These relate to the most fundamental concepts of the constitution of matter, of the transfer of energy, and of the nature of time and space.

Progress in physics results in the first place from the acquisition of any new knowledge concerning experimental facts, but rational interpretation of the facts of experimental measurement, new and old, in the form of consistent and always more and more inclusive theory, is as much a mark of progress as the discovery of new phenomena. The history of physics shows plainly that theory has steadily become more and more inclusive and unifying. The discovery of the law of conservation of energy bound heat and mechanics very closely together. The electromagnetic theory of light connected in an inclusive manner two sections of physics, namely, electricity and optics, that had previously been entirely distinct. To indicate how this process of unification by physical theory has proceeded since 1904 will be a main object of this discourse.

Before we proceed to discuss interpretations and theory a word must be said as to the developments of new facilities for experimental research. To mention only a few out of many, there may be cited the use of electron streams from hot cathodes in many kinds of apparatus, for example, in X-ray tubes and in detector and amplifier bulbs; the equally important developments in vacuum technique through the invention of the molecular pump and the diffusion pump, that have made easy the rapid exhaustion of vessels to extremely low pressures, for much of the recent progress in physics has been the result of the experiments done under the simplified conditions of a high vacuum; X-ray spectroscopy and crystal analysis; and the cloud-track method of observing the paths of high speed single atoms and electrons. The physicist of today uses these and many other aids that did not exist twenty-five years ago and his range of inquiry has been widely increased thereby.

Proceeding now to the main undertaking of this brief survey we shall first try to outline the state of knowledge of physics of twenty-five years ago, particularly with respect to those problems which had then been newly solved and the recognized problems that were still unsolved. Then after recounting advances as they came we shall assume a position a decade later, in 1914, and summarize what had then been accomplished. Going on another decade we shall look back from 1924 at what had been accomplished, and similarly for the next half decade to 1929. From this present stand we may indeed not be able to evaluate most recent progress as surely as we can judge that of earlier years though physical science is fortunate in being able quickly to test and weigh its new developments.

In 1904 the electron, or elementary negatively charged particle, had been clearly visualized and its charge and its mass at least roughly measured. It was seen to be the essential factor in such phenomena as metallic conduction, the reflection of light from metals, magneto-optic effects, and even magnetism, as well as in those phenomena in which it first clearly appeared, such as discharges of electricity through gases at low pressure. On the other hand, the nature of positive charge was not clearly understood. In a lecture on an occasion somewhat similar to this at Columbia University twenty years ago Professor

Ernest Fox Nichols said as to this, "All efforts to obtain a charge of positive electricity free from matter — a veritable positive electron — have thus far failed." As a matter of fact, the unit of positive charge corresponding to the negative electron, which we now call the proton, was at that time well known experimentally as the positive hydrogen ion, but it had not yet been recognized as the elementary atom of positive electricity. Sir J. J. Thomson had made an interesting approach to an electrical theory of atoms by postulating that the positive charge of a neutral atom, instead of being a collection of discrete unitary charges, was distributed uniformly throughout a spherical volume of atomic dimensions, and that the negative electrons of the atom were revolving around inside this region of positive charge. Thomson's theory was of importance as a forerunner, but was soon found quite inadequate to describe atomic phenomena.

The concept of the mass of the electron as arising entirely from its electrical charge was just coming to be widely accepted but the corresponding proposition that the mass of positive charge is due also only to the electrical charge itself was rather beyond the conceptions of 1904. Yet since the time of the study of electrolysis by Faraday it had been known that matter was full of positive and negative electricity, and even in 1904 the advance guard of physicists who were working on atomic phenomena were practically convinced of the necessity of arriving at a purely electrical theory of matter in which all the matter in the universe would have to be regarded as constructed of elementary positive and negative electrons. As to this Nichols in the same address said, "Some of these things and many others have led physicists to suspect that if all electricity were removed from matter nothing would be left, that the material atom is an electrical structure and nothing more."

The disintegration theory of radioactivity, which had been so beautifully worked out by Rutherford and his co-workers, had been of the greatest consequence in hastening the advent of a theory of electrical constitution of the atoms of matter, and in reviving hypotheses of the type propounded many times before, according to which the atoms of the chemical elements would have to be regarded as simply various different compounds of more fundamental units of matter, namely the natural units or atoms of positive and negative electricity. Radioactivity had led to striking confirmation of the general atomic hypothesis because it for the first time gave clear evidence to the eye of man of the effect of single atoms, namely, the production of a tiny spark by each alpha particle as it impinges on certain fluorescent substances. These alpha particles are helium atoms (less two electrons) that are shot off from the disintegrating atoms of a radioactive substance with a speed of about 10,000 miles a second, or one-twentieth that of light.

There had been a serious difficulty in the theory of radiation as developed before 1900. Much success had attended the development of statistical molecular theory by which the ordinary or average properties of matter, such as temperature or pressure, are accounted for as the statistical results of the actions of the individual molecules or atoms aggregated in great numbers. Statistical theory applied to the radiation, visible and invisible, from a body at a given temperature predicted with entire definiteness the manner in which energy should be distributed in the spectrum of the radiation — so much infra-red, so much red, so much blue, so much ultra-violet. The prediction was quite contrary to the measurements on actual radiation. The statistical theory gave entirely too much energy in the short wave, or high frequency, end of the spectrum, too much blue, too much ultra-violet.

Planck in 1900, by a sheer stroke of genius, had shown how to resolve this difficulty. He introduced the idea of radiation by quanta in order to arrive at a theoretical formula for the distribution of energy in the spectrum of the radiation from a hot body which would accord with the known facts. His hypothesis was that whenever an atom radiates energy it must radiate it in a definite amount, or *quantum*, which can neither be fallen short of nor exceeded, unless indeed there is radiated an integral multiple of the unit amount or quantum. Furthermore, this unit amount, or quantum of energy radiated, was to be proportional to the frequency of the wave motion of the radiation, that is, the energy in a quantum of light was to be equal to a constant multiplied by the frequency of vibration of the light. The constant is called the Planck constant and is universally designated by the letter *h*. With this assumption as to radiation by discrete amounts or quanta, calculation leads with entire definiteness to a distribution of energy in the spectrum that agrees with the most accurate measurements. With Planck's discovery, just four years before the beginning of the quarter century we are reviewing, had begun a new epoch in physics. "Classical theory' and "classical physics" are used to refer to nineteenth-century physics, for this introduction of the quantum idea by Planck in 1900 was the start and the root of the modern physics as distinguished from the classical. Classical physics viewed only continuous advance from one state to the other, the quantum is discontinuous and utterly inconsistent with classical or continuous physics.

In 1904 one of the most puzzling of phenomena was the photoelectric effect: light falling on clean metal surface tears off electrons from the surface, the number of such photoelectrons is directly proportional to the intensity of the light, but the maximum velocity of ejection of these photoelectrons is strangely enough entirely independent of the intensity of the light, but dependent exactly on the frequency, or color, of the light. In a faint beam of light it would take many days for enough energy to fall within an area of atomic dimensions on a metallic surface to supply the energy for the ejection of an electron. Yet in such faint illumination it was found that electrons were ejected from the metal immediately upon exposure to the light, and that these electrons, though few in number, left the metal with as great an energy as when the most intense light of the same color fell on the metal.

X-rays had been discovered nine years earlier and had come into wide use. It was pretty confidently believed that they were electromagnetic wave radiations like light, but of very short wave length or high frequency of vibration. They were not, however, known to be reflected, refracted or diffracted like light waves, and no means had been found of measuring their wave length or frequency.

In spectroscopy there were puzzling facts. As far back as the eighties the spectroscopists had analyzed the lines in the spectra of the elements into series, the lines of a series being definitely and rather simply connected as to frequency of vibration, so that on first view they might be considered as arising from some simple mechanism in the atom. But the relation between the frequencies of the lines of a series were not such as would arise from anything except an extremely complicated mechanical or electrical system. A mechanism as complicated as a piano can have its strings tuned so that they will give any desired series of frequencies, but a single string will give only a certain series of frequencies, or overtones, that are not and can not be at all similar to the series of frequencies of the lines of the spectrum. Simple systems will give only those frequencies that can be expressed mathematically in what is called a Fourier's series, the ordinary overtones of a musical instrument. The spectral frequencies can not be expressed by such a series.

Another outstanding question which was not by any means of recent origin was that of the relation of gravitation to the rest of physics. Newtonian gravitation stood out like a lone peak in the midst of a great plain far separated from the connected ranges of electricity, mechanics, and radiation, that constituted the rest of physics. Nichols said, "Gravitation is still unconnected, unattached to anything else in nature. How can he (the physicist) explain a universe when he is unable to give a reasonable account of the cement which holds it together?"

There was also the question, relating to very fundamental views in physics, which had been standing (with no wholly satisfactory answer) since 1887, when the famous Michelson-Morley experiment was made, although the Fitzgerald-Lorentz shortening hypothesis had eased the perplexity somewhat. This famous experiment was an attempt, with a most sensitive optical system cleverly devised for the purpose, to detect the motion of the earth in its orbit through the hypothetical universal ether. No effect of the supposed motion of the earth through an ether, which was postulated as the medium of optical and electrical radiation and fields of force and as furnishing a fixed and universal frame of reference, was detected in this or in subsequent optical and electrical experiments devised for the same purpose.

Summarizing the foregoing we may briefly depict conditions at the boundaries of knowledge of physics in 1904 by stating seven questions that were uppermost in the minds of physicists in 1904. The order of topics is somewhat changed, for purposes of later discussion, from that in the foregoing paragraphs. The seven questions were:

1. Why is it not possible to detect some effect of the motion of the planet earth through the ether?

2. Is all matter composed solely of electricity?

3. How can the photo-electric effect be explained?

4. What is the nature of X-rays?

5. What is the meaning and scope of the quantum hypothesis?

6. What gives rise to the peculiar sequence of frequencies in the lines of a spectrum?

7. What is the relation of gravitation to the rest of physics?

The first of these seven questions was soon completely answered. In 1905 Einstein published his revolutionary paper on what is now called the special or restricted relativity theory. In this and subsequent papers he said in effect that we ought no more to expect any optical or electrical experiment, carried out on the earth as it moves through space in its orbital revolution around the sun, to be affected by the earth's velocity than we ought to expect to find such an effect on ordinary mechanical experiments. Of course no one had ever for a moment imagined that a steady velocity, however great, through space or through an ether would in any way affect the workings of a self-contained machine of any kind, a watch, for example. Einstein simply postulated the same thing for electrical and optical phenomena as has always been intuitively accepted for mechanical phenomena. He postulated also that the velocity of light is constant in whatever system or by whatever apparatus it may be measured, and is therefore independent of the velocity of the source of the light. These simplest possible postulates, which at once did away with all complications arising from conceptions of the intangible ether, brought as an unforeseen consequence an entirely new and unexpected set of relationships between measurements of length, of time and of other physical quantities when the measurements are made on bodies as they move rapidly past the observer, and corresponding measurements in a stationary system — stationary with respect to the observer. For example, if we should try to make the best measurement we could of the length of a rigid metal bar going past us with a high speed, say three-fifths of the velocity of light, we should find its length only four-fifths of what we should find it to be if gradually brought to rest and then measured. These new relations have no importance until the velocity of motion of the body which is being measured approaches that of light. Einstein was necessarily led to a critical examination of the fundamental notion of time as a measurable quantity — whether or not that may be the time of the metaphysician — and more particularly of the concept of simultaneity at different places, and he showed clearly that the question of simultaneity of two events in places far apart is answered differently by observers who have velocities relative to one another. Events in different places that are considered simultaneous by one observer may appear successive to another observer, and successive in the reverse order to still another observer.

According to the relativity theory duration of time and extension in space enter into physical measurements and into the laws expressing the results of our measurements not as wholly independent variables but as related in somewhat the same way as distances straight ahead and distances to the right are related. To a man standing beside me and facing a little to the right from me my straight-ahead is for him partly straight ahead, partly to the left; a distance to the right for me is for him partly a distance to the right partly a distance straight ahead. In this case the difference in what the two observers report is due to the fact that they face in different directions, while in the time-space analogy differing reports as to what is a distance and what a time interval will come from observers who are moving with different velocities. Unless the difference in velocity of two observers is an appreciable fraction of the velocity of light their reports will agree, but to an observer on a swift comet moving past the earth, two events that we would say occurred simultaneously at points a certain distance apart would to his best knowledge occur at slightly different times and a smaller distance apart. The discovery that time and the three components of distance in space enter in a similar way in a general formulation of the fundamental laws of physics, that time and space are but different and varying aspects of a single four-dimensional space-time manifold, is the most significant and astounding outcome of the simple and innocent enough hypotheses of the special relativity theory.

Other far-reaching conclusions followed from the adoption of the relativity postulate. The most important one was the conclusion that mass is directly related to energy and that energy of any kind has a mass or inertia which is equal to the energy divided by the square of the velocity of light. If a body or system of bodies gives out energy in any form its mass decreases. For example, hydrogen and oxygen after combining to form water with a loss of energy as heat must have less mass, and less weight, than the two gases before combining, ordinarily this loss of mass is inappreciable, too small to be detectable in the union of hydrogen and oxygen. In connection with the electrical constitution of the atom and the so-called packing effect this loss of mass and release of energy is very important. For example, the helium atom, composed of four protons and four electrons, has not four times the mass of the hydrogen atom, which is composed of one proton and one electron, but only 3.971 times the mass of the hydrogen atom. Therefore in 4 grams of helium there is .029 gram $\times$ (3×10^{10} cm. per sec.$)^2 = .261 \times 10^{20}$ ergs of energy less than in the same number of protons and electrons in hydrogen. If the protons and electrons of 4 grams of hydrogen (the amount of hydrogen in a little more than an ounce of water) could be packed by fours into helium atoms this amount of energy would be given off. In familiar terms this is 725,000 kilowatt hours, which at the seven cent rate for electrical energy in New York City would cost a little more than $50,000. Millikan and others have speculated as to the possibility of condensations of protons and electrons into atoms occurring in interstellar space and furnishing the energy for the penetrating radiation that comes to the earth from all directions in space.

The relativity theory has influenced the whole framework of thinking in physics by allowing freedom from the entirely hypothetical, yet formerly much respected, unique frame of reference, namely, one attached to the hypothetical universal ether, with respect to which frame only it had previously been felt that the description of electrical and optical phenomena could be set forth with entire confidence. With the abandonment of the hypothesis of the existence of such a unique frame of reference, the stationary ether itself, with its postulated material properties of elasticity, mass and stress, fell into disuse as a necessary mental background. The real achievement of the original relativity theory, which came to be called the special or restricted relativity theory, was the entire unification of all physics excepting gravitation, that is, the unification of mechanics and electro-magnetism. This unification showed that the accepted Newtonian mechanics would have to be modified for cases in which the velocities approach those of light, for by the relativity theory the velocity of light is an upper limit for all velocities of transfer of matter or energy. Indeed the limiting nature of the velocity of light had previously been recognized on account of the fact that all classical electromagnetic theory of moving charges had shown that their inertia must increase toward infinity as they approach in velocity the velocity of light. Since all bodies have been known since Faraday's time to be full of electricity, it was well known that this kind of increase of inertia must occur for all bodies. The relativity theory showed just what modification of mechanics this increase of inertia would introduce.

Toward answering the second of our list of questions above, that as to an electrical theory of matter, developments came as follows: Many experimenters had observed that when a stream of alpha particles, which are positively charged helium atoms moving with a speed of, say, 10,000 miles a second, passes through a very thin sheet of metal most of them come straight through, but occasionally one comes through in a direction off its original course by a large angle. Rutherford in 1911 saw in this occasional large deflection of an alpha particle, by some atom it had approached or struck, a disproof of the J. J. Thomson hypothesis as to the distribution of positive charge throughout a spherical volume of approximately the full size of the atom. In that case the alpha particle would have entered the positive charge and would have gone right through without suffering any appreciable deflection, like a comet going through a great gaseous nebula. To furnish force enough to deflect the positively charged alpha particle it was clearly necessary for the positive charge in the atom to be collected in a small volume so that it could exert its full force of repulsion increasingly as the square of the distance decreased, and produce any angle of deflection even up to a complete reversal of direction of motion of the alpha particle. On the basis of this conclusion Rutherford pictured the atom as consisting of a positively charged and very concentrated nucleus with a group of electrons revolving in planetary fashion around the nucleus. The group of planetary electrons determines the outside contacts of the atom and the forces with which it is held to other atoms, and hence its chemical properties. By this time the positive charge of ionized hydrogen, now called the proton, had become recognized as the positive counterpart of the negative electron, having the same charge, but having an electromagnetic mass 1850 times as great as that of the electron, hence Rutherford conceived each atomic nucleus made of a sufficient number of positive hydrogen ions, or protons, to give the proper atomic weight, together with some negative electrons neutralizing some of the electric force of the protons. The outer electrons are sufficient in number to equal the unneutralized protons in the nucleus. In general about half of the electrons of an atom are in the nucleus and half in the outer region. The number of the outer electrons in the neutral atom is the atomic number for that atom, and the atoms of the several chemical elements have 1, 2, 3, and so on, electrons up to the full list of 92. This atomic number relationship was confirmed by the studies Moseley had made by 1913 of the frequencies of X-rays emitted by the elements, which go up by uniform steps from element to element of successively higher atomic number, thus showing a natural sequence in atomic structure corresponding to a numbering of the elements from 1 for hydrogen to 92 for uranium, with a few gaps for undiscovered elements, which missing elements were now clearly predicted. Rutherford's nuclear atom took care of atomic weights; in a general way it took care of chemical properties. The discovery of the nuclear atom must be rated as one of the greatest discoveries in atomic physics. Eddington rates it as having brought a more "arresting change" into physics than the "rearrangement of space and time by Einstein."

Planck had introduced the quantum solely to enable him to derive a formula that would give correctly the distribution of energy in the spectrum of a hot body. Poincaré and Jeans had shown that Planck's formula could not possibly be derived from the classical laws of electricity and mechanics, that the introduction of the quantum hypothesis — the radiation by packets of energy — was not in addition to, but absolutely at variance with, classical physics.

Our question number 3, the puzzling one as to the photo-electric effect, was another to find its solution, in terms of quantum theory, at the hands of Einstein. Einstein advanced boldly with quantum ideas and showed how photo-electric phenomena over the whole range of radiation from visible light to X-rays could be treated quantumwise with great satisfaction. Assume with Planck not only that energy is radiated in quantities proportional to the frequency of the waves of the radiation, but also that this energy goes out in one direction, not spreading out in all directions, as we usually think of waves doing, but proceeding as a discrete wave bundle of radiant energy — and the photo-electric effect is easily explained. The quantum of radiation can give up all its energy hv, h being the Planck constant and v being the frequency of the radiation, to an electron of the metal or other body on which it falls, hence the energy of the photo-electron is limited to that of the quantum hv, that is, the velocity of the photo-electron depends on the frequency v of the exciting radiation and not on its total intensity. This photo-electric interpretation, which was a little later applied both to the absorption of X-rays and to the converse process of the generation of X-rays, gave great concreteness to the quantum and to the idea of a particle of radiation or *photon*.

The fourth question, as to the nature of the X-rays, received a brilliant answer. Laue, Friedrich and Knipping in 1912 showed that a crystal, rock salt for example, will give diffraction patterns with X-rays analogous to those given by a fine grating for ordinary light. Everyone is familiar with how a series of regularly spaced fine lines or ridges on a surface gives a play of colors when light is reflected by the surface, that is, the light is resolved into a spectrum by the grating of lines. The regular arrangement of atoms in a crystal acts as a three dimensional grating. X-ray spectroscopy quickly became as active a branch of research as optical spectroscopy and in certain ways more productive because simpler. The wave lengths of X-rays were accurately measured and found to range from one two-hundred-and-fiftieth to one ten-thousandth the length of waves of yellow light. The quantum relation applied beautifully to both the generation of X-rays and their absorption. In the generation an electron from the cathode in the X-ray tube is given a certain energy by the voltage applied the tube. The electron (with kinetic energy $\frac{1}{2}mv^2$) strikes the target in the tube and can, if it strikes an atom just right, give rise to a quantum of X-radiation with a maximum energy $hv = \frac{1}{2}mv^2$. This quantum of radiation after going out of the tube may in turn fall on an atom of some element and eject from it an electron with a maximum energy $\frac{1}{2}mv^2 = hv$, just equal to the energy of the electron that struck the target in the tube.

The sixth of the outstanding questions, that as to the meaning and scope of the quantum hypothesis, had of course been in part answered by Einstein's application of his more radical quantum or photon theory to the photo-electric effect and its extension to X-ray phenomena. But the quantum theory was soon to be extended to a whole new domain by Bohr.

Bohr set for himself the answering of the question set down as seventh in our list: what is the cause of the peculiar relation of frequencies in the spectra of atoms? He had the Rutherford nuclear atom to start with and he had the quantum hypothesis as to radiation by discrete amounts of energy. His problem was to combine these in such a way as to account for the frequency relationships in the spectra of atoms. Even aside from accounting exactly for spectral frequencies something had to be done for the nuclear atom with respect to radiation. Planetary electrons revolving around a nucleus would by classical electrodynamics radiate electrical waves continuously. They would do this just as surely as the moving electrons constituting the varying current in a radio antenna radiate waves. In the atom the electrons would as they lost energy by this radiation have to spiral more or less slowly down toward the nucleus, and the frequency of the waves radiated would continuously increase. But atoms do not radiate in this way, the light emitted by them does not show a continuous range of frequencies but on the contrary it shows a series of frequencies each of which is one of the most sharply defined quantities in physics.

Therefore Bohr first denied that atoms can thus radiate

continuously. This he did by postulating, directly against classical theory, certain orbits in which the electrons, without radiating any energy in electromagnetic or light waves, could revolve for an indefinite time under the ordinary planetary laws as to the relations of velocity or kinetic energy, attracting force, size and shape of orbit. A planet could not take up an orbit nearer the sun unless it should lose energy. Similarly in an atom an electron cannot pass from an outer to an inner orbit and have the right velocity for the new orbit without getting rid of some of its former energy, by radiation necessarily. Here Bohr introduced the quantum theory by postulating that this energy radiated as an electron drops from one stationary orbit to another is the quantum of radiation and is therefore equal to $h\nu$. The frequency ν of vibration of the radiation is therefore equal simply to the energy difference between the orbits divided by the quantum constant h. The frequency has thus nothing to do with the period of revolution of the electron in its orbit or any other period of the electron's motion. The frequency of the emitted radiation depends only on the two orbits between which the electron makes its quantum jump. No explanation is offered of why or how the electron goes from one orbit to another.

Further Bohr discovered just how he could specify a series of stationary orbits such that the energy differences between them, therefore the frequencies of the radiation, would correspond to the known series of frequencies in the simpler atoms. This he did by applying the quantum condition again to specify that only those orbits for which a certain function of the momentum of the electron is equal to the quantum constant are stationary or permissible orbits. The Bohr theory at once accounted beautifully for the main lines in the hydrogen spectrum and actually predicted new lines that were afterwards found by Lyman. Calculations on this theory also corresponded quite well with the frequencies in the X-ray spectra of elements. The theory gave a great impetus to the study of atomic physics.

It would be hard to decide satisfactorily what decade of years in physics has been most fruitful, but a strong claim could be brought for the one we have just reviewed. In terms of the subjects of our seven questions of 1904 we may sum up the situation in 1914 as follows, noting that questions 2 to 6 had become much interrelated:

1. The question of motion through a stationary ether had been given an answer by the revelations of the relativity theory.

2. As to the electrical constitution of matter, the nuclear atom constituted of positive protons and negative electrons had become fully established.

3. The photo-electric question had been answered in terms of quanta or photons.

4. X-ray wave lengths had been measured, X-ray spectroscopy developed, and the relation of X-rays to the Bohr atomic structure made clear.

5. The meaning and scope of the quantum hypothesis, theory or method had been extended by its successful application to the photo-electric effect and to the Bohr atom.

6. The peculiar sequence of frequencies in the spectra of atoms had been with good approximation interpreted in terms of the nuclear atom plus the Bohr quantum theory.

7. The question as to the relation of gravitation to the rest of physics had received no answer. It was the only one on which great progress had not been made.

Taking a quantum jump of another decade to 1924 we may look back and see that the theory of the electrical constitution of atoms had advanced by this time to a point of entire satisfaction as to the general features of the nuclear atom theory. The arrangement of electrons in orbits about the nucleus was worked out for all the chemical elements, many elements were found to have isotopes, that is elements with atoms chemically similar, having therefore similar systems of outer electrons, but different numbers of protons in the nucleus, and therefore different atomic weights. Much had been done on molecular as distinguished from atomic theory. The disintegration of atoms of most of the lighter elements had been accomplished by bombarding them with the swiftly moving alpha particles. The paths of the alpha particle and of the parts of the atom in such a disruption had been seen and photographed by the cloud-track method. Even the building-up of an atom, as an alpha particle strikes a nitrogen atom and unites with its nucleus, was soon to be photographed.

Arthur Compton had applied the simplest principles of mechanics to the impact of photons, or light quanta, on electrons and the resultant scattering of the photons. He reasoned that since a photon, or quantum, of X-rays or light has energy and therefore mass, it must have also momentum and hence that the impact of a photon on an electron is similar to the impact of a moving billiard ball on a stationary one. The moving ball gives up to the other ball some of its kinetic energy ($\frac{1}{2}mv^2$). If the impact is a glancing one so that the moving ball is not swerved much from its course it will lose little energy, if the impact is nearly head-on so that the moving ball is much deflected from its course, or sent almost straight back, it will lose much of its energy. The loss of energy increases with the angle of deflection. Compton said, Let us consider the case of a quantum or photon of X-rays falling on an electron as just an ordinary elastic impact, the energy of the photon being hv instead of $\frac{1}{2}mv^2$. Accordingly, if we should let a beam of X-rays fall on the atoms of some substance, and should examine the deflected or scattered X-rays coming from the substance, we might expect quanta reflected by the electrons of the substance to have less energy than the quanta of the original photons, by an amount increasing as quanta are observed that are swerved from the original direction of the X-ray beam through a greater angle. The decrease in energy would have to show up as a decrease in frequency since the energy of every quantum of radiation or proton is always h times the frequency. The frequency would be less, the wave length greater. The wave length of scattered X-rays observed at an angle of 45° from the original beam should be greater than the wave length of the original beam, that observed at an angle of 90° should be longer yet.

This Compton and others verified by experiment, and the verification of the prediction of the simple theory, built on the essential similarity of a proton-electron impact to the impact of two elastic particles, gave further strong support to the conclusion that quanta of radiation or photons are very much like small particles, discrete and localized very closely in space. Of course the photo-electric effect and the Compton effect were now no longer mysteries in themselves, but only a part of the whole quantum puzzle in its antithesis to classical theory. Experimentally the Planck constant h, and the quantum relationship, cropped up in every direction in which atomic phenomena were experimentally investigated, but in making a theory the quantum discontinuity simply would not fuse with classical theory, in which all physical quantities were supposed to vary only in a continuous manner in time and space. It had come to be deeply felt that some new underlying foundation, some new approach, was demanded, that would reconcile the quantum theory necessary for atomic phenomena, and the classical theory applicable to large aggregations of atoms or quanta, either by including them both or by finding something more fundamental than either.

As to spectra, Bohr's atomic scheme of orbits or energy levels carried through with the guidance of his "correspondence principle" namely, that when large quantum numbers are dealt with the quantum results must approach the expressions of classical theory — was seen definitely to be failing to account for facts, since certain lines in the spectra of atoms, even of the comparatively simple helium atom, could not be fitted at all into the Bohr theory.

A more definite guide, as to what radiation a Bohr atom will give, than the correspondence principle had been discovered by Pauli, namely, that no two electrons in an atom can have the same orbit or, more generally, the same set of four quantum numbers, the condition of any one electron in an atom requiring four quantum numbers for its exact specification. But Pauli's exclusion principle was only empirically enlightening. Its fundamental significance could not be uncovered.

As to gravitation, Einstein had brought out in 1916 a marvellous scheme whereby universal gravitation is brought into relation with the rest of physics. The special relativity theory had equipped him with the idea that physical laws ought to be statable in forms independent of the particular system of coördinates or frame of reference used, somewhat as the length of a stick is invariant as properly measured in any three dimensional space frame of reference — $L^2 = x^2 + y^2 + z^2$. Since gravitation affects all mass alike, Einstein postulated that gravitation was not so much a property of mass as of the time-space frame of reference in which physical phenomena are viewed. He succeeded in showing that a certain relationship between time and space coördinates, which could be called a curvature of the four dimensional space-time manifold, would correspond in its effect on the free motion of bodies to the effect of a gravitational field. In short, a moving free body always moves in the straightest possible line, but the space projection of the straightest possible line in space-time near a large mass is a curve, say a planetary orbit, because the space-time itself is curved, just as in the case of the straightest possible line drawn on a sphere, its projection on a two dimensional plane will be a curve. In the space-time

manifold, a planet revolving around the sun is represented
by a helix with its axis in the time direction, a helix very much
elongated in the time direction, so that a small portion of it
is pretty straight, but the projection of the turns of the helix
on the orbital plane of the two space dimensions gives the curve
of the orbit repeated over and over. This generalized relativity
theory not only accounted for gravitation in a general space-
time scheme, but it accomplished formulations of physical laws
of very great generality, and opened large fields of speculation
as to the cosmical meaning of curved time-space.

Thus by 1924 two great divisions of physics — electricity
and mechanics, which had chiefly to do with particles, whether
electrons, protons, atoms or mass particles, had by the Einstein relativity theory and the Rutherford nuclear atom theory
been completely fused. The relativity theory did away with
the fashion of thinking of an ether as the seat of all electrical
forces and actions while thinking of ordinary mechanical forces
and phenomena as complete in themselves, needing no ether.
The Rutherford atom dispensed entirely with any idea of electric charge residing on, or being carried by "gross" matter.
Electric charge is matter itself. X-rays, photo-electric effects,
spectral series and radiation in general yielded to quantum interpretation. By the generalized relativity theory gravitation
had become interpretable in terms of the special nature of the
space-time framework in which the rest of physics is staged.
A high degree of fundamental unity and simplicity had been
attained.

The fundamental questions in physics had been reduced in
number, in that they could no longer be thought of separately
to anything like the extent possible in 1904. But the questions
in their reduced form were none the less difficult for having
been traced and uncovered to a point further back.

There remained unresolved the prime anthithesis between
the discontinuous quantum processes that include all small scale

or atomic radiation or interchanges of energy and the continuous or classical physics that serves where there is no radiation and in general for large scale phenomena. That the classical laws arise somehow statistically from the quantum laws for atoms — as the laws of the steady pressure of a gas arise as a statistical or average result from the multiplicity of impacts of atoms — was thought to be the case, but the nature of the transition was far from clear. The quantum theory of radiant energy had led more and more to viewing all radiation as consisting of unidirectional missiles of energy in wave form, now called photons, corresponding in dimension to our notion of a small particle, but traveling always with the speed of light, and with an energy proportional to the frequency of the wave motion associated with the proton. While the most important feature of the photon is its frequency, the number of vibrations per second, it does not spread out widely like ordinary waves on water or sound waves, it sticks together, has momentum, and exhibits the discreteness and definite localization of a particle. It is both wave and corpuscle. Strangely enough an electron can divide it and according to the Compton effect can reduce its energy, and therefore frequency, by an amount depending upon whether it makes a more or less glancing impact with the electron. The converse is not true, the photon can not split up an electron, it can only change its energy or velocity.

It was in 1924 that new light began to come from several directions on the fundamental problem of fitting together the quantum ideas and the classical physics and of finding concepts underlying both. The developments since that time constitute the new quantum theory, or quantum mechanics. In 1924 L. de Broglie published a paper in which he suggested that the mechanics of particles can be expressed in such a way as to be similar to the description of phenomena that appear in the propagation of a wave group, on water for example. The paper attracted interest but no general use was made of the idea immediately.

In the meanwhile something else developed. For some years, particularly since Einstein examined the question of simultaneity and the nature of measurable time, physicists had more and more realized that quantities have significance in physics only in so far as they may in some specific way be measured, that is, be related to recognizable and reproducible standards. This idea has been most fully developed by Professor Bridgman in his book *The Logic of Modern Physics*. In 1925 Heisenberg applied this principle to atomic phenomena. He reasoned that we do not actually have any measurement of the positions or velocities of electrons or protons in an atom. What we get from atoms is radiation of observable frequency, polarization, intensity, and phase. He therefore made no use of atomic structure as determining interchange of energy between atoms, electrons or protons, but set down quantities compounded of the observable variables and attempted to describe the experimentally observed relations betwen sets of such quantities. Such sets of quantities are what are called *matrices* by mathematicians. The formal laws for their combination are not those of ordinary algebra, but a special type of algebra. For example, if P and Q are matrices, PQ is not equal to QP. The matrix treatment worked out very successfully, nothing was missed by giving up the classical model, because the matrix method included all that is actually measurable. The physical significance of the matrix mathematics is definite enough but it appeared in an unusual form. Hence it was with much satisfaction to physicists that there appeared in 1925 a formulation by Schrödinger, using differential equations of the common algebraic kind, of a treatment of atomic phenomena from the standpoint of the analogy suggested by de Broglie, as to particles being similar to wave groups. The Schrödinger formulation is called wave mechanics and is applicable with great success to computing electronic, atomic, and molecular motions and radiations.

Very gratifying to the proponents of both, it turns out that the Schrödinger wave mechanics is fundamentally the same as the Heisenberg matrix mechanics as regards their physical significance. They are only different formulations of the same relationships.

But this was theory. Did experiment in this field bring out any new facts? It did most strikingly. Davisson and Germer in 1927 published results showing that a beam of electrons, traveling with not too high a speed, is diffracted by the atomic lattice of a crystal in just the same way that X-rays are diffracted. Instead of being scattered at random the electrons are reflected back at certain definite angles. No stream of particles could be expected to show this: diffraction is essentially a wave phenomenon. Electrons must have the properties of waves just as photons have the properties of particles. This has been fully and beautifully confirmed by other experiments, and for protons and atoms as well as for electrons.

This essential dualism in the behaviour of both radiation (photons) and matter (electrons and positive nuclei) is fundamental in the new quantum theory. On the one hand both radiation and matter appear as discrete particles localized in space-time, and interacting in accordance with the ordinary laws of the conservation of momentum and the conservation of energy; on the other hand both radiation and matter behave as waves which are not wholly localized but need infinite regions of time and space for their definition. These two properties are complementary rather than contradictory, since they appear in different types of experiments. In all experiments with radiation in large amounts the wave properties are preëminent and all results are to be accurately described in terms of waves; in experiments with matter in large amounts (large numbers of protons and electrons) the particle properties of localized energy and momentum predominate and there are no phenomena to be described in terms of waves. Conversely, in experiments with small amounts of radiation (single photons) the particle or corpuscular properties of the radiation become very prominent; in experiments with small amounts of matter (single electrons, protons or atoms) wave properties appear very clearly.

Of deep significance and wide implication is the recognition in the new quantum mechanics of a very definite limitation to the precision and completeness with which it is possible to think of describing the motions of electrons and protons. The recognition of this limitation does not arise from a metaphysical hypothesis as to electrons, photons and photons being the ultimate units of matter and radiation, but arises from a consideration of very obvious and inescapable experimental limitations in making any observations of the position and velocity of a single electron, for example. This uncertainty principle, or principle of indetermination, was clearly enunciated by Heisenberg in 1927. The reasoning is as follows: The only conceivable kind of probe or pointer that is fine enough to use in locating accurately an electron is a beam of light. With ordinary light and a microscope the limit of smallness of things that can be seen is soon reached, with light of shorter wave length smaller objects can be seen. Conceive of some microscope that would work with the shortest conceivable waves of radiation, super X-rays we might call them. With this we can conceive the position of the electron determinable with unlimited precision. But each single photon of this high-frequency radiation would contain a large energy by the $h\nu$ rule, and therefore would upon impact with the electron we are trying to locate give it a great kick in some direction or other, with the result that by the very act of observation, the velocity of the electron would suddenly be changed by an unpredictable amount and any simultaneous accurate measurement of the velocity would be inconceivable. On the other hand, by using light of long enough wave length, measurements could obviously be made to determine the velocity of an electron accurately without appreciably disturbing that velocity, but in this case the observations as to its position at any moment would be very hazy. Both objects cannot be attained at once; if we require the position very accurately, the velocity measurement is correspondingly inaccurate, and conversely. Here the Planck constant h crops up again, for it can be shown that the uncertainty in position multiplied by the uncertainty in velocity, or rather momentum, cannot be less than the quantum constant h. Of course this uncertainty is small and beyond the range of ordinary measurements (h is 6.55×10^{-27} erg-second) but it is a perfectly finite uncertainty.

The limit of objectivity of matter is thus reached. The very act of observation changes the external world in a way that cannot be calculated. Of course nothing is lost by giving up the fiction of our being able to specify, in conception at least, both exact position and exact velocity for a particle. We never had the ability so to specify and never can have it unless we are given apparatus and senses beyond the physical. It is agreed that the recognition of the uncertainty principle, or the principle of indetermination, constitutes an advance in physics of not less significance than the relativity theory.

A far reaching implication of the uncertainty principle is that the law of causality fails, at least if we must describe phenomena in terms of space and time. The principle of causality applied to a single electron, for example, requires that the future position and velocity of the electron shall be absolutely determined by (among other things) its present position and velocity. But if the determination of its present position and velocity beyond a certain degree of definiteness is in the very nature of things meaningless, then in any exact sense the sequence of cause and effect in this case becomes meaningless.

If strict causality is meaningless in this simple case it is in all atomic phenomena and finally in all physical phenomena. For atoms position and velocity can be specified only with a certain probability, hence a probability theory plays a large part in the new quantum theory.

As a statistical matter probability was the basis of the classical molecular theory of heat, but in that theory probability entered as a convenience. It was sought to express those results that would be most probable, without having to specify the motion of each molecule, even if it could be found and specified exactly. The new application of probability is not statistical but means that the most elementary of phenomena is affected by an irresolvable uncertainty or chance.

We have reviewed some of the amazing developments of the past quarter century; even a bare mention of others of high importance we have had to omit. A vast store of experimental facts and technique has been gathered that cannot be recounted. A few shining names have been mentioned, many others might justly have been mentioned in this company. If we may stretch our period backward a little to include Planck's inception of the quantum theory in 1900, we may safely say that no similar period in physics excels this in experimental and theoretical advances. As for fundamental influence on practical affairs we may have to place ahead of it the period of about three hundred years ago when Galileo and Newton were formulating mechanics, and the period of nearly a hundred years ago when the conservation of energy was becoming recognized and when Faraday was laying the foundation for a new world of electrical energy.

Progress is marked by questions that are raised as well as by questions that are answered. The unanswered questions are the difficult ones to ask. We venture to suggest a few from among those now being asked.

What constitutes the difference between negative electricity and positive electricity?

How does the nucleus of any atom hold together?

What is back of Pauli's principle that an atom cannot hold two electrons with the same set of quantum numbers?

How far from the foundation of the determinism of classical physics will the Heisenberg uncertainty relations lead us?

How far may the methods of the generalized relativity theory be carried with respect to relating electromagnetic fields to properties of space-time as Einstein has done for gravitation?

Are we in a closed universe, and if so, of what type is it?

Are protons or electrons in the stars or elsewhere in the universe being converted wholly into radiant energy, and does the converse process also take place?

Guided by the principle that in physics regard need be given only to physical quantities, those that can be compared and measured by definitely statable and reproducible methods, the progress of physics will go on in its analysis of the world of things, and along with the analysis into finer and finer elements there is and must be constant effort given to the synthesis of understanding and theory, up from electrons, protons and photons to atoms, molecules, crystals and all the varied aggregations of the material world.

ENGINEERING

William Barclay Parsons

Progress in engineering during the past twenty-five years has been more notable both in a general advance along the whole front and in striking ahievements in new fields than during any other period of equal length. Perhaps the only period that might claim to vie with it in original productivity is that quarter century which ended one hundred years ago, when the foundations for modern engineering were laid, the steamboat, the locomotive and the steam motor car were invented and the use of machinery to supplant manual labor was begun. In fact, the year 1829 was a memorable one in engineering annals, for in that year the celebrated contest between the locomotives "Novelty," built by Braithwaite and Ericsson, and "Rocket," the product of Stephenson & Co., took place at Rainhill in England, when the feasibility and power of the steam locomotive were proved beyond doubt and a new era in transportation was begun. In that same year Horatio Allen, a graduate of Columbia, drove the first locomotive, the "Stourbridge Lion," to be operated in America; and as a result of the Rainhill experiments the diretors of the Baltimore and Ohio, then being constructed, decided to use steam as the motive power instead of horses as at first contemplated.

The two periods of twenty-five years that ended in 1829 and 1929 are in striking political and economic, as well as in mechanical, parallelism. In both periods occurred great wars that shook the social structure of the world to its very foundations. It is not an excessive statement that the recovery of Europe from the devastation and losses caused by the Napoleonic wars was due in no small measure to the work of the engineer, through creating new channels of industry and trade and furnishing the means whereby man's labor became more efficient. To the genius and energy of Stephenson, Fulton, Watt, Telford, Arkwright, Brunel, Rennie and their contemporaries, as much as to the planning and scheming of diplomats and statesmen, is due the fact that the great nations were able to recoup their losses, discharge their debts and start on the great progressive development of the nineteenth century.

In like manner the year 1929 sees the whole world, this time not only Europe but America, Africa, Asia and the Antipodes again the victim of a general war. Young men who should now be in the flower of manhood have, to the awful extent of tens of millions, been killed or incapacitated as industrial producing units. National debts amounting to figures previously unthinkable have been incurred, and individual losses suffered of which no accounting will ever be possible. Old national boundaries have been obliterated, and governments, supposedly all-powerful to resist aggression, have been overthrown. We are still in the throes of readjustment after the catastrophe, and still too close to the events to be able to measure what progress has already been made toward a new order. But we think we can say, and that is all the man of science ever dares venture of the unknown, that if world stability and world peace are again to be established on a sound basis, it will be largely through the work of the engineer devising new means of production to counterbalance the human loss in the war, creating new economies whereby the appalling debts can be discharged, and with science that recognizes no boundaries and no differences in races or people, to weld the nations of the world in closer harmony through new industries and new commerce.

If the man of the street were asked to name the great advances made in engineering during recent years he would probably quote those constructions that by their increase in size catch the eye and so impress themselves upon the mind of the observer, and then point to the taller buildings, more powerful locomotives or larger steamships as examples. But mere bigness, either in size or cost, does not necessarily in itself indicate progress. The investigator is not satisfied as the man in the street might be with an ocular demonstration; he demands to know the cause and actuating reason, and when he pushes his inquiries into these factors, he discovers the element that has pervaded every field of engineering work during the past twenty-five years, which distinguishes it from every other like period and which marks the great outstanding achievement. That element is the closer connection between engineering and science.

The previous generation recalls with amusement, and a future generation will learn of it with astonishment, the controversy that a few years ago was waged with so much asperity and warmth over the broad merits of the practical man as compared with the narrowing limitations of the education of the theoretical man, that is, one versed in the fundamental principles of his art. No longer is progress looked for in the ingenious and estimable mechanic with his monkey wrench, but in the trained man of science. Science has ceased to be regarded as something for metaphysicians and higher mathematicians to wrangle over, and from it to draw finespun theories that are interesting to the inventors but which have no real bearing on everyday affairs of life. Today science is recognized as having a most intimate and important bearing on all that we do, and he who would apply science to the actual needs of man watches with intense interest the researches of the scholar, even those of the astronomer as he studies what is taking place on far-off stars whose distance is measured in thousands and even millions of light years, to seize on some new and unsuspected law of nature that may find application in our engineering activities on the planet Earth.

That is the dominating accomplishment of the past twenty-five years, not that the movement began within that period, but that it then reached unquestioned recognition.

Today the engineer who would become prominent in his profession must know not only what is generally accepted as coming under the designation of engineering but also be a physicist, chemist and metallurgist, and have an understanding of pure science, so as to be prepared to solve his problems, or to have them solved, in the laboratory as well as in the computing room or on the drawing board.

Twenty-five years ago a few large industrial plants maintained laboratories in which their products might be analyzed and new developments studied. In 1929 there is not a single such plant that would be progressive but that employs a staff of men, who, a few years ago, would have been contemptuously described by practical men of business as theorists and, therefore, of little use in actual affairs.

As an example of the scale on which such laboratories exist, the American Telephone and Telegraph Company maintains in the city of New York a research organization consisting of more than two thousand persons and at an annual cost of $15,000,000 in which every theory of telephonic communication is studied and restudied, and every part of the apparatus subjected to experimental investigation with the hope of improving its quality. In this and similar engineering laboratories there is nothing too small or too large, nothing too intricate or too simple to be subjected to intensive investigation if only there be promise, hope or even possibility that by such research there may be found the germ of a thought that with fostering care can be developed to find a useful application.

A century ago, Thomas Telford gave a definition of engineering as being "The Art of directing the Great Sources of Power in Nature for the use and convenience of mankind."

That definition has not been improved, although it is only now through the aid of pure science that its full meaning is being brought out.

When modern bigness is analyzed in terms of the application of science the real truth of the accomplishment becomes clear. Modern engineering structures are remarkable not because they are greatly increased in size but because in their design empiricalness has given place to rationalness, and their functions and composition are in accordance with the outstanding beauties of science. This is particularly the case when those types of construction are considered that may be classed as dynamic as opposed to static, namely, those structures whose parts are in motion and which depend on or generate action; though the field of static engineering is not without its monuments that are not yet twenty-five years old, as for example the Panama Canal.

To recite the outstanding accomplishments since 1904 would weary you on account of its length, so a few instances will be selected here and there that will serve to illustrate the type of progress that so distinguishes the period.

The application of scientific methods has recently evolved many structures that no matter how much they may resemble in form and purpose their prototypes, nevertheless, are really new creations. Thus the huge latest type of locomotive engine weighing 715,000 pounds is possible, not alone because of the experience gained from operating locomotives for more than one hundred years, but because within twenty-five years the working steam pressure has been raised and super-heating and feed-water heating perfected, which have so reduced the consumption of fuel and water as to enable the carrying of power producing supplies within economical limits. Improvement in the quality of metals has rendered possible the designing and proportioning of the parts to withstand with certainty the increased stresses. Stokers and other mechanical devices have been introduced which make possible the operation of these huge units of power over long distances.

Another instance of virtual creation through increase in size, though retaining the original form, is the electrical generator now driven almost entirely by steam turbines to the practical extinction of the reciprocating engine. In 1904 the largest generator was of 5,000 KW. Today there is in existence a single set developing 280,000 HP. The peripheral speed of generators has been increased to 25,000 feet per minute, and by the use of mica insulation on the armature and asbestos on the fields and a method of closed circuit ventilation, there results a machine efficiency approaching 98 per cent, or practical perfection. By raising steam pressure to 1,200 lbs. and superheat to 725°, and using high vacuum condensers, a kilowatt hour is obtained from 14,000 BTU, a heat efficiency of 24 per cent. This last figure is encouraging, being about twice what was realizable a few years ago, but still very wasteful when it is seen to mean that 76 per cent of the power in the fuel is lost.

Typical of the dependence of static engineering structures upon dynamic improvements is the skyscraper, which, however imposing outwardly with its skeleton frame and deep foundations, is possible not by solving those problems but by that of vertical transportaiton.

Twice since 1904 the accepted method of moving elevators has been wholly discarded until there has been evolved a machine whose speed is increased from 300 feet per minute to a possible 1,500 feet. Before this latter rate is reached an elevator is far beyond human capability to operate, so that the engineer has been obliged to replace human agency by mechanical controls. Speed of elevation is now limited not by mechanical considerations but by the power of the human body to adjust itself to a rapid variation in barometric pressure.

Since the introduction of steam to transportation there has been no engineering contribution with like overturning effect on our economic life as the internal combustion engine, reaching into nearly every phase of our existence. It has placed in the hands of the country dweller means of rapidly reaching the cities and market places, tilling his farm and transporting his crops. To the city dweller it has horribly and expensively complicated his traffic problems, but it has also given him the means to go afield. In 1829 the steam locomotive threatened destruction to all forms of highway traffic, while in 1929 through the whirligig of progress the internal combustion engine more seriously threatens retaliation.

Like the locomotive the motor vehicle can boast of an existence for more than one hundred years, since carriages were propelled by steam on the common roads in England in 1824. But a suitable engine was lacking. In the last quarter of the nineteenth century the internal combustion engine was devised but its application lagged until about 1900 when the practicability of replacing horses with an engine-drawn vehicle was recognized. Early progress was slow, for even in 1904 the total output of such vehicles in the United States was less than 14,000. The great success and development that has followed is, therefore, wholly a matter of the past quarter century, during which time the internal combustion engine has found application not only on land but as the means of driving ships of the largest size, as a convenient auxiliary to sail power with promise to eliminate it entirely, and as the essential feature of the airplane and submarine that has made them both feasible.

In engineering, results flow one from another, frequently unexpectedly and nearly always unintentionally. The advent of the motor car with its soft pneumatic tires was hailed as the end of road destruction that had been previously caused by the pounding of iron shod wheels. But alas for prophecy, it soon became evident that the air-cushioned tire was far more destructive than the rigid iron one, because as the power was transmitted through the tire the inevitably small but constant slip, aided somewhat by a sucking action, soon destroyed the best macadam surface. The concrete road, now adopted universally, was the engineer's answer and solution, the only radical contribution to road construction since Roman days, except that of MacAdam in 1815, a Scotch engineer but whilom resident of New York.

The internal combustion engine has, through the rapid increase in numbers of vehicles, seriously complicated the problem of urban transportation. This problem has to some extent been relieved by the improvement in underground transportation, as exemplified by the opening of the New York subway in 1904, the development of the admirable system in Paris and the electrification of the underground lines in London. The New York system extended in cost to $1,000,000,000, coupled with the pre-existing elevated structures, now carries annually more passengers than are carried on all the steam railways of both the American continents.

The engineer, however, is both a creator and wrecker, and in making new, frequently destroys great values. Already there is a cry for the removal of the elevated structures whose usefulness has been so eclipsed by other means of travel that the public sees in them only their columns as an obstruction to surface traffic, and the whole structure, once the pride of New York, a burden on abutting property. As first the cable railways spelled the end of horse-drawn cars, so the electric trolley supplanted the cables; now in the cycle of progress, the motor car and the motor omnibus bid fair to dim the trolley cars into things of memory, a victory to remain only until the engineer in his ceaseless and insatiable thirst for something different shall have devised a new motor, or new means of transport that shall displace the motor car and perhaps the subway.

In 1904 the largest steamer was of 23,876 tons with 15,000 HP in her engines. In 1929 vessels 1,000 feet long, of more than 60,000 tons have been laid down. The United States Navy airplane carriers have turbine-driven electric generators furnishing 180,000 HP capable of developing a speed of 34 knots. Submarines have crossed the Atlantic under their own power and are now built of more than 3,000 tons displacement, and carry an armament of heavy guns as well as torpedoes.

The air, as well as land and sea, has also been a medium for achievement and perhaps more spectacular than either of the last two. Both the telephone and electric light are old, that is, old as recent progress in science is measured, but so newly old that there is a generation still in the prime of life that recalls the inception of both, though their radical developments are of very recent origin. Within fifteen years the tungsten filament lamp has been produced with an economy in illuminating power of four times that of the old carbon lamp, so that it has entirely displaced the carbon and metallized filament lamps and, for all practical purposes, the arc light. It is estimated that $600,000,000 are expended in light annually in the United States. Were it not for the lessened amount of power required and the diminished cost in lamps themselves, the same amount of lighting would cost on the old standards more than $3,000,000,000, which means that the engineer has presented free to the American public nearly $2,500,000,000 worth of light annually.

But even more sweeping has been the progress in the transmission of sound both by and without a wire. As a measure of growth the number of Bell telephones in the United States in 1904 was 1,800,000; in 1929 more than 15,000,000, while the miles of circuits have grown from 4,600,000 to 68,000,-000.

As an instance of the rapidity with which the development has been made, the speaker recalls that thirty years ago in San

Francisco he asked an eminent Columbia professor how soon telephoning from coast to coast would be possible. The answer was a convincing explanation of the electrical complications that would render it forever impossible. But at that very time Professor Pupin was at work developing along purely theoretical lines his loading coils whereby these very insurmountable difficulties were to be overcome. Telephony was established commercially between New York and San Francisco in 1915, and rapidly thereafter between all points in the United States, though in Europe the principal installations have been put in operation during the past five years. By a combination of land lines and radio jumps over water, conversation has lately been maintained between New York and Melbourne. Telephone cables will presently be laid across the Atlantic so that every telephone subscriber in America will be able to secure a connection with every subscriber in Europe with the same ease that he can between any two cities in the United States.

Another achievement, but ten years old, is the carrier telephone and telegraph system whereby three telephone conversations and several telegraph messages can be sent simultaneously over one pair of wires. These outstanding accomplishments have been made by American telephone engineers studying and applying the theory of wave transmission.

Concurrently with wired development has come that of wireless. First proposed by Morse, advanced as a theory by Clerk Maxwell in 1865, and developed through experiments by Heinrich Hertz in 1888, it was not until 1901 that Marconi established long distance communication between England and Newfoundland. As with the sister art of telephony, the radical steps in all forms of wireless transmission are the results of scientific work during the past fifteen years. Today any part of the world's surface can be put in instant communication with any other, ships with other ships or shore stations, and a moving train with other moving trains, all without any physical connection other than the air, while world broadcasting can be caught by simple machines costing but a few dollars. Then for both systems of transmission there is rapidly being perfected television and the transference of pictures.

Automatic tools that can make articles of any shape or nature from the humble carpet tack to an automobile car body have had a multitude of applications for many years. Of late there have appeared machines that take the place of the intellect, instead of the hands, of man. As illustrations of such machines there is the gyro-compass, based on the principle of the gyroscope, that always points due North and is free of all the irregularities and variations of a magnetic compass. This gyro-compass can be attached to the steering gear of a vessel and guide it unerringly on any stated course, no matter how the wind or sea may change in direction or intensity. Other similar machines are: the one that computes the tidal range at any point for any desired date; the automatic telephone exchange that not only does away with human operators at the central office, but is able to care for all irregularities in service and even the mistakes of subscribers; and various forms of heat and electrical controls. The work of these devices is not that of the ordinary automatic tool repeating the one and same process indefinitely, but one that varies from moment to moment with conditions constantly changing, and their work is done with greater certainty of accuracy and dispatch than a human operator could possibly guarantee. As indicating how far machine devices can be carried, a factoring or "congruence machine" recently was perfected to find the factors of large numbers. As an example of its work the factors of the number 9,999,000,099,990,001 were required. After two hours of work the machine gave the answer 1,676,321 x 5,964,848,081.

Of all the fields of engineering it is perhaps aviation that most fires the imagination, the whole of whose extraordinary development has been created during the past twenty-five years, because it was only in 1903 that man put his foot on the first rung of the ladder, though he had not begun to climb.

Since early times man has had the ambition to wing his way through the air with the birds. Early in the sixteenth century that versatile engineering genius, Leonardo da Vinci, investigated the possibility of flying and made designs for wings to be attached to the body and operated by the arms and legs, and pictures published during that century of both gliders and balloons are extant, though neither type of machine was actually made. Montgolfier made the first ascent at Versailles in 1785 in a balloon supported by hot air. In this condition the art languished for a century except for an effort by Giffard who designed a sausage-shaped dirigible balloon in 1852 propelled by a steam engine. But as Giffard's balloon could not advance against a wind blowing as gently as seven miles per hour, it was but a gesture.

During the last quarter of the nineteenth century the whole subject was taken up seriously as to machines both heavier and lighter than air. But the former experiments were confined to gliders through lack of a suitable propelling engine. Among those adventures should be named Pilcher, Chanute and Lilienthal, the last sacrificing his life in his experiments. Simultaneously Santos Dumont was developing a lighter-than-air machine and in 1898 was awarded a prize for making the first directed flight.

At the same time two men were quietly at work studying the problems of aeronautics at the core, Langley an American, and Zeppelin a German. The story of Langley is deeply pathetic. Seeing the possibility offered by the newly developed internal combustion engine, he boldly struck out to construct an aeroplane that of its own power could carry a man aloft. Langley built a plane, and in 1903 ventured flight. To get initial motion, he relied on a launching way. On the eventful day some-

thing failed in his incline and the plane, instead of gaining the
necessary momentum, hesitated, staggered and plunged like a
wounded bird into the Potomac River. Langley, overcome by
grief at his supposed failure, died soon afterward not knowing that his plane would rise as he had intended, a fact later
demonstrated with the same machine.

In December of the same year another American, Wilbur
Wright, made an actual flight for 852 feet, recording for the
first time that man had risen into the air by means of an engine. This flight at Kitty Hawk passed almost unnoticed; in
fact, the Wright brothers, who had done it behind an enclos-
ure, made no great claims, not being as yet satisfied. On
October 5, 1905, or twenty-four years ago, the Wrights made
a sustained flight, this time covering 24¼ miles in 38 minutes,
and aviation became an actuality.

From that beginning progress was rapid and unchecked. In
1906 Santos Dumont, believing that the heavier-than-air
planes offered better promise than a balloon, gave the first
public exhibition. These dates are interesting as showing in
what a short space of time this aeronautical revolution has
been accomplished. In 1908 Glenn Curtis, another American,
won the Bennett prize at Rheims with the unheard of speed
of 20 kilometers in less than 16 minutes. Curtis brought out
the hydroplane and was the first man to take off from and
alight on water, as he had been the first to leave the ground
on a wheel machine, all previous starts having been made by
the aid of a catapult. Of the pioneers abroad in this development, mention should be made of Bleriot, Latham and Far-
man.

While the problem of the heavier-than-air machines was being worked out, the lighter-than-air type was receiving no less
attention. Zeppelin built the first rigid dirigible in 1900, but
it was only an experiment. He made his real beginning in
1905. In 1908 he made the first long flight, 260 miles in 9

hours. In 1910 there was the first commercial flight, and in 1911 the first regular service was established.

Dirigibles have not only crossed the Atlantic successfully and in both directions, but the latest Zeppelin has made the circuit of the earth. In England there has just been completed an airship designed to carry 100 passengers with every convenience and comfort. Airplanes have also crossed the Atlantic, and in races have attained a speed of 357 miles per hour. An amphibian machine was recently tested that rose with 169 passengers. The natural corollary of this advance is the establishment of regular routes for passengers, mail and express matter. Such routes cover Europe with a network, and the same is rapidly becoming true in the United States, in fact, there being now in this country 29,227 miles of commercial air routes. This is the result after only three years of development, whereas it was thirty years after the first railway was opened in the United States before there was an equal number of miles of railway routes.

Many other illustrations can be noted showing how progress has resulted solely by the application of science, but it would be but a case of piling Ossa upon Pelion.

After considering these high spots in the record of achievement during the past quarter century, the question naturally arises: What of the future? Time has been annihilated and space has been reduced to very small dimensions; air, earth and water have been conquered, and power is developed in huge units. Has the end been reached, or is it possible that there are other fields now unknown that the ingenuity of man can enter and turn to his use? This is an important question, for of all human activities engineering is the one that enters most into our lives, that gives us our means of living, and permeates every fiber of the social fabric. To this question the answer is unhesitatingly that until the well of science has been drained dry the engineer will draw from it new sources of inspiration and new thoughts for accomplishment.

That question answered, there follows a second: Along what lines will advance take in the next few years and what are the unexplored fields remaining? The response to the second question is more difficult than the first, and perhaps it would be well, as it certainly would be safer, to leave the whole matter with a calm, broad statement of confident optimism rather than to attempt the very risky venture into the prophecy of details. But certain lines of advance seem to be clearly indicated.

The steam locomotive that was deemed, and rightly so, a great achievement is doomed to go the way of the trolley car. The developments in electrical engineering during the past twenty-five years clearly point out that from present knowledge the machine to draw fast passenger and heavy freight trains is not a reciprocating engine wastefully carrying and burning its own fuel, but a rotary electric motor taking its power from a distant station. The day is rapidly coming when the traveler will no longer be annoyed by smoke, dust and much shock, and the roadbed of the railways will be relieved of the uneven pounding of occasionally unbalanced drive mechanism.

The dirigible and airplane will be brought to a state of perfection whereby they will be freed of the danger due to the instability that now attend them, and will play a great part in fast express service. The steamboat is now considered practically danger-proof as being open only to rare and unforeseenable accidents, and yet in its early days it was regarded much as the timid passenger views the airplane today. To give him confidence, early steam lines on the Hudson River advertised that passengers would be carried in barges towed by steam tugs and so be protected from the risk of boiler explosions.

Great as has been the contributions of science to engineering, only a beginning has been made. With a more intimate knowledge of the composition of matter there is opening a new field of research of extraordinary promise. Already the celestial mechanic and astronomical physicist, studying the great laboratories of nature in those far-away universes now in the process of forming, feel that there is a possible realization of the alchemists' dream of old and that elements are actually being transmuted. What do these and other similar startling observations portend? No one can answer; and yet they signify laws, actions and reactions of great force. As they come to be understood may we not believe that the scientific engineer of the future will some day turn them to the use of his fellow men?

But the outstanding consideration for speculation is: power.

The modern condition of culture, frequently and erroneously referred to as civilization, depends for its creation and maintenance on power. Almost everything that we consume is affected by power, certainly in some stage of its production or delivery. All means of transportation, of communication, of recording and disseminating knowledge, and in fact all our needs, are met by power. Our whole economic and social order of living results from the use of power, for by it man's productivity has been so much increased and at such an accelerated rate during the period under review, that his needed hours of work to provide for his maintenance are in progress of sharp reduction. Curtail the quantity of power available to operate machines and we would find ourselves drifting towards the darkness and the direful condition of the Middle Ages, and yet that is the course we are pursuing today.

Power is derived mainly from two sources, the weight of falling water and the consumption of fuel. The first is far less important than popular fancy pictures it. Were all hydro-power sources fully developed as power generators, including such great falls as Niagara and Victoria Nyanza, the existing world's demand for power would be met only in part, without any allowance for the inevitable future increase. To the consumption of fuel the world looks and must continue to look for its chief source of power supply, unless some new means of generation be applied.

The existence of fuel, coal and oil is fairly definitely known, both as to location and extent. Its quantity is absolutely limited, no more being produced by natural processes, so that when a ton of coal or a barrel of oil is burned the supply is permanently reduced. If we keep on using it as we are and at the same increasing ratio, a limit of consumption will be enforced within less than one hundred years, a short space of time in the world's history, and it will all be gone so far as a source of power is concerned, within a comparatively short period afterward. The adventures of men like Byrd may disclose unsuspected deposits in the inhospitable regions within the Arctic or Antarctic circles, but such discoveries if made, and if the deposits be so situated that they can be utilized, will but postpone for a few years more the days of reckoning.

Does this mean that our boasted mechanical culture that has done so much to alleviate the condition of mankind is doomed? Perhaps it is doomed to go as other great cultures of the past have gone, but if it does, it will not be through lack of scientific assistance to support it.

As the pressure of shortage comes to be acutely felt the engineer of the future will come to the rescue. We of this generation are indefensibly wasteful and will be terribly blamed by the generations to come for squandering the most precious of nature's gifts. In the most efficient power-generating plants, to which we point with so much pride, we are utilizing less than one-quarter of the heat units contained in the fuel, the remainder being discharged into the air or otherwise lost. The ordinary power plant is much less efficient, locomotives notoriously so. If we include domestic use of fuel we utilize probably not over one-tenth of the contained energy, the balance we throw away never to be recovered. Not a pretty picture for the man of science to contemplate, but one that by its very awful character is full of promise.

Since 1904 the output of power from central generating stations in the United States has increased more than tenfold, or from 3,000,000 KW to 32,000,000 KW, thus decreasing part of the waste of fuel through the elimination of inefficient plants. This tendency to concentration is certain to continue, and with further improvements in transmission we may look forward to the establishment of a network of transmission lines covering the country, as do telegraph wires, delivering power generated from many sources, both hydro and steam, to consumers both large and small. Such a unified system will permit the installation of large economical units which running continuously will take advantage of differences in local load factors and variations in time, and so save fuel.

To develop hydro power fully and economically, the produced energy must be stored against future demand, because the flow of streams is neither regular nor coincident with the consumption of power and much water is necessarily lost. The only means of storing power today is the battery which is both expensive and wasteful. If power could be converted into some inert form that could be transported and kept as coal, and the energy released as needed, a great advance would be made, and a very large amount of possible power, now wholly wasted, would be saved for use. This is one of the greatest single items waiting discovery.

But even with hydro power completely developed, with power stored, and the consumption of fuel raised from a maximum efficiency of 24 per cent to a mean of 98 per cent, or better, that is, to put the boiler or its equivalent on a footing with the electric generator; the limited supply of fuel in the world will still hover on the horizon as a threatening cloud, and the breaking of the storm would be only postponed, not averted. To do the latter, some new source of power must be found. Will our successors raise fuel by intensive growth, aided by irrigation, will they draw from the central heat of the earth, will they secure heat that is contained in the sun's rays, or will they find it in some undiscovered source of energy. The heat in the sun's rays that fall on the waste desert spaces is in amount sufficient to meet industrial demands, but such heat will have little practical value until some way be found to store the latent energy.

While we are thus building castles, which, however, may have much stouter substance than the proverbial ones of air, why not go one step further and carry the development to the ultimate conclusion? The supply of copper like that of fuel is limited, and like the latter must some day be conserved. Moreover, in wire transmission there is a serious loss. Can we foresee the day when power, like speech, will be broadcast, and when all wires will be eliminated, and when all the great sources of power in the world will be combined into a single generating agency, and from it distributed widely to world consumers? Then we will be able to heat, cook and light, to operate our industrial plants, and run trains, ships, airplanes and motor cars by power generated across the seas and transported by no visible means. At our present central stations no power is generated unless there be a consumer ready to take it. May it not be so with broadcasted power, the air acting in place of the land wires, and no power be actually generated and consequently lost until some consumer somewhere on land or sea or in the air opens a switch to receive it?

Is all this a dream? Certainly it is, but a dream no more unsubstantial than once were like visionary dreams of motion at three hundred miles per hour, of far-flung speech, of picture transmission through air, of man flying around the earth, or of broadcasting concerts in New York to be heard at the South

Pole. Is any feature of the dream possible in the present state of the art? Not one. Will any be realized? Who can tell.

The engineers in the nineteenth century started a movement that has been tremendously accelerated in the first quarter of the twentieth century. It cannot long continue at the present rate of acceleration, but there is ample opportunity to save, preserve it and develop it for more than one thousand years. To do this is the problem that the engineer of the future will inherit from him of today. What he will do with this heritage some of you may see. Man through science applied to engineering has, during the past quarter century, made one of the greatest intellectual achievements of all time. It is without reason or justification to believe that he has reached his limit, because we know there remain vast fields of science unexplored. We, therefore, with all our sins of ignorance and wastefulness can regard the future with calmness and assurance.

GEOLOGY

Charles P. Berkey

Nearly twenty-five years ago the late Professor James F. Kemp of Columbia, drew a picture of the development of geologic science to that time. He pointed out that this field had been developing as a distinct branch of natural science for only a little more than a hundred years. This is rather astonishing considering the fact that the raw materials of the science were always within easy reach for observation and actual handling, and because many of the fundamental principles now seem to be so simple. It is true that here and there an individual in earlier times did see the significance of certain special features or phenomena, but the fundamental things were not understood, and their historical aspect was wholly unappreciated. It has been pointed out by others that the reason for such slow development lay chiefly in the fact that the science of geology depends to a large degree on the principles of physics and chemistry, and consequently it was not until those basic sciences were well established that the foundations could be laid for a great deal of modern geology. Until such understanding was reached, the processes that operated in the earth, and the products that were made, had no better explanation than that they came to be so by chance, or that they came from, and were controlled by, the supernatural.

Geology continues to benefit from the progress made by the other sciences. In so far as their progress establishes a better understanding of the nature of earth materials and of the forces and processes by which changes in them take place, geology also is enriched. In so far as astronomy may have reached a better knowledge of the constitution, behavior and life history of the heavenly bodies, that science also throws light on the origin and early stages of the earth. Such contributions are fundamental not only in their own fields, but also in the field of geology, because physical matter is the stuff with which the geologist has to work. The earth is to him a great laboratory in which there is much apparent confusion to be sure, but the laws governing matter apply as rigidly there as they do in the laboratories of a scientific research establishment, and have been operating much longer. We now believe that there are no happenings whatever in the making of the whole complex exhibit of minerals, ores, rocks, geologic formations and even the landscapes of the surface and the hidden structures of the depths of the earth, that do not conform in every minutest detail to the requirements of these laws. It was not until some such conception of the earth and its making had been grasped that the features and phenomena dealt with in the field of geology began to take on meanings that have made the science of geology what it is today.

It is quite true that the earlier geologists were not as fully convinced of the orderliness of all process, and the inevitableness of the results, as are geologists of the present day. Greater confidence in this generalization has come with more extended observation and experience. For a very long time after some of the fundamental principles were well established, it was still believed by a large proportion of the geologists of the world that occasional cataclysmic world-wide revolutions upset the whole program of orderly processes and events, and that the earth had to start making all over again. It is now fully accepted that every structure and form, every condition and quality, every change and happening can be accounted for by the operation of normal processes, and the work of natural agents. Therefore they can be interpreted in terms of origin and history.

As a matter of fact, the science of geology had reached such convictions more than a quarter of a century ago. The principal agents and forces responsible for the building of the structure of the earth as it is were known. The major steps that have marked the development from the beginning to the present time had been mapped out and have not been greatly changed. All supernatural and abnormal elements, whether agents or forces or processes, were finally rejected. There was nothing left of magic or the supernatural, unless it be in the origin of matter itself, out of which the earth was made, and the origin of life, both of which to this day are as mystifying as they were when it was written that "in the beginning the earth was without form and void."

In the beginning of the nineteenth century, a student or investigator of any kind of earth lore was regarded as a geologist, but within the century specialization had reached the stage where it was practicable to make subdivision into branches occasionally referred to as sciences themselves. Investigators devoting themselves to special fields came to be distinguished by such terms as physiographer, paleontologist, petrographer, mineralogist or stratigrapher. By 1900, therefore, it had already come about that geologists were of different kinds, and it was possible then as it is now for one to specialize too narrowly to appreciate fully this very comprehensive science which purports to be the study of the earth and its history.

The beginning of a new century made no change whatever in the trends of that time. Specialization has continued, emphasizing still more limited fields. A paleontologist may now be a specialist within his own branch. He may be a micropaleontologist or an invertebrate paleontologist or a vertebrate paleontologist, and as such have little to do with the other branches of the general subject or even with the other fields of his own branch. A similar tendency, though not in all cases on such a scale, may be seen in other branches of the science.

Occasionally an entirely new branch has been established as interest and activity centered about some new method or new resources or demand. Thus it happens that within the last few years great interest has been attracted to geophysics, concerned with the subterranean condition and structure of the earth. Such determinations as are now made were considered quite beyond reach a quarter of a century ago. Data are accepted now as reliable that would have been regarded at that time as the claims of an impostor.

Applied geophysics has come as an entirely new subject, emphasized because of the information it is able to give about the underground. In addition, one of the older lines of investigation, that covering earthquake phenomena, has risen to great prominence. The phenomena of earthquakes, apparently the most erratic of all earth phenomena, have lost the glamor that belonged to them when they were regarded as visitations of the divine wrath, and have descended to the common level of other earth happenings. Even the earthquake wave is being subjected to observations, measurement, classification and interpretation. Out of these studies has grown the science of seismology; and, by means of its methods and observations, more light has been thrown on the structure and condition of the interior of the earth than was ever thought possible before. The zonal internal structure of the earth is no longer pure assumption. Seismic waves reach them, are affected by them and the modification can be interpreted in terms of depth and quality of earth structure.

In several important respects the geology of the last quarter century has registered new trends. It has become decidedly less speculative; it has developed a quantitative aspect; and it has been put to service. It is both less speculative and less picturesque, but is also more definite, more reliable and more useful.

Unbridled imagination has given way to a much more conspicuous matter-of-factness and there is evident effort to bring even the contributions based on the farthest reaches of imagination within the rules of law-abiding behavior and logical consequences. The imagination has been set to work instead of being allowed to roam without purpose. It has become the principal supporter of a most useful method, that of multiple hypotheses. There was a time when it was considered appropriate for a geologist to let his imagination run wild, especially in painting word pictures of the far-distant past, wherein the vividness of the description and the unusualness of the scene portrayed, were relied upon to create interest, excite admiration and suggest a certain geologic ability.

There is still enough left of the spectacular and unusual, and there is exercise for all of one's imagination; but it is put to direct use in helping to suggest possible ways in which different groups of data can be interpreted, and in discovering the different results that certain combinations of factors should be expected to produce. In such a program imagination serves the purpose of scouting the field and outlining possibilities, so that the few scattering observations, which may ultimately be made, can be more readily evaluated and fitted into various alternative explanations to the end of reaching the correct one.

There is a very decided difference between this and the earlier objective. Instead of the imaginative description being the chief end, the present effort is to make the imagination serve as an explorer of possibilities, so that it becomes the servant of subsequent observation and reason.

Geology has always been a qualitative science. Most of the phenomena do not yield readily to measurement and most statements are given in general terms.

In later years, however, a good many geologic phenomena have been found to be reduceable to quantitative statement. With this trend greater definiteness of statement has resulted. Coincident with this change, geology has become more useful.

The quantitative system of rock classification is the most outstanding single example, but the trend is not by any means confined to petrologic work.

A second marked trend, not more important but much more apparent than the one just noted, is that of the trend to the practical. Geology has become to a marked degree an applied science. The main objectives have not shifted, but, without losing sight of them, the principles of the science and its stores of knowledge have been turned to direct practical use on a large scale. This is doubtless the most important change in relation and outlook of the last quarter century.

Up to that time, as pointed out by Dr. George Otis Smith of the United States Geological Survey, there were only two kinds of openings for a geologist — a state or national survey, and a college or university. There were virtually no other places. Now, in this day, after the usefulness of geology has been established, there are many other openings for men trained in this line. Most large mining and exploiting companies have staffs and departments of geology in their own establishments. Many investment houses and organizations requiring advice on natural resources and reserves or about values of properties involving mineral rights, have geological advisors.

Whole new industries have sprung up, based directly on special mineral resources, which absorb literally hundreds of geologists, where not a single one was employed twenty-five or thirty years ago. The petroleum industry alone requires a larger number of geologists than were attached to all other services combined before that industry was established.

The discovery that geology has practical use is not new, but appreciation that it has so many applications and that so many of its principles and established data have an important bearing on practical affairs is a very late development. Geology always had its applications to mining and engineering, although the geologist was not always recognized or differentiated from the engineer in charge. In fact a large part of geology as we now know it grew out of the experience of men who worked in these fields, but the new science accomplished little in the beginning beyond the classification of minerals, the identification of ores, the description of rocks and an attempt to group the different rock formations. The history of the formations themselves came in due time.

It is a comparatively new thing to attempt to read the origin and history of an ore deposit from the deposit itself. In later years this kind of investigation has accomplished much more, because it has helped to a better understanding of the reasons for the deposit, and from that vantage point has aided materially in judging its distribution and probable extent.

Geology was slow in finding its place among the applied sciences, partly because of the latitude given to speculation. There was much too great tendency to write elaborate descriptions without apparent object, or long historical dissertations not too well founded in fact, while the few evidences that might have some significance in practical affairs were passed over as of too little scientific interest to warrant critical attention. Not until geologists of the mental attitude of the engineer, with his sober insistence on fact and his strict curb on hasty or ill-considered conclusions, entered the field of advisory work, did they and their science come to have a better standing.

Many modern engineering projects depend for their success in large part on meeting fully the requirements imposed by natural physical conditions. Some of them depend for their safety on rightly judging the behavior of the ground under the process of construction and after the new abnormal conditions imposed by such construction are established. As soon as it was found that geologic science could be applied in a form that was helpful to this problem, and that a geologist could detect questionable conditions and predict changes and behavior suc-

cessfully enough to serve as a reasonable guide, his service soon
replaced the questionable method of taking a blind risk or
blundering through a program of construction both more
dangerous and more expensive than necessary. As a result the
applied geologist is called in now to help plan and give preliminary advice, instead of being called in after failure to suggest
an explanation. In this field Columbia men, beginning with the
late Professor James F. Kemp, have taken a leading part for
more than a quarter of a century and have aided materially
in gaining for applied geology a good reputation and a record
of widely extended service.

Despite what has been said about great matter-of-factness in
geology and putting imagination to work, speculation has
flared out in surprising activity in certain directions. These
bear on the origin of the earth; the condition of the earth's
interior as suggested by the newer studies in seismology; and
the problem of continental instability or the shifting of continents.

These speculative fields deserve some consideration. How
much truth there may be in them, it is not possible to say at
the present time, but they demand a vigorous resifting of the
evidence for our former beliefs. Out of the investigations
prompted by these speculative hypotheses there is certain to
come a better understanding of the structure of the earth and
its history.

The origin of the earth has claimed the best effort of our
ablest American geologist. Chamberlin's Planetesimal Hypothesis had already been proposed at the opening of the
quarter-century. It was particularly satisfying to geologists,
who found an earth made up by accretion of particles gathered
from surrounding space, and welded by metamorphism and
volcanism into its present condition, quite satisfactory for the
geologic program. He believed that he could see the processes

that prevail now establish themselves in this growing mass, and thus originate the program of change and development that we call geologic history.

The tendency through most of this quarter century has been to accept the major elements of his hypothesis which pictures the earth as originating through an accident to the sun, beginning in disruption and a scattering of matter through adjacent space and ending in the gathering of it into units which now constitute the planets of the solar system. The original hypothesis assumed a comparatively insignificant nucleus for each of these planetary units, into which was gathered, in the course of time, the rest of the surrounding material, chiefly in the form of particles of solid matter. The tendency in the most recent contributions is to regard the primary units as larger physical masses probably still maintaining a super-heated condition carried over from the sun itself, and much smaller credit is given to the accretion of particles in the building up of the total mass of the earth. The whole problem is as much astronomical as geological, and it is not at all likely that geologic observation in itself can ever contribute much to prove or disprove the hypothesis.

Evidence is accumulating from geophysical methods and from seismology, as already noticed, especially from interpretative studies of earthquake records bearing on the condition of the interior of the earth and its structure. The interior does not have uniform effect on earthquake waves. It is possible to determine within reasonable limits the boundaries between certain structures of different behavior which it is convenient at the present time to think of as zones or spheres of different quality and condition. It is true, of course, that zones and shells and internal spheres have been much discussed before; but they were almost wholly speculative concepts. We have now come to something more real. The earthquake wave searches the depths of the earth, and by recording the vibrations coming through from these depths, it is possible to discover differences that require explanation.

Certain margins of continents facing each other, such as Africa and South America, are so strikingly similar in outline that they readily suggest the possibility of once having been a single mass that was broken apart. It is virtually proven that the continents are made up of lighter materials than the ocean basins. In the so-called Taylor-Wegener hypothesis, it is claimed that the continents are actually floating masses on a subjacent sphere of heavier material rigid enough to prevent rapid or erratic movement, but not rigid enough to prevent the continents from slipping or shifting their positions on its surface in the course of long periods of geologic time. By the great majority of geologists this is considered wholly speculative, other explanations being given for the considerable array of facts that have been used by the sponsors of the hypothesis to support it. At the present time however it is not possible to say how much of truth there may be. Steps can be and have been taken which, in the course of time, will enable the geologists of the future to determine from actual measurement and observation whether the continents shift their positions. It ought to be as easy to tell whether continents have moved as it is to tell that a ship has changed its position. If they do, the hypothesis is in its essential features correct and it would help to explain a number of puzzling phenomena, such for example as former glaciation within the tropics and temperate climatic conditions in polar regions. Otherwise, it will become simply another one of these interesting speculations affecting the make-up and behavior of the earth, that has grown out of a zeal for new explanation and which is willing to question the permanence of the only fixed things left on the face of the earth, the great continental masses. In geology, it is accepted that the truth can be only one way, whether it can be explained or not. The continents either do or they do not shift their positions. In the next quarter century perhaps we shall know.

At the opening of the quarter century it was well established that there had been extensive Pleistocene glaciation, and most attention was being devoted to possible causes for this effect. Not much was known, although evidence was accumulating, about glaciated regions in much earlier time.

The great problem still facing glaciologists is why there have been glacial epochs at all. It is certain now that there have been several epochs of great glacial advance, separated by epochs of warm climate and almost complete disappearance of the ice. These individual epochs must have lasted tens of thousands of years. Perhaps a hundred thousand years is a fair estimate. Many explanations have been given, none of which is entirely satisfactory, and the only advance of any definite character made in the last quarter century toward this solution has been to discredit some of the explanations of earlier time, and to add one of seeming importance. Geologists have always recognized the importance of elevation and subsidence in changing the climatic conditions of any region. But this does not seem sufficient to account for the behavior. The additional thing that would make a more satisfactory explanation is either some modification of the atmosphere, or some long continued change in the amount of heat received from the sun. This latter is the most interesting suggestion made in recent years. It is not simply a suggestion, for there is evidence that there is variation in the amount of heat reaching the earth from the sun. In line with that fact, geologists are inclined to believe that for some reason or other not fully understood and perhaps not wholly determinable, Glacial and Interglacial epochs register changes in insolation as well as changes in relief due to elevation and subsidence. Whether there is a rhythmic change in the heat thrown out by the sun, or whether instead the solar system occasionally passes through regions of space containing sufficient matter to interfere to some extent with the transmission of heat and light rays, it is quite impossible to say. Either of these conditions would tend to produce a part of the effect that is registered in the glacial epochs.

Geologists have come to believe on further acquaintance with all of the phenomena involved that the present Post-Glacial epoch is in nowise different from the Interglacial epochs immediately preceding, and, if this is true, it is entirely possible that a new glacial advance will be experienced again in the course of time.

Evidence of glacial conditions in earlier geologic time, much earlier than the Pleistocene, was a discovery of revolutionary portent. These events have been multiplied in recent years and it is now known that in several places on different continents and representing different geologic ages, there are authentic glacial deposits. The most comprehensive contribution assembling these data, is that of Coleman in his *Ice Ages Recent and Ancient*. The erratic distribution of these ice deposits, especially their occurrence in sub-tropical areas, together with their wide distribution in time, makes the problem of accounting for glacial epochs still more difficult.

The problem of glaciation is related to that of climate in still other ways. It is entirely possible that strong zonal climates are rather characteristic of glacial epochs. The present climate, which is distinctly zonal, may be so because of the ice caps of the polar regions. If they were wholly removed, doubtless there would be an entire change in the climatic conditions of much of the earth.

One of the most interesting of all glacial relations is that connected with man. Most of the remains of ancient man on which his history is based, come from glaciated regions. It is clear that man lived close to the borders of the ice and occupied territories in interglacial epochs that were occupied by the ice of the previous glacial advances. It is this association with glacial history that enables one to date the different finds made in Europe. Some of these belong far back in the Pleistocene time scale and indicate an age immensely greater than was formerly assumed.

Outside of the glaciated regions of the world, finds of this kind are much more difficult to determine with respect to age. The usual method is to judge from the other associated content, particularly extinct species of animals that lived at the same time. The chief difficulty with such occurrences as that recently reported from China in the finding of the so-called Peking Man is to determine the age. Some progress, however, is now being made, even in those regions lying outside of glaciated territory, through application of the principles of erosion and deposition in their relation to large changes of climate. It must be that climates of regions beyond the ice border were modified in much the same manner as were those of the ice-covered regions themselves. There must have been epochs of warm dry climate separated by epochs cold and comparatively humid. In certain regions, nicely balanced with respect to erosion and deposition it has been found practicable to detect evidence of these changes and interpret the dominance of erosion or of deposition forms in terms of time and climatic cycles. One of the earliest attempts of this sort was that made by the Central Asiatic Expedition in Mongolia, and others are being made in Africa and other outlying regions. There is reason to believe that criteria may ultimately be found that will enable geologists to unravel the history of Pleistocene man in other regions as well as in glaciated territory.

There was some reason to believe, twenty-five years ago, that the chief methods to be employed in investigation of geological phenomena had been devised, but as a matter of fact, since that time there has been a good deal of progress in this direction. Not only have the methods formerly used been greatly improved, but entirely new ones have been invented or adapted, and, by their means, determinations far beyond the reach of earlier investigators are now the product of daily experience.

The most outstanding of these new methods must be briefly described.

The use of X-rays enables the mineralogist to determine definite facts about the internal structure of crystalline mineral substances, and detect differences in make up and composition that can not be learned by any other method. The method is destined to be an important determinative aid and promises to throw more light on crystal structure and mineral difference than any other yet used. Such difficult and obscure and confused groups of substances as the clays are found to yield to this method. For X-ray studies Columbia is particularly well equipped, and is engaged in active investigation under the direction of Dr. Kerr in mineralogy.

Several different kinds of tests, all known as geophysical methods, have been devised to throw light on subsurface structures and conditions. It is now practicable to detect changes in character and structure of the rock floor quite beyond ordinary reach, and even where all ordinary evidence is completely buried. Structural facts determined in this manner have the greatest practical economic significance.

Four such methods are in constant use. These are: the magnetic, the electric, the gravitational and the seismic methods. The magnetic method is the oldest and in principle has been known and practiced for more than fifty years. The others are all comparatively new. The electric methods depend for their usefulness on the fact that different kinds of rock formations offer different resistance to an electric current. The application is made by sending a current through certain stretches of ground, and interpreting the minute differences noted. Some surprisingly good results have been secured, and there is no doubt but that the method has come to stay.

The gravitational method relies on the fact that different rock strata and other structural units have different densities and therefore have a gravitational pull that can be measured. The torsion balance, an extremely sensitive instrument, was designed to detect these minute differences. Changes in the normal succession of rock formations or normal structural relations affect the reading, and these readings yield to interpretation. It has been extensively employed by petroleum geologists in problems connected with structures seemingly hopelessly buried beyond reach.

The seismograph has been used for many years as a recorder of earthquake vibrations, but its use in detecting the presence of hidden rock structures is a late application. Refinements of this instrument make it possible to record the artificial earth shakings caused by planting explosives and by this means detect differences in the transmission of vibrations through the ground in different directions. It is a rapid and very valuable method. Large areas have been explored by this method and it has earned a high place among the methods of geophysics.

All of these methods are successful as physical detectors of certain facts, but the data have to be interpreted in geologic terms. They are usually capable of many different interpretations and it is in this field that the geologist brings into play his keenest powers of discrimination.

The application of aerial photography to topographic mapping is wholly new. This is a method that now enables the topographer to make relief maps of the most complicated and difficult surface configuration with an accuracy and detail never attained in any other way. It has proved enormously valuable and is both more rapid and more economical than any of the methods of ground mapping. Such a map in its simplest form is essentially a mosaic of photographic patches or fragments so assembled as to make a continuous picture. It carries both relief and geographic detail as well as many surface cultural exhibits never recorded in any other form of map. Some of these aid greatly in practical service, not only in locating one-self in the field but also wholly eliminating mistakes of original observer, draftsman and printer alike.

Although the petrographic microscope long ago proved to be of great use with rocks and non-metallic minerals, ways had not been found until within the last twenty-five years to determine with similar satisfaction the mineral composition and structure of the opaque metallic ores. They do not respond to the regular methods applied to thin sections. For this pur-pose a polished plate is examined in reflected light, and this method has done for such ores what the petrographic micro-scope and the thin section did for rocks. It has done more to unravel the intricate structural relations of complex ore aggre-gates and, as a result, their genesis and history, than any other method yet discovered.

Improvements in the petrographic microscope also have made it possible to make the required determinations on smaller and smaller particles of minerals and rocks. This has been of immense service in working with minute samples of material and has extended materially our knowledge of fine-grained aggregates and aphanitic rocks.

From the side of applied geology, especially in engineering, methods of exploration have been borrowed that help greatly in the accumulation of accurate quantitative data. It has always been considered the privilege of the geologist to draw a gener-alized geologic section intended to represent the underground structure of a district or locality. But the depths of the different formations, their physical condition, and the occur-rence of special features or qualities, were always matters of crude estimate or even of mere speculation. It is the diamond drill and other devices of similar purpose, introduced by engineers for the penetration of the subsurface, that have given the needed data. Some of these devices recover an almost

continuous column of rock from the surface to whatever depth
the boring is made. Thus one can work with the actual material,
and know that it came from a particular depth, even though
that be hundreds or thousands of feet, below the surface. With
this help, the engineering geologist is enabled to present his
structural representations with a reliability of interpretation
and plotting that meets the exacting requirements of the engineer in modern projects.

Thus far the effort has been to present a general picture of
development. Because of the wide range of the subject, it will
be more convenient from this point on to discuss such progress
as has been made in specific terms under heads corresponding
to the recognized branches of the science.

Recent years have seen many of the objectives of geographical exploration attained. The most spectacular, of course, are
those which have entered the polar regions and have, during
the quarter century, reached both the North and South Poles.
Peary's expedition to the North Pole proved that this part of
the earth belongs to the sea rather than to the land areas of
the globe. The south polar regions visited by Scott and Amund-
sen are land and are even as I speak the scene of persistent and
very successful exploration under Commander Byrd.

Much more extensive exploratory undertakings have been
carried out in the Arctic regions of North America from
Alaska to Greenland, and the interiors of continents hitherto
untouched by modern exploratory work have been crossed and
recrossed until their general geographic features have become
a part of general knowledge. Such accomplishments as those
of Sven Hedin in Central Asia and of Stefanssen in Arctic
America and of numerous others in Central Africa and in
South American have made their contributions in this field.

In addition to work of rather strictly geographic nature
there have been a still larger number of reconnaissance expeditions and more elaborately organized scientific researches in

limited regions and on special problems. Among these must be mentioned the researches in China by Willis and Blackwelder which laid the foundations for all the later geologic work of Eastern Asia. In saying this, I do not overlook the reconnaissance expeditions of Von Richtoven, the German explorer, many years before, and of Obruchev, the Russian geologist, who also spent years in reconnaissance travel in Asia. An exploration of quite another type directed to a special problem rather than a regional reconnaissance was that of Pumpelly in Asiatic Turkestan in which he showed that the varying fortunes of certain cities, even to the point of repeated abandonment and subsequent reoccupation, synchronized with cyclic changes of climate.

Another example is the Central Asiatic Expeditions of the American Museum of Natural History, organized for reconnaissance of North Central Asia, especially Mongolia. These expeditions have maintained active field organizations for several years and have added greatly to geologic and paleontologic knowledge of Central Asia. Other somewhat more specialized exploratory investigations are the Princeton Patagonian Expeditions devoted largely to paleontologic and stratigraphic studies, and the expeditions led by Mr. Barnum Brown of the American Museum of Natural History, into Southern Asia.

Yet another type of organized investigation is represented by the Scientific and Natural History Survey of Porto Rico and the Virgin Islands by the New York Academy of Sciences in coöperation with the Porto Rican government. Comparatively detailed surveys covering the whole island, with the production of geologic maps and reports as well as contributions in other scientific lines, have been carried on there for the last fifteen years, the geologic work, largely by Columbia men, being virtually completed.

Most survey undertakings the world over have been supported and operated with purely governmental support. Extensive territory has been covered in many different countries, the most notable and successful new work, considering the enormous difficulties involved, being that done in South Africa. Similar work, however, has been carried on by many other countries; the work of the United States has been pushed forward in a systematic manner continuously through the whole period on a program that will take many years more to complete.

The International Map of the World on a scale of 1:1,000,-000 grew out of the need for a map of uniform scale covering all countries. A little over twenty-five years ago Professor Albrecht Penck, the German geographer, proposed a map of this type at the International Geographical Congress in Berlin. As a result there is now a Central Bureau located at the British Ordinance Survey Office in Southampton.

The Millionth Map, as the name indicates, is published on a scale of 1:1,000,000 which is about 16 miles to an inch. The different sheets, which are of convenient atlas size, cover areas 4 degrees in latitude and 6 degrees in longitude. The original plan was to have the different countries of the world prepare millionth maps of their areas in accordance with the standard symbols and colors. But during the war the need for a set of maps on uniform scale for Europe and the Near East caused the Geographical Section of the General Staff of the British War Office to compile and publish maps of those areas. The value of these maps was demonstrated by the fact that the various peace treaties included these sheets as base maps upon which the new boundaries were indicated. At the present time about three hundred maps have been completed, covering all of Europe, North Africa, Central Africa, India and Western Asia. The United States Geological Survey has put out four sheets. Canada has published one. In South America the American Geographical Society of New York has, as a non-governmental but nevertheless as an official agency, taken up the project of publishing maps for the whole area. Ninety sheets out of 125 have been completed or are under way. This work is done in coöperation with the various South American governments and commercial companies. Taking the land areas of the world as a whole, about one-quarter of the earth has been completed in the Millionth Map series.

The great development of aviation has encouraged the preparation of an International Aeronautical Map of the World. This is being done on the Mercator projection, and for the middle latitudes has a scale of about 1:3,000,000. Much of Europe is covered as well as North Africa and Western Asia as far as India.

The United States Geological Survey has been pushing forward the completion of the topographic map of the United States on the usual scale of 1:62,500, about an inch to a mile. The pressure from many sides for an earlier completion of this map brought about the passage of the so-called Temple Bill which provides for the finishing of this map within twenty years. The mapping program of the United States is now about half completed.

The most recent contributions to glacial studies is a series of world maps by Antevs depicting the extent of glacial ice in the different epochs of the Pleistocene.

Considerable progress in oceanographic surveys may also be noted. The Prince of Monaco's well-known Bathymetric Map was revised in 1920. There are thirty sheets, covering all the oceans of the world, on the Mercator projection. The revised map shows the relief of the ocean floor as well as many other details and is the standard of reference for all students of oceanography.

The most notable study of the oceans during the past twenty-five years has been carried on by the Germans. In 1927 the ship "Meteor" made a complete oceanographic survey of the Atlantic and the published report was the first treatment of an ocean along geographic lines. The use of the echo sounder with complete crisscrossing of routes made it possible to prepare maps which showed in far greater detail the configuration of the ocean floor than had been possible before that time.

The recent catastrophe to the non-magnetic ship "Carnegie," now interrupts the work of that famous vessel which has been under way for the past twenty-five years. This ship, built and supported by the Carnegie Institution of Washington, has voyaged over all the oceans year after year, making a magnetic survey of the world. Its latest trip, covering the past two years, was much wider in scope and included soundings and other observations not attempted in the earlier surveys.

Because of the fact that each large maritime country of the world has up to the present felt obliged to prepare hydrographic charts of all the oceans and coasts by compiling all available information, a great deal of duplication of effort resulted. To avoid this duplication and to correlate the preparation of hydrographic charts for all parts of the world, an International Hydrographic Bureau has recently been established at Monaco.

In general it may be said that recent years have seen a tendency toward much greater coöperation between governments as well as between non-official bodies in the preparation of maps, in the making of surveys which are not of purely local interest.

The fourth quarter of the last century saw the birth of modern geomorphology, with the work of Powell, Dutton, Gilbert and others; and the codification of its principles by Davis. It saw also the firm establishment of the so-called Davis method of describing and analyzing surface features. There has been a growing appreciation of the value of this simple way of approach dealing first with rock structure or foundations, then with processes, and finally with the stage of development of surface configuration. In this method of approach there is logical application of the processes of erosion to areas of definite rock structure carried through from the very beginning to mature development and finally to old age stages. This point of view has probably been more helpful and enlightening to students of land forms and landscapes than any other contribution ever made to the physiographic side of geology.

The method had been fully developed by the beginning of this quarter century but it was almost wholly confined in its application to the stream erosion cycle. The peneplane was the logical end product of such erosion and all peneplanes were believed to have had subaerial origin.

Since that time and within the quarter century the same method has been used with like success in the study of other cycles of development of earth features, such as the marine cycle in the development of shore forms and coastal features. One may therefore speak of the last quarter century as the "marine period" in geomorphology. Both in this country and abroad greatly increased attention has been given to the geomorphology of coasts. The possible marine origin of some peneplanes, a proposition almost universally denied after Davis rejected the marine theory, is again asserted by competent investigators like Barrell and others; while extended accounts of shore forms and shore-line evolution appear in many languages.

This Davis method has taken such a firm hold on the investigators in this branch that one can detect a growing tendency to present the results of investigations in the same manner, first the general principles with deduced consequences followed by citations of actual conditions and argument. A good example of this manner of presentation and at the same time the most advanced study of the marine cycle on the lines already emphasized, is the study of shore lines by Professor Johnson of Columbia.

The arid cycle has been studied in a less systematic manner but with similar suggestiveness in the desert regions of Africa, America and Asia, some of the latest contributions coming from the reconnaissance studies of the Central Asiatic Expeditions of the American Museum of Natural History manned in part by Columbia men.

Probably the greatest service of physiographic studies is in making surface features intelligible by reading into them the same orderly development and history that one expects from other branches of geology. A landscape has as definite a life story as a rock formation or a fossil bone. Physiography has become to a marked degree the historical geology of surface features.

The surface features or scenery of the states, and the geological histories back of them, are now recognized as matters of wide public interest. Such bulletins play an important rôle in public education. Professor Lobeck, of Columbia, has prepared contributions of this kind which are models of what such publications should be.

The beginning of the last quarter century found crystallography with precise theoretical designs showing the possibilities of classification for all crystalline substances. These had been thoroughly demonstrated mathematically but no practical method of testing their validity had yet been found. The work of the physicist Laue in 1912, accomplished under the inspiration of Groth, the mineralogist, provided a practical method for testing the theoretical concepts already proposed. As far back as 1895 Schoenflies had shown 230 possible arrangements of points in space consistent with the symmetry of crystals. With the aid of the new X-ray methods developed since Laue's time mineralogists together with physicists and metallurgists have been busily engaged in cataloging crystalline substances according to these various groups.

Methods of investigation have improved in other directions. The range of observation has been extended downward to include the most finely divided masses of mineral substances produced in nature. Fine ores, mixed aggregates of minerals and even clays, which formerly defied all attempt at determination, are no longer to be classed as obscure masses. The opaque ores have yielded in the same manner to better methods. An enormous number of mineral occurrences have been studied, and possible uses have been investigated. As a result, many minerals previously considered worthless have been found to be useful and have become objects of commerce. The total production constitutes a vitally important contribution to economic stability and prosperity.

Mineral resources are of prime importance in this modern industrial world. They and their products are in large part the physical foundation on which the present-day civilization is built. Revolutionary changes in the relative importance of individual resources come with bewildering suddenness as discovery and invention introduce new competitors or find new uses. Within the quarter century, one of the greatest of modern industries, that of petroleum, based on a single resource, has sprung up. Geologists have had heavy responsibility in it from the very beginning because of the demand for geologic guidance in the finding and development of new supplies. In return, the support given by this industry has enabled geologists to make stratigraphic and structural studies in immensely greater detail and to extend them much beyond the usual scope of such studies. Vast areas have been investigated in detail, which would otherwise have been passed over with simple reconnaissance. Some of this has been done with a minuteness that can only happen when there is immediate practical application of the information secured and where the knowledge gained in this way pays.

Corresponding progress has been made in the study of ore deposits, although it has not made a new industry or developed so great a demand for geologic service. The dominant note in this last quarter century is that of genesis. There was a time when form of deposit and the kind of metallic content and occurrence were considered fundamental; but, with improved methods of investigation and new insight into the general problem of petrogenesis, interest has swung strongly to studies of origin. In like manner and to similar purpose special attention has been given to structural changes and to chemical alterations that have affected deposits since their original formation.

All this is parallel to the changes that have come about in petrology, where now the life history of a rock is the principal objective. In ore deposits this same tendency appears in the form of determinations of genesis and secondary changes. This latter, in some deposits, leads to the addition of metallic content, thus making ores workable that were not before. This is the so-called "secondary enrichment," of many deposits — a term to conjure with in present-day mine promotion. It is necessary, therefore, in such studies not only to read the origin but to distinguish between primary and secondary contributions to the deposit itself, for on the accurate determination of this point may rest the whole case of distribution of values and workability.

Coincident with this trend in the study of ore deposits there has been a strong swing in favor of igneous or magmatic sources of supply for a great many of the ore substances. A quarter century ago greater emphasis was placed on the work of percolating meteoric waters, on their competence in gathering metallic substances from the rocks through which they pass and on their task of precipitating them in concentrated form at some convenient point as an ore deposit. Better understanding of the behavior of a magma, especially the separation of different substances as the fused mass cools down, has greatly increased confidence in the competence of volcanism to provide the very conditions needed to extract and carry mineral substances and initiate the complex reactions, replacements and precipitations that belong to ore deposits. In it all one can trace the influence of physical chemistry. Ore deposition is recognized as operating on the same principles. For these views, which have now won high regard, the late Professor James F. Kemp was a stout champion from the beginning.

One of the most useful of the newer concepts in ore deposits is the zonal theory. It has been established beyond question that where complex ores are genetically connected with magmatic sources there is a direct relation between mineral character and relative distance from the igneous body. Certain ore substances are carried in solution much farther than others beyond the borders of igneous contact. Their deposition must depend in part on changes in temperature affecting the escaping mineral-laden solutions.

The same theory applies to depth. By depth in this sense is meant distance from the original surface at the time the deposit was made, rather than present depth which may be very different due to subsequent erosion. This principle has been formulated and discussed in detail by Lindgren and others specializing in this field. It has been found that the character of mineralization differs greatly with depth, certain minerals being formed only under conditions of great pressure and comparatively high temperature, whereas others are characteristic of shallow depths with low pressure and temperature. Still others have been formed at intermediate depths with correspondingly moderate temperatures and pressures. The principle is so well established that criteria based on the mineralogy and petrology of deposits are constantly used in interpretation in terms of physical condition and relative depth of original deposition.

On account of the great importance attached to magmatic sources of supply, the differentiating batholith is a body of prime interest to the student of ore deposits. Here the student of ore deposits and the student of rocks join in the task of unraveling the life history of a magma through all of its stages to its final solidification and rejection of the "end products" or last dregs. Sometimes these last dregs are most important of all.

Interest in rock classification and description was at its height twenty-five years ago. Fifty years earlier the petrographic microscope had been invented, and, with its further development, it had become possible to examine and identify the internal constituents of a rock with as great ease and certainty as the crystals of a mineral cabinet. With the aid of such a microscope it was possible to magnify the structures of the fine-grained rocks that had formerly defied determination, and it was found then that these also were made up of identifiable minerals of the same character as those of coarse grain. This broadening of the scope of rock examination led to great advances in knowledge of rocks and to much more satisfactory classifications.

This field was originally cultivated largely by men of special training in mineralogy. They brought to the subject the mineralogist's enthusiasm for identification, for distinguishing between the different elementary substances, and for classification and description. The petrology that grew out of this kind of investigation therefore was a descriptive and classification petrology.

Then a new principle was introduced, the quantitative principle. Its maximum development was reached with the publication of the quantitative system of rock classification sponsored by the four leading American petrographers — Cross, Iddings, Pirsson and Washington. Theirs was a refinement over the rock classification then developed through the use of the petrographic microscope, for it was based on a much more elaborate series of determinations and analyses ending with the recasting of the chemical analysis. This kind of petrology obeyed a definite trend in emphasizing the quantitative principle. Neither this method, however, nor the earlier one, gave much of an understanding of the meaning or history of the rock. Description, classification and detection of new combinations and proportions, and naming of new types or varieties based on these characters constituted the petrology of that time.

In recent years the whole point of view has shifted. It was soon appreciated that all of these refinements of classification still left the rock in certain of its aspects quite unknown. A new point of view had been reached already by students of ore deposits, who had begun to see that in the study of ores it was much more important to determine the origin and history of the deposit than to have a detailed physical description or a classification of its different combinations of mineral proportions. They also had discovered that the petrographic microscope was helpful in the study of ores and that a succession of events could be made out in that way.

This was a new point of view and petrographers who came in touch with the same problems soon adopted the new point of view for the study of rocks also. They soon came to see that all aggregations of mineral substances, even the ores, are essentially rocks. As geologists they saw that the chief object in studying them should be to determine their origin and the sequence of events that mark the various steps in their history. This is the new petrology whose major purpose is not so much to classify or to distinguish one mineral proportion from another, and not so much to discover some new type and variety, but to read from a rock its life story. Thus the new petrology has become a part of geology proper. It has become a method of unraveling geologic history, and throws light on obscure fields that formerly were thought to have no story to tell. In this development Columbia men have had an important part.

This kind of petrology has its applied side, and its value in that field is measured largely by the success attained in solving the life history of the materials on which it works. Thus the petrology of the present day is as different from the petrology of a quarter of a century ago as the petrology of that time was from the lithology of 1850.

In the field of dynamic geology one should not fail to note the progress that has been made toward proving the validity of the principle of isostasy. It appears to be well established that relatively elevated regions are deficient in mass, whereas low-lying regions are heavier. Thus the continents stand above the sea because they are lighter than the corresponding portions of the crust of the earth that form the ocean basins. The same principle applies to subdivisions of the continents and ocean basins themselves. These results favor the view that the major continents and ocean basins are permanent features of the earth.

But it is a plain geologic fact that they have changed in level repeatedly, and many less extensive areas have been both above and beneath the sea several times. It is not yet clear how these changes of behavior are inaugurated, but most geologists are confident that the principle of isostasy holds good, even under these circumstances, and that deep seated volcanism is probably the principal factor in accomplishing the necessary modifications of mass and the accompanying transfer of material.

Views of diastrophism have changed somewhat. It has become clearer from seismic evidence that the earth is essentially solid to great depth. This is consistent with recent views with respect to volcanism. There has been a tendency in later years to regard surface volcanic activity of the present time as a very local phenomenon. As pointed out by Chamberlin, this relation seems to favor a kind of internal structure that ought to be expected under the accretional theory of earth origin. Active volcanoes are being made the object of special investigation. Geologists have become more and more convinced that igneous activity is a unit, but with different expressions, dependent on the control of physical conditions and registering different stages in the life histories of subterranean igneous masses. The processes related to volcanism have been given immensely more prominence in the development of the structure and make-up of the ordinary geological formations, even those of sedimentary origin, than was prevalent a quarter century ago. Some of the silts and sands of former times are now known to be beds of volcanic ash and ashy tuff.

Perhaps the most revolutionary modification of view has come about from the contribution of physics in the discovery of radium, and the evidence that large enough quantities of such substances exist in the earth to add materially to its heat. There is indeed a question whether the earth loses heat by radiation as fast as it is developed from radium, and therefore whether the earth is actually cooling off at all. A speculation based on this principle sponsored by Joly assumes that there has been periodic increase and decrease in the internal temperature of the earth due to lack of balance between heat losses and heat evolution. The hypothesis has certain attractive features but for the present is purely speculative.

There is as yet no satisfactory explanation for much of the dynamic behavior of the earth, especially its large scale movements which must originate in some way from the deeper interior. To say that they are due to isostatic adjustments only moves the difficulty one step farther back, for one must still account for the changes that disturb an isostatic equilibrium already established. Geologists of the present day find a considerable number of such problems of fundamental character which must carry over to the next quarter century. It is to be hoped that new sources of information may be found or new methods of investigation may be devised that will serve the next generation, as others have served the past to reach a better understanding of the earth.

In the field which has to do with the underground structure of the earth and the relation of the different formational units, a great deal of attention has been attracted to the old problem of the origin of mountains. A reasonable understanding of the structural differences between the different types of mountains has been reached, but less success has attended consideration of origins and causes, especially for those extraordinary products of side-crowding, the great thrustfolds, such as seem to be represented by the Alps in Central Europe. An explanation that calls for the movement of a continental mass, such as a crowding northward of Africa, appears to be much too speculative. Perhaps there is as yet too incomplete knowledge of facts to warrant an explanation. The same thing can be said of the festoon structures around the borders of Asia. It is hard to believe that thrusts could be transmitted to such distances through rock structures of this kind, even if the continent of Asia could move, to account for some of these great bordering ranges and island arcs, much discussed in recent years.

There is much better understanding of the modifications that take place in rocks under deformation in the depths of the earth. Adams' experiments made by subjecting different types of rocks to great deforming pressures under enclosed conditions, simulating those of deeply buried strata, have given definite experimental results. They show that common rocks, such as granite or basalt, or marble, may be molded into new form without losing their cohesion or essential unity as a solid structure and that the deformations inside of the rock itself, due to the artificial pressure, are very similar indeed to some of those seen in certain rock formations that have at one time been deeply buried in the earth. Such experimentation aids greatly toward a better understanding of the possibilities of intimate deformation. Accompanying recrystallization, which takes place on a grand scale in nature, will account for most other structures seen in metamorphic rocks.

Coincident with this improved understanding of the effect of deformation, there has been a growing appreciation of the work of volcanism in producing modifications of, and making contributions to, already existing strata. The banded gneisses have long been known, and it is becoming increasingly clear that most of these complicated and obscure rocks are essentially a complex of materials of different origins, partly metamorphosed sedimentaries and partly igneous materials introduced from magmatic sources. These are the so-called mixed rocks forming the injection gneisses and similar types. We are now confident that a double or even a triple genesis is largely accountable for the exceedingly great variety of compositional and structural peculiarities that characterize these so-called injection gneisses. This principle has been of immense value in working with very ancient strata in the Pre-Cambrian systems, which, for many reasons, are the most obscure and difficult of the whole geologic column.

In the field of paleontology many great monographs based on studies of particular groups of organisms with their stratigraphic and age relation have been published. In invertebrate paleontology those by Bassler, J. P. Smith, Walcott and Raymond on Tertiary and Recent Bryozoa, the Mesozoic Cephalopods and the phylogeny of the Trilobites are the most prominent. In no special field, however, has there been such great activity as in that of micropaleontology. Revival of the study of foraminifera and ostracods has been encouraged by their usefulness as horizon markers in refined stratigraphic studies. These particular microforms have proved to be enormously abundant and varied. Special impetus has been given because of support from the petroleum industry. Greater accuracy of correlation and identification can be attained by means of these microforms than by any other method or content thus far discovered. Since this fact has been demonstrated, virtually every important petroleum company engaged in exploration and development of petroleum-bearing lands maintains a staff of specialists working with these forms.

Greater and greater interest in vertebrate paleontology has resulted from the various field explorations and a better understanding also of what their discoveries mean. There has been intensive collecting in many fields, and a technique has been devised that insures the preservation of such material much more successfully than anything formerly known. In the last thirty years probably approximately 75 per cent of the collections of the American Museum have been gathered. In other American institutions of like character, the percentage is likely to be even higher.

The trend of recent work has been to make closer contact and correlation with stratigraphic geology. There is much more exact reference to field occurrence and stratigraphic sequence. The contribution to stratigraphy lies in the establishment of life zones within definite geologic formations. There is a better correlation of the strata of later age which have always presented much difficulty.

Some of the great contributions are those on the fossil fishes of the Silurian, Devonian and Triassic of Spitzbergen and Norway by Stensiö and his colleagues; studies in the Permian and Triassic of South Africa, Russia, Texas, New Mexico, Brazil and Australia, with attempts at correlation. One should mention also the South African studies by Broom, Watson, Haughton and von Huene; those of Russia by Amalitzky and Sushkin; the Permian and Triassic of Texas by Williston Case and Romer; the Mesozoic reptilian horizons of Europe by von Huene, and of East Africa by Jannesch, and of America by Gilmore, as well as the studies of Mesozoic mammals by Simpson. Investigations in the Cenozoic mammal horizons of North America have been carried on persistently under the leadership of Henry Fairfield Osborn and W. D. Matthew of the American Museum of Natural History. Pleistocene mammal horizons have been summarized in North America by Osborn and Reeds of the American Museum, and by Merriam and his school in California. Similar studies have been made for Central Asia by Granger and by European geologists. A long list of significant contributions could be made which it is not practicable to do at this time.

Studies made by the vertebrate paleontologists in the mammal horizons of western North America led W. D. Matthew long ago to challenge the interior lake theory of deposition referred to in another connection. Out of his work and others, there was developed the aeolian and flood-plain theory of origin for many of these deposits, a much more acceptable explanation than prevailed before.

Vertebrate paleontologists have been more vitally concerned with paleogeography than any other group of geologists. For land vertebrates, migration routes are required including land connections between continents, some of which do not now exist. This situation has led to many special studies which have been summarized by Osborn and Matthew.

The vital significance of changes of climate has attracted special attention from this group also and has led to suggestions with regard to the relation between climate and evolution and the effect of changes of climate on migration and persistence of species. There is a tendency among vertebrate paleontologists to regard climate and the physical conditions that depend thereon as of vital importance in some way in providing the proper environment for evolutionary development. It is even suggested that the succession of glacial and interglacial epochs may have been of primary importance in the development of modern man. Much of this is speculative, but not wholly so, for there is evidence that many an organism has not been capable of adjusting itself to marked changes of that kind, and has either been compelled to abandon the region affected or succumb to the inhospitable conditions. Perhaps the tax that is laid on the organism to adjust itself, in case sufficient adjustment can be made, is a mark in itself of organic superiority, and it may be that this very test is required to bring out dormant capacities that would not otherwise develop. It is idle to postulate climatic changes to account for paleontologic effects, unless they are supported by geologic evidence of the same significance. One of the most marked accomplishments of closing years of this quarter century, therefore, is the coördinated study of problems of this kind by the paleontologist of biologic training and the geologist together.

The most fundamental contributions to the field of stratigraphy have had to do with continental deposits and with the processes and products of sedimentation. These two are mileposts in better understanding of sedimentary strata. A quarter century ago it was assumed that nearly all bedded deposits were laid down in water and for the most part in the sea. They were regarded as marine even when there was no special evidence of such origin. Later, as it became evident that fresh water rather than marine fossils characterized them, they were credited to great interior lakes. Such bodies of water were postulated largely because it was still unbelievable that sedimentary beds should be deposited elsewhere than in water. The efficacy of rivers was not yet recognized.

In more recent years abundant evidence has accumulated to prove that a large proportion of these formerly questionable deposits are of continental origin, laid down on exposed land surfaces largely by streams and by rain wash. Associated with them are other deposits accumulated by wind. In certain regions, in fact in most continental areas, such deposits form a common and now well-recognized type, making up a considerable proportion of the total sedimentary column. Recognition of these facts has established an entirely different viewpoint for the study of life content, stratigraphy, and paleogeography. Such splendid contributions to the paleogeography of North America as those of Grabau, formerly of Columbia and of Schuchert of Yale, could not have been assembled under the older interpretations of sedimentary strata.

There have been also many important regional studies. Some of these have added greatly to the detail of stratigraphic subdivision and to knowledge of the life of the periods represented. No work of this kind stands out in greater prominence than that of the late Dr. Walcott involving both Cambrian and Pre-Cambrian stratigraphy of the Cordilleran region. Perhaps the most pretentious of these adventures in stratigraphy, in that it proposes an addition to the geologic column, is that of Ulrich, whose study of the Cambro-Ordovician column of the Mississippi Valley led him to propose the interpolation of an entirely new system to be known as the Ozarkian. It is too early to judge of its validity or general acceptance.

To no portion of the geologic column, however, has there been more consistent contribution than to the Tertiary. These later strata have come into great economic prominence and the detailed study of their stratigraphy has gone forward with marked success fixing their boundaries and defining their characteristics and content to much greater perfection than had ever been done before.

Within this quarter century most of the contributions to the structure and stratigraphy of Africa, South America and Asia have been made, so that the general stratigraphic history of much larger proportions of the earth are now known, at least in reconnaissance outline.

To write the history of the earth is, of course, the central objective of the whole science — this despite the fact that in some of its other relations it is not historical at all. In addition to its reach farther and farther into the past, the geologic story has taken on greater definiteness in the successive periods as the stratigraphers have developed clearer ideas of the procession of changes from one period of time to another. Fifty years ago the Pre-Cambrian was almost an uncharted territory — a wilderness of confused scraps only remotely suggesting the operation in that far-off time of the same processes that have prevailed throughout Paleozoic and Mesozoic and Tertiary history.

In this last quarter century the story of the Pre-Cambrian has been read much better. It is now well established that the stratigraphic systems still preserved in the Pre-Cambrian cover as long a period of geologic history as all subsequent systems together. The longer portion of geologic time is doubtless the Pre-Cambrian. Out of these later studies has come an orderly statement of the sequence of events compiled from the fragments of formations uncovered by erosion of the later cover in different parts of the world. Nowhere is there a complete story, and nowhere is the beginning found. There is no question, however, but that the same program of development that has marked the transformations of the earth throughout its later history has prevailed in the Pre-Cambrian. The same processes were operating; the same types of strata were formed, the same kinds of changes and transformations occurred to them, and interpretation of their genesis and life history give us for that time as intelligible a story as is furnished by other sections of the geologic column.

Even with this extension, however, of sedimentary history into the past, geologists are compelled to admit that they as yet have not reached the beginning. Indeed, it is unlikely that the ordinary processes of geologic investigation which depend on interpreting preserved geological strata will ever unravel the very earliest chapters, even the earliest sedimentary chapters, in the history of the earth. It is more than likely that every vestige of such original records has been utterly destroyed. The rock formations that were made, and probably existed in perfectly readable condition in the early eras of geologic time, have been swallowed up in the fusions and destructions that belong to the occasional reworking of portions of the earth by volcanism. The materials of the earliest rock formations have been melted and redistributed to become for the time being constituents of magma masses and then take the form of igneous rocks to begin the whole long cycle over again.

It is quite understandable, therefore, that there must be portions of the earth's story that cannot be read. Some of them there is no hope of ever being able to read in the manner of other portions of the record. This is in keeping with observations in every region thus far examined on the face of the earth. The oldest, underlying, most obscure formations, formed way back toward the beginning, lie not on other formations of like character, which in their turn might add another chapter to the story, but are fused off and caught up and invaded, by igneous material coming from the depths of the earth long after these strata were laid down. Therefore they lie on nothing that preceded them.

Clearly a part of the record has been destroyed. There must have been other formations beneath. How many were there? what were they like? how long time did their making represent? No one can tell. It is the hope of every geologist working in new regions or exploring uncharted territory, that he may find remnants of some of these still more ancient rocks by the interpretation of which he might carry the story back another era. It is also his hope that he may find new strata so little modified by the changes of time that better exhibits of the life of those far-off eras in the Pre-Cambrian may be preserved.

At the upper end of the column geologic chronology has taken a definiteness that formerly was considered impossible of attainment. There were estimates of geologic time based on a variety of different methods of computation, none of which was satisfactory, and none of which was capable of translation into the exactness that characterizes human history. Human events are recorded in terms of years, whereas the geologist must think in terms of eras and periods and epochs, seldom in years. A great step was taken, therefore, when that epoch known in geologic history as Post-Pleistocene or Recent time, could be measured almost as definitely as one may measure the width of a valley with a foot rule. It was a triumph of keen observation when Baron de Geer of Sweden and his staff of student investigators were able to determine the number of years that it took for the ice of the Glacial period to retreat from the Scandinavian peninsula. They were able to count the years by the number of annual laminae of silt laid down in the transient lakes impounded at the front of the retreating ice, matching them up from one retreatal position to another until the whole of Post-Glacial time in that region was accounted for. Then for the first time it was possible to say that Post-Glacial or Post-Pleistocene time for the north temperate regions must be of the order of magnitude of twenty or thirty thousand years instead of five or six thousand years, as was formerly maintained, and this has become the yardstick by which certain other estimates are now made.

No single question has been of greater interest to the geologist himself than that of geologic time. No problem has been more baffling, and no estimates have differed more. It was the geologist, however, who continued to claim, ever since he became convinced that the formations of the earth had been made in an orderly manner by the same processes now prevailing, that geologic time must be enormously long, and probably should be measured in hundreds of millions of years. He attempted to estimate it by the rate of erosion and deposition, using the thickness of known sediments, as the basis of estimate. Although there is no doubt of the applicability of the method, there is no good quantitative basis for translating the data into years.

Physicists and astronomers have made their contributions to the same field, and for the most part have argued for shorter time than the geologist required. Thus matters stood until recently, when the discovery was made that the rocks of the earth carry rare substances that suffer atomic disintegration at determinable rates and that they produce other substances in measurable quantity with such nicely adjusted relations between time and amount of transformed matter that they yield to interpretation in terms of time. It was then possible to make an entirely new estimate of the length of geologic time and to date certain definite events in the distant past.

Now for the first time the work of the physicist is consistent with the demands of the geologist and adequate time is allowed for the whole complex program of earth building that characterizes the geologic structure of the earth. The hundred million years of a quarter of a century ago has been stretched to a thousand million years and more, distributed quite unevenly through the geologic column. Post-Pleistocene time may stretch out to a maximum of fifty thousand years. It is probably at least a million years back to the beginning of the Pleistocene or the end of the Pliocene. Each preceding period stretches out into longer and longer vistas of time, with Post-Mesozoic time placed at fifteen million years, and Post-Paleozoic time at fifty million. According to revised estimates, the length of time since the beginning of the Cambrian is of the order of magnitude of five hundred million years. The measurable Pre-Cam-

brian is as much longer. One may say, therefore, that geologic
time, represented by the formations of the earth which record
the operation of the same processes that now prevail, reaches
back through a vista of more than a thousand million years.

If there are geologic problems of more interest to the general public than others, they are doubtless those of geologic
time and the relation of man to geologic history. There was a
time when it was objectionable, if nothing worse, to speak of
ancient man and discuss his origin as belonging to the regular
program of development of the other creatures that belong to
the earth. There was a time when the mere finding of a skeleton
that showed great antiquity was considered more or less of an
offense, and led, if to nothing worse, to denial of the validity
of the foundation principles of geologic science.

Geologists had become somewhat accustomed, however,
long ago to an occasional discovery that indicated great antiquity for man. The Trinil man of Java had been discovered
in 1891. The Neanderthal man of the Fourth Glacial epoch
had been discovered in 1864. The Cro-Magnon man of Post-
Glacial time had been discovered in 1823. In more recent years
some of the blank spaces have been filled in and former evidences have been more definitely supported by additional finds,
proving the existence of man on the face of the earth in very
ancient times, indeed times measured back into the past in
terms of not only thousands of years, but surely many tens of
thousands, and as we now think, some hundreds of thousands
of years.

In the field of prehistoric archaeology, for which the time
interpretations all come from the field of geology, this
quarter century records the discovery of the Grimaldi races
belonging to Post-Glacial time, the discovery in England in
1913 of the so-called Piltdown man, belonging to the Third
Interglacial epoch, the Heidelberg man in Germany in 1907,
belonging to the Second Interglacial epoch and going back to

a time that probably must be of the order of magnitude of five hundred thousand years. Finally, as the latest and one of the most interesting of all, just the other day, in December, 1929, came the discovery in China of the so-called Peking man, whose exact age is not yet determined, but which has certain characters that may make this one of the most instructive and scientifically important discoveries yet made bearing on the problem of prehistoric man.

The existence of Pleistocene man is thoroughly established, and unless the ordinary principles of geologic science are unreliable, these discoveries must mean that man has been going through a development that reaches back at least to the beginning of Pleistocene time — a time that cannot be measured very accurately in terms of years, but which is of the general order of magnitude of a million years of our time.

If the geologic history that we now claim to be able to read covers a thousand million years, as we think it does, man has been present for about a thousandth part of that time to observe events and help in the recording of the story.

INDEX TO AUTHORS AND TITLES

COLUMBIA UNIVERSITY PRESS
COLUMBIA UNIVERSITY
NEW YORK

FOREIGN AGENT
OXFORD UNIVERSITY PRESS
HUMPHREY MILFORD
AMEN HOUSE, LONDON, E. C.

Date Due
